Save Me,
A Study of Psalm 119:89-96
by C. Matthew McMahon

Copyright Information

Save Me, A Study of Psalm 119:89-96, by C. Matthew McMahon
Edited by Therese B. McMahon

Copyright ©2022 by Puritan Publications and A Puritan's Mind®

Some language and grammar are updated from any original manuscripts. Any change in wording or punctuation has not changed the intent or meaning of the original author(s) and has been made to aid the modern reader.
Published by Puritan Publications

A Ministry of A Puritan's Mind® in Crossville, TN.
www.apuritansmind.com
www.puritanpublications.com

All rights reserved. No part of this publication may be reproduced, stored in a retrieval system or transmitted in any form by any means, electronic, mechanical, photocopy, recording or otherwise, without the prior permission of the publisher, except as provided by USA copyright Law.

This Print Edition, 2022
Electronic Edition, 2022

Manufactured in the United States of America

ISBN: 978-1-62663-439-8
eISBN: 978-1-62663-438-1

Table of Contents

Introduction 4

Chapter 1: The Eternal and Immutable Nature of God and His Word 7

Chapter 2: God's Promises are Perpetual and Unalterable 34

Chapter 3: God's Governing Providence Over the World 55

Chapter 4: All Things Serve God at God's Pleasure 85

Chapter 5: Immoderate Sorrows of the Sinking Soul Crushed by Delight in the Word 111

Chapter 6: Christian Resolve Set in Remembering the Word 135

Chapter 7: God's Election of His Own Special People . 161

Chapter 8: Election in Christ, the Ground of the Sinner's Safety 187

Chapter 9: Assurance of Election in Christ Considered by Spiritual Fruit 215

Chapter 10: Interest in the Word a Means of Divine Encouragement to the Soul 239

Chapter 11: Worldly Affliction Arrested by the Comfort of the Word of God 269

Chapter 12: The Fallen Material World Rejected in Light of the Mysteries of the Gospel 291

Other Works by Dr. McMahon at Puritan Publications 320

Introduction

I *very much* enjoy Psalm 119. If you have ever doubted whether you are truly converted or not, this psalm is for you. Collectively, the psalms are like a little bible in and of themselves. Independently, Psalm 119 is like a little bible in and of *itself*. It is the longest of them all, in fact, the longest "chapter" in the Bible. It contains in it a *thesis* that God's word is to be *preeminent* in the believer's life, and it houses in it everything that a growing Christian would need to draw closer to Jesus Christ if they would but take time to consider it, to *meditate* on it, even in the midst of the worst afflictions. The psalmist displays this *meditation* over and over. 119:15, "I will meditate in thy precepts, and have respect unto thy ways." 119:23, "Princes also did sit and speak against me: but thy servant did meditate in thy statutes." 119:48, "My hands also will I lift up unto thy commandments, which I have loved; and I will meditate in thy statutes," (*cf*. vv. 78 and 148). He loves God's word. He contemplates it as the marrow of his life. Certainly, other psalms speak out such contemplating as well, (1:2, 63:6, 77:12, 143:5). And this psalm is not unique in the idea of meditation and thoughtfulness, yet, it is *filled* with it, and *overflows* with it.

This psalm is also an *acrostic* divided into sections. Each section of the psalm is divided into seven verses, and each section of those seven verses begins with a consecutive letter of the Hebrew alphabet. This was for memorization purposes (which we will *consider* in the first chapter). In light of this, why did I choose this particular section of the psalm to study? I have chosen the section of vv. 89-96 for this study, more *particularly* because it houses the verse, "I am thine, save me; for I have sought thy precepts," (Psa. 119:94). This little phrase, "save me," was the springboard in which this study began. To understand how *being saved* occurs, and what the psalmist meant by it. As we will see, this psalm was also very pivotal in the great reformer's life, Martin Luther, where he relied heavily on this little phrase "save me" during his initial ministry. As with Luther, so with us, my hope is that you will be encouraged to pray along the same lines as the psalmist did, in desiring God *to save you*.

You may think, "I'm already saved. I'm a blood bought believer in Jesus Christ!" That's excellent! But know, Scripture provides *saved and transformed* believers with the biblical truth that, 1) they *were* saved, that, 2) they are *being* saved, and that, 3) one day they *will be* saved. "Savedness", as we will come to find out, has a past connotation, a present reality, and a future hope; and all this on account of the work and merit of Christ, God's *Fellow* who has come to seek and save that which was lost. And there is great comfort to be mined out of these verses for the believer to understand *how* God accomplishes this "saving" through Jesus Christ, and in light of this section and teaching of Psalm 119. It houses in it comfort, hope, help, and importantly, the need to have a true assurance in one's eternal position of "savedness" before God. What Christian has not, at some point in their walk, questioned their assurance? Most Christians, *most* of the time, seem to have doubts. This psalm is a great remedy for such doubting, and demonstrates how and why the Christian can have a blessed assurance in the work that God has done on their behalf. And the psalmist expressed this when he said, "save me!"

So let's get started in our study!

Chapter 1: The Eternal and Immutable Nature of God and His Word

"For ever, O LORD, thy word is settled in heaven," (Psalm 119:89).

The title of the book of Psalms is "praises" or "book of praises," Tehillim (תהלים), or Sepher Tehillim (ספר תהלים). In this book of praises, is found one of the most superlative psalms, and it praises God by praising his eternal, abiding and steadfast word; and all Christians know that his eternal, abiding and steadfast word is seen in its height in the Son of God, who is the eternal *word* himself. The writer in this Psalm was clear to convey that God's word meant more to him than "all riches" (Psalm 119:14), "gold and silver" (Psalm 119:72), all the "fine gold" of the world (Psalm 119:127), and any "great spoil" that could be taken from his enemies or surrounding enemy countries (Psalm 119:162).

The author exemplifies an attitude toward the word of God which is to be the perpetual attitude of God's beloved people. To be in love with the word! Over and over and over again he confirms his great love for the word, (vv. 47–48, 97, 113, 119, 127, 140, 163, 167). He declared his faithful obedience to it (vv. 17, 44, 55–57, 60, 67, 69, 88, 100–101, 106, 112, 115, 129, 134, 145–146, 166–68). He chooses it as his own, remembers it (v. 52), longs for it (vv. 20, 40, 174), seeks after it (vv. 45, 94), holds fast to (v. 31), meditates on it (vv. 11, 15, 23, 27, 48, 78, 95, 97, 99, 148), delights and rejoices in it (vv. 14, 16, 24, 47, 70, 77, 92, 111, 143, 174), speaks of it incessantly (v. 46), and he found immense comfort in it. He stood, as it were, in utter awe of it as God's law (v. 120). He would not forget it, (vv. 61, 93, 109, 141, 153, 176), he would never forsake it, (v. 87), he could not in good conscience depart from it (vv. 102, 110, 157). It guided him through affliction and tribulation. No matter what was happening in the temporary world, the fleeting world, the word was a comfort and a solace to him. Troubles abound, but God will save him and deliver him from all his enemies, both physical and spiritual. For the psalmist, God's word was more valuable than all the material wealth of the whole world, (vv. 72, 127) and even in view of contemplating everything about the temporary nature of the world, found that the depth of the word stretched into eternity tasted sweeter than honey, and was more satisfying than any other thing which exists (vv. 94, 103). Do Christians today think this way about God's word?

  The Hebrew text gives the reader an exactness to its structure and poetic composition in relaying these sentiments. It is divided into twenty-two parts, according to the number of the Hebrew letters, this is called an *acrostic*. Psalm 25, 37, 111, 112 have parts of their composition using this poetic tool. But Psalm 119 is complete in this regard. Every part contains eight verses. Every part begins with a corresponding letter of the Hebrew alphabet in order. This has nothing to do with mysterious codes, or reading between the lines. It is more relevant in such a long Psalm, to aid the reader in retaining its meaning by memory work, memorization. Yet, it is the longest of all the psalms containing 176 verses.

This psalm speaks of God's word as *preeminent*. It gives a number of synonymous uses for the word of God. His law or laws (119:1, 7, 13, 18, 20, 29–30, 34, 39, 43–44, 51–53, 55, 61–62, 70, 72, 77, 85, 91–92, 97, 102, 106, 108–109, 113, 126, 136, 142, 150, 153, 160, 163–165, 174–175). His people must keep, not break, his laws—for their own good. His decrees (119:2, 14, 22, 24, 31, 36, 46, 79, 88, 95, 99, 111, 119, 125, 129, 138, 144, 146, 152, 157, 167–168). They provide them with discernment as it relates to his providence in their lives. Light (119:3, 105): God's word provides light for their way. Light often referring to the purity of the truth. *Not a light at a distance, but a light for the feet*, for *every step* one takes before God. Commands (119:4, 6, 10, 15, 19, 21, 27, 32, 35, 40, 45, 47–48, 56, 60, 63, 66, 69, 73, 78, 86–87, 93–94, 96, 98, 100, 104, 110, 115, 127–128, 131, 134, 141, 143, 151, 159, 166, 168, 172–173, 176). Loving them, keeping them, never forgetting them. His principles (119:5, 8, 12, 16, 23, 26, 33, 48, 54, 64, 68, 71, 80, 83, 112, 117–118, 124, 135, 145, 155, 171). Rules (119:9), ways (119:15), statues, (119:59), and judgments (119:120, 137); so *many* designations for the word of God.

According to the Psalmist, *the word* has a number of theological and practical benefits seen in this Psalm. It brings blessing and happiness (119:1–2, 122). It promotes purity (119:9). It hinders the righteous from sinning (119:11, 29, 121). It renders the godly wise (119:24). It encourages, (119:28), shows God's promises (119:38), and provides answers for daily living, (119:42). It is a bearer of freedom in God, (119:45) offers hope (119:49) revives the weary and enlightens the mind (119:105). It protects (119:114), sustains true hope (119:116), brings spiritual delight (119:70, 111), peace (119:165), and demonstrates God's mercy to all those who love his holy name (119:132).

Among most reliable commentaries, the psalm is considered as written by David. There is no title to this psalm. This view is built on its Davidic tone and expression. It also seems to comply with David's experience in many places, as it is compared to other psalms which have his name attached to them. It has been called, "David's pocket book," being a royal diary that David wrote down over a long period of time, throughout his life. The longer one reads the psalms of David, the more one sees this psalm as fitting his temperament and style.

Considering the various verses in this book, my aim is to look at verses 89-96, beginning now only with verse 89. "Forever, O LORD, Your word is settled in heaven," (Psalm 119:89). "Forever," the Hebrew idea revolves around, not a philosophical concern about what "forever" means, but a practical concern, and that for all time. The word of God is boundless, as God is boundless. It is *his* word, which is answerable to *his* nature. The speech which has been given by God, that which comes out of his mouth so to speak, is *forever*. He is forever and his word is forever. It is literally, firm-standing, or settled; for it cannot be broken. It is settled in heaven, in his eternal counsel. What is this word, that is forever settled in heaven, that belongs to God? As seen throughout Psalm 119, such pertains both to the Law of God, and also secondarily, to all the word of God; both are equal and the same.

There have been three classes of laws published by God to this point. The first is the *Moral Law* as given in the Exodus 20. We know that this Law was not simply written for the Israelites, but for all Christians for all time. "For whatever things were written before were written for our learning, that we through the patience and comfort of the Scriptures might have hope," (Rom. 15:4). "Now all these things happened to them as examples, and they were written for our admonition, upon whom the ends of the ages have come," (1 Cor. 10:11). Not one breathing mark or tittle of this law will ever fail, be cast out, or voided. Why? It is the exact representation of the character and nature of God. Only the *moral law* had attached to it capital offenses. Break it and *God breaks you*.

Christ fulfilled this word, and the apostles established this law as ratified, (Rom 3:31). "Do we then make void the law through faith? Certainly not! On the contrary, we establish the law," (Rom. 3:31).

But then, God also gave the *judicial law* in Exodus 21-23, and that law does not belong to the church as a theocratic country. And, there was also given the *ceremonial law* in Exodus 24-31. This was in types and shadows showing Christ *to come*. It pointed to the Christ being once offered to bear the sins of his people. The ceremonial law was in fact utterly monotonous in its application because the priests stood daily ministering and offering the same sacrifices over and over. But when Christ had offered *one sacrifice* for sins, he forever sat down at the right hand of God (Heb. 9:28; 10; 11; 12), and finished and completed and fulfilled God's word and promises.

David, then, is concerned with the established word of God, that never changes, that continues for all time, and is that which is settled in heaven, which includes the importance of the word as the directive for all men for all time, *especially* for believers.

Doctrine: God and his word are eternal and unchanging. When it is said that God is without limits, that means he is infinite; he is not finite, he is not limited. When that infinite attribute is applied relative to duration, to time, this considers his eternity. God is free from all the limitations of time. He does not exist during one period of time more than in any another. For God all things are at an instantaneous now; he experiences all things in one point. There is no distinction between the present, past, and future for him. "Before the mountains were brought forth, or ever thou hadst formed the earth and the world, even from everlasting to everlasting thou art God," (Psalm 90:2). "Of old hast thou laid the foundation of the earth: and the heavens are the work of thy hands. They shall perish, but thou shalt endure: yea, all of them shall wax old like a garment; as a vesture shalt thou change them, and they shall be changed: but thou art the same, and thy years shall have no end," (Psalm 102:25-27). God is "the high and lofty One that inhabiteth eternity," (Isa. 57:15). For God, "a thousand years in thy sight are but as yesterday when it is past," (Psalm 90:4). And as the Apostle Peter echoes, "One day is with the Lord as a thousand years, and a thousand years as one day," (2 Peter 3:8).

Even as it applies to the God-man, Jesus Christ, he is "the same yesterday, and today, and forever," (Heb. 13:8). The Bible teaches that God is called the eternal or everlasting God. God is infinite, and so is also immutable; he cannot change. The Bible says, "He is the First and the Last," or "Alpha and Omega," or "the same yesterday, today and forever," or "They shall be changed, but thou art the same," and such language. God is exalted above even the possibility of change. Infinite space and infinite time (duration) cannot change. They must forever be what they are. So, God is absolutely unchangeable in his *essence* and *all* his attributes. He can neither increase nor decrease. He is not under any type of development, or evolution. His knowledge and power can never be greater or less than they are right now. He can never be more wise, holy, righteous, loving or

Chapter 1: The Eternal and Immutable Nature of God and His Word

merciful than he ever has been and ever will be. James 1:17 says, he is "the Father of lights, with whom is no variableness, neither shadow of turning."[1] Isaiah 56:9-10, "I am God, and there is none like me, declaring the end from the beginning, and from ancient times the things that are not yet done, saying, My counsel shall stand, and I will do all my pleasure." Blatantly, Malachi 3:6 states, "For I am the LORD, I change not; therefore ye sons of Jacob are not consumed." If God is infinite, and does not change, and God has a will, and his will flows from his eternal and unchangeable nature, it is settled in heaven. So, as God is, so God's will and word are in their character both eternal, and unchangeable.

Next consider, the doctrine that the Word of God is eternal and immutable. God's word holds the same characteristic as God's attribute of eternity. If God says it, it is as eternal as he is. It is applicable and good for all time; it does not change, and will never go out of style. It's odd that many professing Christians look at the Old Testament and want to throw it out because they feel it is outdated in some way; no, *it is eternal.* It is eternal and unchangeable in its nature and function. Well, one thinks, it does not mean the same things that the New Testament means because there were sacrifices in the Old Testament and there are no more sacrifices now so God must have changed his mind. This is incorrect. In fact, the New Testament is the *explanation*

---

[1] See my work, *Sparks of Divine Glory*, for a full study on the attributes of God.

of the Old Testament which is enduring; the new is in the old concealed and in the new the old revealed. In this way the New Testament is *also enduring*. This is because, God's word is settled in heaven forever and Christ comes to fulfill what God says and to ratify it, to make it abide.

God's word is eternal. If God is eternal, his wisdom, power, love, and goodness are also eternal. The expression (or outward working) of those attributes in his *willing anything*, is *also* eternal. Such acts are found in the will of God; and for people to see these, the will of God is found in the word of God. In this way, the word, an expression of the mind of God, is eternal; it is *settled forever*, the psalmist said. The Law and word of God are eternal, "settled" and "forever" as God is forever. For example, "With an everlasting love have I loved thee, and therefore with loving-kindness I have drawn thee," (Jer. 31:3). God loves, and his love is everlasting. Again, it's odd to find professing Christians thinking certain aspects of the Old Testament are everlasting, until they get to the New Testament and then things seem to change for them. "And I will establish My covenant between Me and you and your descendants after you in their generations, for an everlasting covenant, to be God to you and your descendants after you," (Gen. 17:7). Abraham has an *everlasting* covenant, but then in the New Testament it is *no longer everlasting*? No, Jesus fulfills it *so it remains everlasting*; such things are everlasting because Christ upholds all of it and God's word is settled in heaven.

Chapter 1: The Eternal and Immutable Nature of God and His Word

Whatever God is, so is his word. Jesus said "the Scripture cannot be broken," (John 10:35), and he was speaking about *the Old Testament*; the Old Testament cannot be broken because it is God's settled word. To take this a step further, Jesus Christ is the eternal Word which communicates God's mind perfectly to humanity, and he is infinite and unchanging forever. Scripture affirms that Christ is the eternal word, the settled Word (the logic of God himself) in heaven (read John 1). Jesus claimed this for himself, and the Apostles claimed this about Jesus throughout the New Testament. John 1:1-3 states, "In the beginning was the Word, and the Word was with God, and the Word was God. The same was in the beginning with God. All things were made by him; and without him was not any thing made that was made." The word is Christ. The word is God. The word came from God and created all things. He is the everlasting *logic* of God, the *mind* of God himself, who came to earth in covenant obedience taking on human flesh to save his people by an everlasting covenant, settled in heaven.

Further along in the passage of John 1 we find verse 14 stating, "And the word was made flesh, and dwelt among us, (and we beheld his glory, the glory as of the only begotten of the Father,) full of grace and truth." John not only says that the word is God, but explains that the word holds *the glory of the Father*, and is *begotten* of the Father, which shows his *eternal* nature. The word came down from heaven, dwelt among men, and his glory, the glory of God alone, shone among men for a time. This eternal word is God himself. Philippians 2:6-7, "Who, being in the form of God..." Paul speaks of Jesus Christ here. The Messiah is God, equal with God. To be equal with God is to *be* God. Only God can be equal with himself. And God is the word and the word is God, and both are *eternally settled*. Scripture then, as Christ says, is the eternal and abiding truth of who he is, and what he has done. "And beginning at Moses and all the prophets, he expounded unto them in all the scriptures the things concerning himself," (Luke 24:27). The eternal testimony of Christ the word is found in the eternal and immutable pages of the word.

    Equally, then, God's word is unchangeable. It cannot change; it does not evolve; it cannot get better. It cannot become less; it cannot become more. It can only be made more clear to the fallen mind of men by responsible heralding and study. It is settled, in Christ, the Living word, for all eternity, settled in heaven. *The 1647 Westminster Confession of Faith* (1:6) says this, "The whole counsel of God, concerning all things necessary for his own glory, man's salvation, faith, and life, is either expressly set down in Scripture, or by good and necessary consequence may be deduced from Scripture: unto which nothing at any time is to be added, whether by new revelations of the Spirit, or traditions of men." This applies to the words Moses recorded of God, "What thing soever I command you, observe to do it: thou shalt not add thereto, nor diminish from it," (Deut.

12:32). Observe the Scripture, do them, to regain lost ground of knowledge, righteousness and holiness lost in the fall, to have the fall reversed; and what believing Christian doesn't desire that? The *Covenant of Works* in the garden was "do this and live" to Adam. He *did not do it and died*, and sent all humanity plummeting into the abyss of hell. However, there is a blueprint for escaping hell, "According as his divine power hath given unto us all things (*how many things?*) that pertain unto life and godliness, through the knowledge of him that hath called us to glory and virtue," (2 Peter 1:3-4). Where are such things found but in his eternal and unchanging word? This is where God's *knowledge* is found. All things that pertain to godliness are found in Scripture which never changes, and Peter again is speaking of *the Old Testament*. Everything one needs to know, in order to please God, and know they have eternal life in Christ, is found in Scripture. It is not found anywhere else. It is not found in an extra biblical book, in someone's dream, in a hunch, or in the mouth of false prophets who pop up from time to time on TV who think they can tell you God's secret will. The function of the words is to first demonstrate the character and glory of God, revealing God, that God can be known; and then secondly, to press born again believers into a conformity to his character in their conduct according to his will by his Spirit. Laws of a given country or city or town ebb and flow. They change, grow, reduce, are replaced by fickle men; you can see that in the various presidential administrations in America; laws change, and often not for the better. In contrast, God's word is always and forever *settled* in heaven. It *never* changes, and the word stands as a witness to the character of God so that men may constantly look to it as settled in God's mind, demonstrating his will for all men. He will never change his views on sin, his wrath, his love, his mercy, his will, *etc.*

This word demonstrates the mind and will of the Most high as expressed in the condescension of his covenants. Not only is the Lord forever, so his word is settled in heaven in the same manner, but the whole of the Bible is set in the context of the *everlasting* covenant of God; it does not change. God's decree, his abiding will set down, unchangeably and eternally so, can be found in the pages of the Bible in the manner in which he speaks to men, and requires their obedience to what he has given them. He stoops down to bring men that which they need and is his mind on all matters.

In the *Covenant of Works* with Adam in the garden, what did God at first reveal to man as the rule of his obedience? The rule of obedience revealed to Adam in the estate of innocence, and to all mankind in him, besides a special command not to eat of the fruit of the tree of the knowledge of good and evil, was the *moral law*. God told Adam, *Do this and live*; a settled word that would bring happiness; but Adam fell and *did not do this*.

In the *Covenant of Grace*, the Moral Law is lovingly given in Exodus 20 in the Ten Commandments.

Chapter 1: The Eternal and Immutable Nature of God and His Word

Question 93 of the *1647 Westminster Larger Catechism*, "What is the moral law? Answer: The moral law is the declaration of the will of God to mankind, directing and binding everyone to personal, perfect, and perpetual conformity and obedience thereunto, in the frame and disposition of the whole man, soul and body, and in performance of all those duties of holiness and righteousness which he oweth to God and man: promising life upon the fulfilling, and threatening death upon the breach of it." It's, *do this and live*, but men can't, so instead, *come to Christ* and he will show himself as Savior, and then lead men back to the law by taking their hand and filling them with his Spirit that they may *then do it*. David the sweet psalmist uses the terms commandment, law, word, statue, *etc.*, interchangeably throughout this psalm for that very purpose. The word, the law, is settled, because it is eternal and unchangeable.

What does God look like? Children sometimes will ask the question. The Law is a perfect picture of God, the word is a perfect picture of God. If one keeps the Law perfectly, which God requires, he will be like God. Why do you think the psalmist loves the word so much? Does he love it because it is burden, or a taskmaster? No, the word is a *mirror* of God. It demonstrates God's mind and will. It makes renewed image bearers bear God's image the way it's supposed to be, in knowledge, righteousness and holiness. Adam did not keep the word of God perfectly in obedience in the garden, and so God cursed him and all men in him. But graciously, God promised to send Christ to keep it for his people. The righteous requirement of the character of God expects justice when it is sinned against.

As much as God is eternal and immutable, he is eternally just and immutably just. He will never allow a transgression of his word to go unpunished. He will never allow anything against his law, against his character to thrive without consequence. Why would men want to disregard what God says? Why would they disregard what is settled in heaven by an unchangeable decree? To redeem men, he sends a perfect sacrifice for sin, Christ, sinless in and of his own accord, infinite in his being, yet veiled in human flesh, to satisfy his justice for the apostasy of his people against his settled word, broken in Adam. Christ fulfills it for the believer.

As previously studied,[2] Christ does not do away with the Law. How could the settled word be done away with? It's settled! There are so many in the last 200 years of the church, that have so misunderstood this to their own demise and damnation, throwing out great portions of the bible to make their Antinomian lives easier. Paul answers them in Romans to such thoughts and acts, with "God Forbid." Christ fulfills the Law, completes what God requires in it on behalf of his people, and then leads all his people by the hand back to it in order to keep it by the power of the Spirit. He

---

[2] See my work, *Reformation of the Heart, Soul and Mind*, as well as my work, *The Ten Commandments in the Life of the Christian*.

empowers his people by his Spirit to fulfill the fruits they should bear as those engrafted in him, and bearing fruit, demonstrating God's settled will which he has written down for all his people to know. People in the church are able, then, to point to another person, and say, "There is God's word in action!"

Now some may object and say, "But if you are led by the Spirit, you are not under the law," (Gal. 5:18); this would be the same as saying, you are not *under the word* as they consider it that way. You are not under the commands? You are not under the precepts? Of course one is not under *the condemnation of the Law* if they are in Christ. Of course people are *not under the Law to work salvation by their own righteousness*. Moses wasn't, neither was David, nor Paul. There is, however, a great difference between legalism and obedience. Legalism is a work to save one's self; doing works to be justified before the Lord according to his law. This is *impossible* being fallen in Adam. Men cannot fulfill the law. They already have a bad heart, and a bad record in Adam. Obedience, though, is what Christ requires of *every* Christian; and this applies directly to his word in the moral law which points out to Christians God's mind and will in the word. Is the word not settled in heaven? Is God not eternal and unchanging in his will and word? Is his word not eternal and unchanging that believers might conform to it? The Psalmist *reveled* in this truth. If God's covenant and word are settled in heaven, he has set the way of godliness before the face of the Christian. The very Gospel of Jesus Christ was settled in heaven. It was settled long before anyone existed. It was settled before creation existed. It is an unalterable decree, which cannot be reversed. So, when men try to earn salvation on their own by the law, they are legalists. But when Christians come under the blood of Christ's work, they are no longer under the condemnation of the law, to keep it for salvation (which is impossible), but instead, now use it for holiness.[3]

God promises Christ to those who believe and trust in him by faith. And God requires those who believe to continue to believe (to use the Apostle John's words) and work works worthy of true repentance. Is this not the Savior's preaching of the Kingdom in Matthew 4? Is this not the psalmist's words as we will see in these verses? Evidences of true faith are bound naturally to Christ and the eternal and unchangeable word. Evidences of true faith? What are they? They are: conviction of the believer's obligation to keep the word for holiness; that believers *practice* the rules of godliness and righteousness out of love to the Father and the Savior in the power of the Spirit; that obedience to the Law runs in the right channel of faith in Christ as they bring Christ to every good work. This is outlined in the

---

[3] Many times, Christians want to *reject* this idea because holiness requires them *to keep the law* (not for justification, but for obedience), and they would rather feel as though they have the choice to do or not do whatever they think they ought to do for God. This is wholly contrary to the nature of the divine character and word of God.

Chapter 1: The Eternal and Immutable Nature of God and His Word

Sum of Saving Knowledge attached to the *1647 Westminster Confession of Faith*.

Sum is defined as the totality, saving knowledge, of the will of God found in Scripture, *settled* in heaven. Jesus pronounces curses on those who throw away the word and moral law. "But whoever causes one of these little ones who believe in Me to sin, it would be better for him if a millstone were hung around his neck, and he were drowned in the depth of the sea. "Woe to the world because of offenses! For offenses must come, but woe to that man by whom the offense comes!" (Matt. 18:6-7). When one throws away the word they are law-less. "The Son of Man will send out His angels, and they will gather out of His kingdom all things that offend, and those who practice lawlessness, and will cast them into the furnace of fire. There will be wailing and gnashing of teeth," (Matt. 13:41-42). They are without the law, without the settled word. Why is this? Why is God so adamant about this unchanging and eternal word? It is because God is eternal and immutable, forever, and so is his word, which is as his word states; it's settled in heaven. God says it, *that settles it.*

Let us make a practical note, now, about residing in eternity. In general, man's future condition shall be *eternal*. It will be eternal in its happiness or eternal in its misery. One will apply *to you*; either happiness or misery. Forever is a long time; you will either be eternally happy, as the psalmist, in Christ; or, you will be eternally miserable without the loving presence of Christ in hell's misery. God's word opens up both of these truths to you in Scripture. What are you, then, to think about this settled word in light of eternity?

First, God's Word will never fail you, and you must trust it. What does *that* mean and why is it important to you? Scripture, being God's mind and will to us, can never fail us. This means little to nothing to you, like the content of this chapter, if you don't know what the word says. If you don't know *what* the Bible says, or what it means when it says something, it will not matter to you. It won't matter to you that Scripture is unfailing. You must trust that it is by *knowing* what it says.

The Scriptures are unfailing. What a horrible thing it would be for you to trust in something that could *fail* you. Not long ago people were riding a roller coaster and the ride failed, and they were stuck on it for six hours, very high up, until the fire department came and rescued them. They were stuck on the loop. It *failed* them, and trust in it was lost. None of them would ever go on it again. To have the word of God *unsettled*, would cause you to be very unsettled yourself; those people on the coaster were afraid, and very unsettled to say the least, and they would not ride it again because it failed them. What is true, what is false, what if I believe something that isn't true in the word, such would be a very *unsettling* view of God's will. In biblical contrast, as God is forever, so his word is *settled* in heaven. And unless you *know* the word you won't *know* that truth, and

Chapter 1: The Eternal and Immutable Nature of God and His Word

you will be *unsettled* in your life. You may even think you are a Christian without knowing what it means *to be* a Christian. That God's word is settled is a great comfort because the eternal God has so ordered all things (not some things) that not only does he stand over you as a Strong Tower in expressible love as a Christian covering you by Christ's *everlasting* covenant, but he has given you a rule by which you can know his mind and please him in Jesus Christ in response in all things; that is a great concern to all Christians. Is it not interesting about what Jesus says in John 4 concerning what the Father seeks? He does not say God seeks *saved individuals* (though he saves people). He says that the Father seeks *worshippers* who *worship him in spirit and truth.* Salvation is certainly implied, but the emphasis is on *truth bearing* (a form of the ninth command) from a sincere heart as God so prescribes, is what Christ is teaching the Samaritan woman. Those who are settled *in him* by his word to *worship* the Father with a right heart and in the truth, comply with the reality that God's word is *settled*.

When the world changes, God's word is still settled in heaven. When you set your eyes on the things of the earth, such things deceive and bombard your emotions with thoughts that betray you because they are fleeting and do not give you assurance. In this you become *unsettled*; we call this *discontentment*; you think in some form, "I wish I had what he has, what she has. I wish I was not in this situation." This is because the temporary things of the carnal world are fleeting and passing. That is *very* unsettling. But *Christ* is the same yesterday, today and forever (Heb. 13:8). His word is settled in heaven. He is settled in heaven on your behalf as the great King enthroned.

One of the most perplexing questions you will ever face or ask is this, "What is God's will for My life?" Verse 89 of Psalm 119, speaks to that *very* question. The answer to "life and godliness" for you is found in the *settled word*. It is *settled*. It is trustworthy. It will never fail you. It will help you choose a spouse. It will aid you in a choice of an occupation. It will direct you how to live in affliction, or live during times of ease. It will direct you how to think, how to talk, how to live well, how to die well, how to use your finances, how to order your family, how to love people. Have you lost your assurance, or never had any? The eternal and settled word will guide you to it. Have you felt overwhelmed in affliction? The eternal and settled word will calm your spirit. Have you sinned against Christ and his blood *again*? The eternal and settled word assures the penitent Christian of pardon. What myriads of questions could be asked in this way, and yet the answer for comfort is always the same – the eternal and abiding and enduring and permeant and unshakable and steadfast and settled word is your comfort, *if you know it*. But if you don't, you don't understand the substance of this chapter. Comfort for the Christian in this unfailing word, showing this eternal and unchanging God, is not about the adequacy

Chapter 1: The Eternal and Immutable Nature of God and His Word

of Scripture. It really is the adequacy about *what you know to be true in Scripture*. How much of Scripture do you know? It was said of John Bunyan that if you cut him he would bleed the bible. Consider what flows through your veins and what you hope in and on? Consider what takes you through each and every day.

Secondly, God's word gives you the comfort of a blessed eternity. Not just comfort, but the comfort of a *blessed* eternity as a believer - the eternal God has settled his word, his eternal decree, in heaven. This was a great comfort to the psalmist and it should be a comfort to you as a Christian. Can you say with the psalmist, You are forever, and your word is settled, and this is a great comfort to me? Maybe you wonder how it can be a comfort?

You should consider your life in serious contemplation of eternity, both to consider the God you love, and his word which shows you how to love him. In considering that word it is eternity you are thinking about weighed in the balance. Now, this life is a preparation for eternity. Whatever you do now counts forever; or whatever you do not do. Thoughts of eternity can be terribly scary for those who are outside of Christ, but a great comfort for those who are in Christ. Thomas Manton said, "Nothing makes Christ precious but serious thoughts of eternity, he being the only means to deliver us from wrath to come."[4] Only Christ is able to

---

[4] Thomas Manton, *The Complete Works of Thomas Manton*, vol. 7 (London: James Nisbet & Co., 1872), 399.

give you comfort through the eternal word, settled in heaven. He is the eternal word interceding on your behalf; what a comfort this is. What a comfort it is for the Christian to gaze into eternity and say, "You are forever Lord," and be comforted by such a thought as God's eternal being, knowing his word is settled in his character and *you* are a partaker of that eternal word in Christ by the Spirit; for those lost, sentences like this, are gibberish; they get *nothing* from it. Listen to the Apostle Paul, "...while we do not look at the things which are seen, [*do we, I hope you don't rest in things seen*] but at the things which are not seen. For the things which are seen are temporary, but the things which are not seen are eternal," (2 Cor. 4:18); set your minds *there*.

    Thirdly, God's beloved children live on grace for all eternity. You must be so emptied of yourself, as to live on God's alms of grace for all eternity. You are to live on nothing but mere free grace, and on a principle of life that is outside of yourself; where shall you find that truth? God's word is settled in heaven, and in his word he tells you the means by which you can live. It is not uncommon for people in the church to rest on something they do, something they have, something they muster, something they pour into a salvation work. The psalmist did not do this. David rested on the eternal God and his settled word, his promises, his directives, his power to save, as we will see in later chapters in these few verses. This is a mighty work that God enables in sinners of emptying yourself and living a life of self-denial and

Chapter 1: The Eternal and Immutable Nature of God and His Word

humility before his settled word in his covenant, and in light of his eternal grace. Conversion shows you that self-denial is the very ground on which you live. Now you might say here, "I don't understand why we are suddenly talking about self-denial when we have been speaking about God's eternal and unchangeable character and word?" I'll tell you, the ground on which the psalmist exclaimed "You are Forever Lord," and that "your word is settled in heaven" was due to a complete and utter *emptying of himself* from any boast or raising up of his own person. What did he say about himself in this regard? Where are his works? Where are all his duties laid out... nowhere here in *this* verse. When God brings you to himself, you are emptied of yourself and filled up with his Spirit. You are emptied of all that which would exalt itself in the place of Christ, and Christ fills you up and makes residence in your heart and mind with the Father. The very act of believing and coming to the Lord Jesus Christ is THE act of the greatest self-denial in the world because such an act if truly done, empties you of anything you could ever bring; you trust in his word, and his Son, in this. Jeremiah Burroughs said, "the wicked heart must be emptied of itself in that which is so much against the pride of man's heart, to live eternally on mere free grace and nothing else."[5]

What else will you fill your heart up with? What pleased the psalmist? You are unable to be like the

---

[5] Jeremiah Burroughs, eBook, *Christ Inviting Sinners to Come to Him for Rest*, (Crossville, TN: 2017) Chapter 20.

psalmist in praising God for his eternal and unchangeable character, and his eternal and unchangeable word, unless God implants in you that principle of belief that you are brought to nothing, and the work of Christ is exalted. Those not humbled after that principle do not see God's word as *settled*. Something must be added, they think. Some *work* must be added. Some infusion of man's effort or exertion. Something they think they must do in order *to be saved*. Something must be added. But what could possibly be added to God's settled word in heaven for your saving good? Those who have been emptied of themselves, and have the residence of Christ in them, see God as the beam of divine glory that is highly exalted and loves to live by his settled word; his sure word, that they trust and know is unfailing because all God's promises are settled. You can never "do this and live" on your own accord; wicked people try this all the time. They cannot live on their own to please the Father. They cannot achieve eternal peace by their own hand. They cannot achieve happiness with the curse of the fall lying on them. They cannot keep the Law on their own merit or accord. Adam was perfect, and he didn't do it.

    Instead, you are to be emptied of all vain glory, and rest in the gracious eternal covenant of grace which promotes your self-denial, held in the pierced hands of Christ's work. You must lay the whole weight of your soul on Jesus Christ and the sure and steadfast testimony of his word as true and right; but how will

Chapter 1: The Eternal and Immutable Nature of God and His Word

sinners ever do this if they do not know what his word says? Be moved to meditate on the eternality of God and the word: Think to yourself, *"O Lord, you are forever, eternal, everlasting, without beginning and without end. You are the great I AM. The unchangeable one. You have made yourself known in your eternal decrees, and in your eternal and unchangeable word settled in heaven. You are before and after all beings, without any limits of time, past, present, and to come. You exist at all times, but without respect of time, an everlasting, and immortal God, before, and after all times, and in all times forever and ever. You are the King of ages, the Maker of times, the Inhabiter of eternity. "Before the mountains were made, and ever Thou hadst formed the earth, from everlasting to everlasting Thou art God." Everlasting in Yourself, in love, in the fruits of Your favor, towards Your people, which You have chosen. And so, your word is everlasting, settled, without respect of time, and is my guiding light and path, not at a distance, but at my very feet step by step."*

We must stir up ourselves to magnify the Lord, and his word forever this way. Great is the Lord, and worthy to be praised. Great is our Lord, and of great power, his understanding is unchangeably eternal and perfect, and so is his settled word. Say to yourself, "O my soul, sing aloud of the praises of God, whose greatness and word are eternal, and unchangable." God is that unbounded eternal, goodness, in high majesty, for he is a great God, and terrible, a Great King and God above all gods. At his presence the earth trembles, the mountains quake, and the foundations of the world are shaken. The angels cannot behold his glory, and they cover their faces in worship to him. He has given us his gracious word, now settled in heaven, which directs us to the Son of his love. Nothing can hinder God from doing us good. There is no distance, there is no difficulty, there are no impediments. God is freed and set in his decrees where his unfailing word is settled forever, even into eternity for the good of his people. His Son is eternal in his never-ending mediation on behalf of sinners who look to him and his word for guidance. God speaks to his people, as with the psalmist, that all he does is settled, his redemption is eternal. The life he gives is eternal life. The Spirit in which he empowers his people is his eternal Spirit. For his word instructs us of such eternal mysteries.

Be stirred up to behold and rejoice in the Lord's eternal and unchangeable nature, and his eternal and unchangeable word. By this grounded faith in Christ, go to him, contemplate him and his word, that you might feel the power of his resurrection quickening you to newness of life through his word, day by day, and find comfort in the pages of the word which never change, in which you can trust. This will then lead us to consider in the next verse, that God's promises are perpetual and unalterable.

Chapter 2:
God's Promises are Perpetual and Unalterable

"Thy faithfulness is unto all generations," (Psalm 119:90a).

Considering the various verses in this series, the aim in this chapter is to look at verse 90, just the first half. The Psalmist moves from praise to the God who is forever, who by eternal decree has set his word and established it in truth for all time, that it is settled in heaven, to its present application in time, with men. The word "faithfulness" can be translated "fidelity". It refers to the steadiness, and steadfastness of God in what he says and what he does. *Faithfulness* means God is the Great Promise Keeper. When the Lord says something, he keeps his promise and does not lie; this is because his word is *settled* in heaven. His word, like his character is perpetual and unalterable. William Spurstowe said, "A promise is a declaration of God's will, in which he signifies what particular good things he will freely bestow."[6] They have particular practical application to the life of the believer.

That God makes many promises to his people is scripturally evident. They are not given for God himself,

---

[6] William Spurstowe, eBook, *The Wells of Salvation Opened*, (Coconut Creek, FL: Puritan Publications, 2012) chapter 2.

but for them. The promises of God are a great steadiness and comfort *to a child of God*. They are the foundation of the saint's comfort. They are free, full and firm in the word settled in heaven. They will bear up the soul in all affliction, in times of difficulty, in times of ease, in all times. There never was any ashamed that rested only on God in his promises. This is because God is eminently faithful in Jesus Christ, and all his promises are yes and amen in him.

Faithfulness excites the psalmist because it not only remembers what God has done, because he is faithful, but it also sits in eager expectation of what he will do based on the word he has fixed and settled in heaven. This musters up hope in David. Scripture demonstrates that faithfulness is tied directly to God's *promises* in his covenant. "Know therefore that the LORD thy God, he is God, the faithful God, which keepeth covenant and mercy with them that love him and keep his commandments to a thousand generations," (Deut. 7:9). Is this not what David considered? David is an excellent exegete of the Scriptures. The text in most bibles is translated with a desire to help the reader understand what the verse is saying rather than translating it word of word. *Thy faithfulness* or *steadfastness* is *toward all generations*, is even more accurate. Even the idea of steadfastness in this case is used seven times in the psalms and once in Lamentations speaking of God being faithful. In 6 of the 7 contexts, it refers to salvation, God's promises and his covenant, and of those 6, 5 of

Chapter 2: God's Promises are Perpetual and Unalterable

them are by David. "For I have said, Mercy shall be built up for ever: thy faithfulness shalt thou establish in the very heavens. I have made a covenant with my chosen, I have sworn unto David my servant, Thy seed will I establish for ever, and build up thy throne to all generations," (Psalm 89:2-4). Such wonders are all bound up in Jesus Christ, the *spiritual* David.

The statement made by David in this psalm is toward all generations, which in and of itself is a covenant concept, where God is very faithful to keep his people intact; he generally does this in families. The continued nature of the settled will and word of God, forever establishes the fidelity or faithfulness of God's promises toward his people, and sustains them. For some odd reason when Christians come to the New Testament, they think *everything* changes, and these promises, that are unchangeable, eternal and steadfast, settled in heaven, somehow don't count anymore in light of the coming of Christ; however, it is wholly the opposite. The Messiah will come, and exemplify the promises of God in the reign of the kingdom in the Covenant of Grace, and he will fulfill all God's promises perfectly. He will ratify these promises and demonstrate their settled nature, and perpetual truth and unalterable reality.

Let us consider an *excursus* on fidelity – God's *faithfulness* in the Covenant of Grace. It is impossible to understand what David is really getting at here without understanding faithfulness in light of God's promises in his covenant. God condescended in the Covenant of Grace to love and save his elect; David will mention this coming down to save men in this psalm. In the *Covenant of Works* in the garden of Eden the parties were God and Adam. Adam by one sin failed in upholding this covenant (*cf.* Gen. 3). God sent Christ, the Word, settled in heaven, to come and save sinners by the Covenant of Grace. In this Covenant the parties are Christ and his church. This psalm is filled with these covenantal ideas.

Here, in the *covenant,* David is thinking about, God's faithfulness for generations is in fact his Covenant of Grace. The Messiah of God, God's only *fellow*, meets all the necessary stipulations required, to fulfill salvation for the elect. In this way he represents them as one who has fulfilled the settled decrees of God in heaven. This agreement was between the Father, Son and Spirit so that men would not go to hell, but be saved by the Redeemer. As a result, the elect have the ability through the Messiah, to draw near to God and worship God acceptably; which is the whole of their life; they will be received by him, enjoy him, be eternally and unwaveringly loved by him. The promises of God to them throughout the word point this out, and give the psalmist great comfort, in fact, comfort to all generations. The elect are to see God in this agreement as all sufficient in himself for saving sinful man. Genesis 28:3, "God Almighty bless you and make you fruitful and multiply you, that you may become a company of peoples." Genesis 35:11, "And God said to him, "I am God

Almighty: be fruitful and multiply. A nation and a company of nations shall come from you, and kings shall come from your own body." In this covenant is found the promise of Christ and salvation. Ephesians 3:20-21, "Now unto him that is able to do exceedingly abundantly above all that we ask or think, according to the power that worketh in us, unto him be glory in the church by Christ Jesus throughout all ages, world without end. Amen." Here is the same idea and the same wording.

The 1647 *Westminster Confession* says in 7:3, "God freely offered unto sinners life and salvation by Jesus Christ," as a result of this Covenant of Grace; and this to all generations. God is to be seen in this covenant as merciful and gracious to sinful man who deserves nothing so gracious. Exodus 34:6-7, "The LORD passed before him and proclaimed, "The LORD, the LORD, a God merciful and gracious, slow to anger, and abounding in steadfast love and faithfulness, keeping steadfast love for thousands, forgiving iniquity and transgression and sin..." This is God's Covenant of Grace which Moses held unswervingly to. Could it be imagined what he heard in God proclaiming such glad tidings to him on the mount? God is "just" to enter into a relationship with sinners. He alone is wise to be able to enter a relationship with them in a manner which does not thwart his character, and renders not only good but *eternal* good to men, *settled* in heaven. Ephesians 3:10, "...so that through the church the manifold wisdom of

God might now be made known to the rulers and authorities in the heavenly places." His people in this covenant are considered as lost, miserable sinners, and yet, a gift to his Son, saved by grace, because they are beautified *by him*. Titus 3:4–5 says, "But when the goodness and loving kindness of God our Savior appeared, he saved us, not because of works done by us in righteousness, but according to his own mercy, by the washing of regeneration and renewal of the Holy Spirit." They are chosen by God to grace and for glory. They are those for whom Christ died as a *Surety* of this salvation. They are equally those who are presently on the mind of Christ, who are being continually interceded for by Christ's heavenly intercession, because he is so taken with them, and finds them beautified as filled by his Spirit. They were on his mind as he hung on the cross. They were on his mind after being raised from the dead. They are on his mind now as he rules in heaven. He gives them great gifts and lavishes his eternal, unchangeable love on them demonstrated in his perpetual and unalterable covenant of grace. They are empowered by Christ's sending the Spirit for them, and they bear much fruit as his servants and disciples and children and heirs, adopted of the Father to glory. All this is part of the *Covenant of Grace*.

    The entire Triune Godhead is involved in this wonderful faithfulness of settled, perpetual, unalterable truth. The Father is the principle Author of salvation. 2 Corinthians 5:19, "that is, in Christ God was reconciling the world to himself, not counting their trespasses against them, and entrusting to us the message of reconciliation." The Father appointed the elect to be heirs of himself and co-heirs with his Son. Romans 8:17, "...and if children, then heirs– heirs of God and fellow heirs with Christ."

The Son is the Mediator, Testator and distributor of all the blessings of the *Covenant of Grace*. John 10:28, "I give them eternal life, and they will never perish, and no one will snatch them out of my hand."

The Spirit applies, signs, and seals the blessings to the elect. John 3:5, "Jesus answered, "Truly, truly, I say to you, unless one is born of water and the Spirit, he cannot enter the kingdom of God." 2 Corinthians 1:22, "...and who has also put his seal on us and given us his Spirit in our hearts as a guarantee."

So, what is David thinking in all this? *Your faithful promises, Oh God, your fidelity, your firmness, your steadfastness, the settled word in heaven, forever as you are, decreed before time began, is toward all generations in your elect, in your chosen generation and royal priesthood.* All this is summarized and packed within just 3 ½ Hebrew words. What an eternal and unchangeable and perpetual and unalterable word this is to his people. The psalmist *celebrates* this.

Doctrine: God is faithful in the perpetual and unalterable promises he makes to his covenant people. God says all through the Scripture, "I shall establish My covenant;" "I shall make a covenant;" "I will bring you into the bond of the covenant," and such things. It is a glorious covenant, filled with the sweetest promises showing forth God's Mediator, the benefits of the saints, and their exaltation in glory. In the Old Testament? Of course in the Old Testament! In the New Testament? Of course in the New Testament! All of God's word is settled in such promises that are perpetual and unalterable which compliment one another and are all fulfilled in Christ. It is a faithful covenant made by God that began immediately after the fall. "Although my house be not so with God; yet He hath made with me an everlasting covenant, ordered in all things," (2 Sam. 23:5). Some of the *last words* of David.

    Its orderliness is so precise that the purity of its righteousness, its unspeakable goodness, and its irresistible power shine forth from Christ's throne. "To perform the mercy promised to our fathers and to remember his holy covenant," Where is that Scripture found? (Luke 1:72 speaking of his promises)? It is found here in Psalm 119. The Lord is faithful to promise a Savior, and bring the Savior to light right at the perfect time. "But when the fulness of the time was come, God sent forth his Son, made of a woman, made under the law, to redeem them that were under the law, that we might receive the adoption of sons. And because ye are sons, God hath sent forth the Spirit of his Son into your hearts, crying, Abba, Father. Wherefore thou art no more a servant, but a son; and if a son, then an heir of God through Christ," (Gal. 4:4). In all this is found a faithful God, and God's promises are seen as steadfast, settled in heaven, set down by his unchanging decree, perpetual and unalterable. John Brinsley said, "God's promises are the ground on which a Christian stands."[7] Such Christians, then, ought to know what God says so they can find his promises sweet. If a person has religious faith on the promises of God, such faith rests upon the faithfulness of God as promised in his settled and supernatural revelation. Yet, it simply does not reside in the pages of a book, but on the evidence of spiritual illumination, personal experience of the power of God's promises, and the witness of the Holy Spirit, in the heart of the Christian. It is not merely theory, it is active, and practical, and changes God's people into a Christ-likeness over time. It is a practical Holy Spirit work and power, not just a theoretical one. God's faithfulness, then, rests on the truth of God, his perpetual and unalterable promises. Faithfulness rests on God's truthfulness (or *veracity*). God says it, so it's true. He does not promise things and then take back those promises, or make those promises to a meager degree, less than what one thought those promises meant when he said it. When God is called *truth*, he is the epitome of truth, and as a result, he is faithful in all he says. He is *light*, in him there is no darkness at all, and when light is used of him, it means purity in truth. His truth in being faithful, is where he is forever mindful of his covenant and fulfils all the promises which he has

---

[7] John Brinsley, *Stand Still*, eBook, (Coconut Creek, FL: Puritan Publications, 2013) section on God's Promises.

made to his people. This is of the utmost significance to the church of God because it is the ground of their confidence, the foundation of their hope, and the cause of their rejoicing; they follow the psalmist in this course. They are not, then, to change what God says, but to highly esteem what he says and conform to it. It is because the truth is *not* subjective, it is *objective*. It is not relative, it's settled, perpetual and unalterable from before the earth was made. People do not get to change it, they are not allowed to misunderstand it, they are never to be indifferent to it, and they are always to follow it. These perpetual and unalterable promises of the covenant made with his people, are like a marriage. Generally, people do not choose disgusting people to be their husband or wife, do they? People, for all intents and purposes, based on their own outlook for what they love, will choose what they deem the best; the most handsome man, the most beautiful woman, the richest, the most famous, and such things. They hope to gain a better life by such a union.

    What did God do in marrying the church? He chose that which was disgusting, filthy, abominable, and *beautified* her through his Christ in the union, "Now when I passed by thee, and looked upon thee, behold, thy time was the time of love; and I spread My skirt over thee, and covered thy nakedness: yea, I sware unto thee, and entered into a covenant with thee...and thou becamest Mine," (Ezek. 16:8). The church was a disgusting filthy mess lying in its own blood in the field.

And yet he says, "And I will betroth thee unto Me," (Hosea 2:19). "Thy Maker is thine husband," (Isa. 54:5). This is where the bride and bridegroom imagery comes in. "I will say, It is My people: and they shall say, The LORD is my God" (Zech. 13:9). "My Beloved is mine, and I am his," (Song 2:16). There the promise of covenant turns to marital ecstasy. All in just three and a half Hebrew words from the psalmist?

This covenant marriage between God and his people is set on an everlasting faithful promise. It does not merely last for ten or twenty years, or for the duration of one's life, but it is a faithful promise without end; it is eternal (Jer. 31:33–34), to all generations; referring to the perpetual and unalterable seed of the woman. It is eternal and unchangeable, or might it be said, steadfast, with all fidelity, and unbreakable on behalf of God, toward all generations, perpetual and unalterable. Isaiah 54:10 says, "Neither shall the covenant of My peace be removed." It is founded on God's character, which is unbreakable in its faithfulness, "My covenant will I not break," (Psalm 89:34; Rom. 9:11). Here the psalmist was clear in expressing the faithfulness of God, "which keepeth truth for ever" (Psalm 146:6). God is faithful because he swears by himself, "wherein God, willing more abundantly to shew unto the heirs of promise the immutability of his counsel, confirmed it by an oath," (Heb. 6:17), which is synonymous with being faithful to his word. Which speaks directly to Psalm 119:89-90. Hear the words, faithful, oath, promise, immutable, confirmation? They are the same as forever, settled, perpetual and unalterable – this is to say, faithful. This made the psalmist more than happy...do people want to be happy? Happiness for the believer concerns the *right understanding* of this marriage relationship in covenant with God resting on his faithfulness in sending the Christ to save that which is unlovely and disgusting. God's righteousness is his faithfulness in fulfilling his covenant promises to his church...and such promises are forever. These are great and precious Promises of the Covenant of Grace, promises which endure for all generations; they are perpetual and unalterable.

When one ponders the salvation found in the Messiah, Jesus Christ, and the means to that salvation, there lies the promises of God. Korah said in Psalm 48:9–10, "We have thought of thy lovingkindness, O God, in the midst of thy temple. According to thy name, O God, so is thy praise unto the ends of the earth: thy right hand is full of righteousness." This is *a pondering about God* in church, about loving-kindness, the right hand of power, ability to reverse the fall and save his people. Salvation itself and the means leading to it are promised by God to his people all through the Bible. Jeremiah 31:33, "But this is the covenant that I will make with the house of Israel after those days, declares the LORD: I will put my law within them, and I will write it on their hearts. And I will be their God, and they shall be my people." Jeremiah 31:31–34 often is the cause for many people that believe that regeneration is a New Testament concept. However, heart-change, or regeneration by the Spirit is taught by Jesus Christ in John 3 to be an *Old Testament* concept. You are Israel's teacher and you don't understand these things of the covenant and Spirit? (John 3:10) "Circumcise therefore the foreskin of your heart" (Deut. 10:16). "Circumcise yourselves to the LORD, and take away the foreskins of your heart," (Jer. 4:4). "And I will give them one heart, and I will put a new spirit within you; and I will take the stony heart out of their flesh, and will give them an heart of flesh: That they may walk in my statutes, and keep mine ordinances, and do them: and they shall be my people, and I will be their God," (Ezek. 11:19-20). The Old Testament and New Testament are different only with respect to "circumstantials." When old and new are referred to, this is the difference between the Old and New Testament. It is a respecting of *testaments*, and those who are the *Testators*, but it is one *Covenant of Grace*. What is the difference? Think of this like the will of the richest man on earth. The man dies, and all things are bequeathed to his wife, who is now the testator of the will. She is very old, not able, really, to take advantage of the wealth of her family, but still, quite understands the *value* of the will. When the wife dies, the will is passed to the *son*, and so, the energetic young son is *now the testator* and is able to put the force of the entire estate to good use. It does not change the will, but the circumstantials change because the testator changed, those in charge of the will. In the Old Testament Moses is the Testator of the *Covenant of Grace* (the old woman) and in the New Testament Christ is the Testator of the *Covenant of Grace* (the young vibrant man). Moses provided the *scaffolding* that stood around the building while it was being built, but could not bring the promises to pass in their fulfillment, but could only *point* to them. Christ is the capstone itself that holds the whole building together. He is the invigorating power of God, that brings his *testating* with efficacy and fulfillment. There is only one Gospel and one Covenant of Grace; one good news, one glad tiding, one Lord, one faith, one baptism. It is the same Covenant of Grace that all saints have forever been part of from Adam's restoration in Genesis 3 until today. What kind of covenant is the Covenant of Grace? Steadfast. Eternal. Everlasting. Perpetual. Unalterable. Filled with God's fidelity to all generations. It rests on the promises of God. Hebrews 13:20, "Now may the God of peace who brought again from the dead our Lord Jesus, the great shepherd of the sheep, by the blood of the eternal covenant." Jesus, though, in the New Testament, is now the testator, and has fulfilled all the righteous requirements of God's Law, that his people may live more freely, and in his spiritual energy his people may suck virtue from him in this fulfillment of God's promises that never change. The worth of the promises of God, demonstrating his faithfulness, are called the, "unsearchable riches of Christ," (Ephesians 3:6, 9). That

Chapter 2: God's Promises are Perpetual and Unalterable

is how amazing they are, unsearchable; this assures the reader of the bible that God is indeed very rich toward all generations in his covenant. *Rich in grace.* This is why the Apostle Peter says that they are, "great and precious promises," (2 Peter 1:3) which God has given to his people. Nicholas Byfield said, "Promises in our hearts, are better than pearls or precious stones in our treasure chests."[8]

Such promises are the inheritance God gives to his people in this life, and therefore they are called the, "heirs of promise," (in Romans 4). Toward all covenantal generations. This is a greater portion than the richest man on the planet can give to his heir, or his children.

And did you know that God has been very meticulous in keeping records of these promises? They are found in the pages of the bible and are the very ideas that the psalmist was after in contemplating God's faithfulness to his people. God cannot lie, being eternally unchangeable, and he is faithful to tell his settled truth. He not only says these things, but has them written down towards all generation to see. "Thy faithfulness endures to all generations..." They are perpetual and unalterable, and so believe what he says; and this is application of the idea.

First, generally, consider that we must believe these perpetual and unalterable covenant promises. When we come to these promises to possess them, to

---

[8] Nicholas Byfield, *The Promises of God*, eBook, (Coconut Creek, FL: Puritan Publications, 2013) chapter 1.

believe them and make them our own, we must renounce all our own merits. We renounce opinions of our own worthiness and take up self-denial. We acknowledge from our hearts, that all the grace we find in the promises, is in and through Jesus Christ. All the promises are yea and amen through him, and only him. What do you bring to this? You bring but faith to believe what God says, and that too is a gift, to believe him.

Second, more particularly, God being faithful in his promises to his people contains an enormous amount of applications. The promises themselves can be systematized for us to better understand them. They show the privileges of the godly above other men. God many times will enlarge and invigorate the hearts of his people by showing them the precious promises and benefits of the *Covenant of Grace* that apply only to them, and these he will confirm on them, and on none but them. He promises you the fullness (not the shadow or scaffolding) of the Savior, Deliverer, the Christ. He promises deliverance from this present evil world. He promises you deliverance from sin. He promises you the indwelling of the Holy Spirit. He promises you the power of being a new creation. He promises to you a kingdom. He promises you entrance to all the means of grace. He promises you an immortal, incorruptible inheritance, that does not fade, reserved for them in heaven, which passes all that the eye of man saw, or the ear of man heard, or the heart of man can conceive. And they are wonderful promises because they are perpetual, and unalterable in his covenant.

In Genesis 17:7 God said, "And I will establish My covenant between Me and you...for an everlasting covenant, to be God to you...and your children after you." This is what David has in mind. What a stupid and foolish man David would have been to rejoice in something that was *temporary*. David knew its meaning as *perpetual*, and *unalterable*. What did this mean to Abraham?

The ratification of the covenant was a confirmation of what God had already promised to do for Abraham in chapter 15. What makes Abraham the father of the faithful? What makes you as a professing believer, children of faithful Abraham. I'll tell you, it's a concept every dispensational Christian that has ever lived misses entirely to their detriment. Abraham believed what God said because *God said it*. To you and your children. Toward all generations, as the psalmist said. Well, it can't mean that, can it? The continuity of the covenant, of God's faithfulness, absolutely means that. Believing God at his word was the foundation of Paul's argument in Romans about Abraham being justified by faith. Do you believe the great and precious promises of God like father Abraham did? This is such a simple question. Do you believe God who speaks in his settled word, his perpetual and unalterable word? Do you believe he is and will be faithful according to his word? Many do not. In Genesis 15, Abraham had believed God's promises, and this belief was credited to him for righteousness. That is no small thing; it brought him to heaven. This was the Lord's free gift of grace to Abraham – and he is the father of the faithful who believe in the same way the same things that father Abraham believed. And when you believe that God is your all, this will comfort and establish you in his promises because you take him at his word. "Thy faithfulness is unto all generations," (Psalm 119:90). Do *you* believe that? God's promises to you breed and enlarge faith in Christ and make your Christian walk sweeter, because the promises are sweet. Scripture is a storehouse of perpetual and unalterable promises in Christ for the glory of the Father to all generations in the everlasting covenant. Augustine described God's promises as *gifts firmly fixed without change;* that is a very nice way of saying it. Are you fixed on them? Do you know them? If someone promises something, and takes back that promise, it calls into question their reliability, their trustworthiness. God never does that to you. He promises and fulfills those promises by the eternal Word, who is the Christ, in the fullest degree possible. What good will it be for you to know popular pieces of the truth such as Adam, Noah and the Flood, Samson and the jawbone, David and Goliath, Jonah and the Fish, but then, not know the substance of his promises in Christ? That he assures us, "his elect shall enjoy the work of their hands, and shall not labor in vain," (Isaiah 65:22-23). That he assures us, "The smoking flax shall

Chapter 2: God's Promises are Perpetual and Unalterable

not be quenched, nor the bruised reed broken," (Isaiah 42). That he assures us, "Not one of them shall be lacking" in the whole flock, (Jeremiah 23:4). That he assures us, "God will build them, and not pluck them down, he will plant them, and not pull them up," (Jeremiah 24:6). That he assures us, "He will confirm us," in and to the end, "that we may be blameless in the day of our Lord Jesus Christ. For our God is faithful, who hath called us to the fellowship of his Son Jesus Christ our Lord," (1 Corinthians 1:8-9). That he assures us, "God will not cast off his people," he will never forsake his inheritance, (Psalm 94:14, 1 Samuel 12:22). That he assures us, "For the Lord loveth good judgment, and forsaketh not the saints, and therefore they are preserved forever," (Psalm 37:28). That he assures us, "He will not turn away from them to do them good, and he will put his fear into them, that they shall not depart from him," (Jeremiah 32:40-41). That he assures us, to make us all the more sure, he will put his Spirit into them, which shall lead them into all truth, and cause them to keep his statutes, and to do them, (John 14, Ezekiel 36).

Does not Christ, "keep us from evil," (John 17) is he not able to "save us to the uttermost, because he ever loveth to make intercession for us," (Hebrews 7:25), is he not the Finisher of our faith, as well as the Author of it, (Revelation 21:6, Hebrews 12:2), is he not all powerful to do it for "None can take us out of his hand," (John 10), being "born again to a lively hope of an immortal inheritance reserved for us in heaven:" our new birth entitles us to heaven, and it is kept for us, and our, "hope is lively," (1 Peter 1:3). Are these promises and others *worth* knowing? That which breeds and increases your faith in God is not a magical zapping of the Spirit on you while you sleep, but and exercising of your belief in the "revelation of God's promises" by his Word and Spirit. The assurance of faith is greatly increased and confirmed in you by the sight of those signs of the truth of your faith, and other graces of God in you, as the word reveals them. Robert Rollock said, "...the sacred Scripture ... alone ... properly breeds faith by the Holy Spirit teaching us in our hearts to believe and apprehend the truth of God."[9] It is God's *settled* word, Scripture, that breeds faith, to believe what God will do from generation to generation, for his covenant is perpetual and unalterable, as his word is, as his faithfulness is. For, "Faith cometh by hearing, and hearing by the word of God," (Rom. 10:17). Faith doesn't come by *feeling*. Faith doesn't come by what you like or don't like. Faith comes by God in believing what God says, and that he is your exceedingly great reward because he has made perpetual and unalterable promises in Jesus Christ for all generations. It is Scripture that feeds faith, and causes it to thrive, "I hope in thy word," David will say in verse 114 of this psalm. Hope is a degree of faith. "Establish thy word unto thy servant, upon which thou hast caused me

---

[9] Robert Rollock, *Select Works of Robert Rollock*, vol. 1, (Edinburgh: Woodrow Society, 1841) 99.

Chapter 2: God's Promises are Perpetual and Unalterable

to trust." That should be your prayer, to trust his word at every point and rest and lean on him as one faithful and true. Faith and assurance of eternal life must be valued indeed, by you who find its blessings, follow Peter who calls such a faith, "precious faith." And this is the way, truly, to believe in God, though we do not see him but by the word, through the Christ, in the Spirit, that by this confidence in him we may have joy and peace as the psalmist did. He had high and lofty thoughts set down in just three and half words.

Do you need some further proof? This pressed the psalmist to consider the latter portion of the verse, "thou hast established the earth, and it abideth," (Psalm 119:90b, as a conclusion to his thoughts about God's gracious covenant, which we will look at in the next chapter.

Chapter 3:
God's Governing Providence Over the World

"...thou hast established the earth, and it abideth," (Psalm 119:90b).

One would think, *so, God created the earth, why is that important in the grand scheme of things?* God has made the earth firm and established it. It remains and stands firm and sure, it abides. This abiding is directly related to the faithfulness of God. This in turn is directly related to God's covenant, Christ, and the Kingly rule of Jesus. If there were no theater of God's works, no creation, there could be no outworking of God's providence in creation in any way. Creation is a very important subject as it relates to God's faithfulness, his settled word, and his saving covenant.

This verse is *contrary* to Atheism. Where God is absent, men desire to remove themselves from the fear of God's divine attributes and invisible qualities; his providence and power. They do this because they want to overthrow what God lays out in his word. They do not desire, as those who are captive to sin, to follow the settled word of the Great King Jesus, and at every turn they attempt to cast away his laws; as Jesus said, to be *law-less*.[10] They want to follow their own inclinations, and do what they like without any reverence to God, without any reproofs and terrors to their conscience, or the possibility of endless punishments and torments in the world to come. They do not want to think about such last things in light of eternity. Atheists deny God by suppressing the truth, which in turn denies the judgment, which in turn denies hell; how convenient for them; *though*, they know God exists and they hate him for it.

    This verse is contrary to Deism. The deist, which is somewhat fashionable today, thinks that he believes that there is a God, and that the soul is immortal, and that good men shall be rewarded and bad men shall be punished in the world to come; whatever *that* means to them. But he is unaware as to how any of these things occurs. He believes that the world is fashioned and created by a Creator, but this Creator has not made himself known. It is in essence a form of Agnosticism (to not really know what exists, though the conscience cannot rid itself that something exists), because though the deist believes a Creator exists, for who could fashion such a world, he has not told men what he is, who he is, what he has done, and such things. Man can't *really* know God. This position is very contradictory overall. How does the deist know, except he assumes based on what he feels, and what he likes, that anything exists?

---

[10] Matthew 7:23.

He likes the idea of some kind of higher power. What is that but being relative in his view of truth. He is *not* after truth, but being pacified and appeased in his conscience by a god of some kind of his own making; something pleasant for his own comfort. *What is good for me is this, and it might not be good for you, but that's okay because we can all believe what we want.* This is in direct opposition to the Christian Religion because the psalmist gives, in this verse, the reason why the earth abides, and the world was created. It is as in the first part of the verse, as we've studied, the faithfulness of God. And it shows, by God's divine revelation that such things are true, and that God is involved in his creation. The deist thinks, that since the fall, God does not manifest himself to man with any clearness, or expression of his will, which is an attempted denial of the very passage in the text, and the whole of Scripture, not to mention the very work of the Redeemer, Jesus Christ, to declare and make known the Father (John 1:10).

What this verse is pressing, is the establishment, and continuance of the earth and everything created in turn giving witness to the settled decree of God's word, of God's faithfulness, of his settled word and his promises which are perpetual and unalterable. "For ever, O LORD, thy word is settled in heaven. Thy faithfulness is unto all generations: thou hast established the earth, and it abideth," (Psalm 119:89-90). From this second half of the 90th verse, it is seen that the earth bears a testimony to God's word in that it abides, it is upheld, it continues to exist in God's overarching providence, and will of God, for they are settled in heaven and continue in the exact measure of God's desire. God will gain glory from his creation, and it has been created for a purpose, according to his plan, will and decree.

Doctrine: That the continuance or preservation of the earth and everything created is a witness to the truth of God's settled word and faithful promises. God is the One who creates and establishes the earth, and that the earth abides. Things done by God always abide because he is faithful, and he works and acts in it. In God's external works, creation houses things that are done *by* God, that is, not only actions working and operations, such as creation, redemption and the like, but also things or works *made*, which are affected and done by those actions that God has ordained before the world began, or anything was ever created. One may say, "God created the world," or "God saves people by Jesus Christ," as general principles, but things such as heaven, earth, angels, devils, and other things *created*, are particularly made by God in his working and all things are preserved in their created place and order by God's providence for his glory.[11] All these things are fashioned by God under things he has made, and works he has done. In turn, they all bear witness to the heavenly truth of God's faithfulness in this way; creation is a marker to

---

[11] God made angels who turned to devils because of sin. He did not create them in sin, or delighted that they sinned. But God is the first cause of all things as they are part of his creation.

God's omnipotent power and sustaining hand. And, creation is the context in which God works his saving power through Jesus Christ that some sinners may be saved, and go to heaven. God has done, or *has made*, which the Hebrew text signifies, the *earth*, and it *abides*. That God's outward works consist in doing things; we call this God's providence or governance. "We have heard with our ears, O God, our fathers have told us, what work thou didst in their days, in the times of old," (Psalm 44:1). "For the LORD shall rise up as in mount Perazim, he shall be wroth as in the valley of Gibeon, that he may do his work, his strange work; and bring to pass his act, his strange act," (Isa. 28:21). God works in doing works, even does strange works, and strange acts as the prophet states. "Things" are done by God. Make note that the author of all these works is *God*. He is the Lord Jehovah, the infinite, eternal God in three persons, the Father, Son and Holy Spirit. This triune God has revealed to men in his word, the works he does is common to all the Godhead. God considered as Triune, is the Author of all these works of creation, and they are all common to the Father, Son and Holy Spirit. Every person in the Godhead has a part in creating, sustaining, preserving, working, doing, acting, saving ... in *his* creation. The word *Jehovah* or *Yahweh* used plainly shows, where it is said, Psalm 115:3, "Whatsoever Jehovah pleased or was willing to do, that he hath done." And how does God work in this way? The Father works by the Son and the Son by the Father with and by the Spirit.

They all work together for one unified and common end that reflects the settled word in heaven, and the faithful promises to bring them to pass in their fullness that he would have the most glory. Even this first great work of creation, which sometimes is attributed to the Father, sometimes to the Son and sometimes to the Spirit, we see the Trinity working. "By the word of the LORD were the heavens made; and all the host of them by the breath of his mouth," (Psalm 33:6); or by the Spirit. "The Spirit of God hath made me, and the breath of the Almighty hath given me life," (Job 33:4). The Son took part in creation. "In the beginning was the Word, and the Word was with God, and the Word was God. The same was in the beginning with God. All things were made by him; and without him was not any thing made that was made," (John 1:1-3). "For by him were all things created, that are in heaven, and that are in earth, visible and invisible, whether they be thrones, or dominions, or principalities, or powers: all things were created by him, and for him: And he is before all things, and by him all things consist," (Col. 1:16-17). That by "the eternal word, the Son," all things were made. So that in this creating and working, these external works of God are *not* divided by these persons, but are common to all the persons and proceed from that one common essence which is God.

      The Lord Jesus plainly said, "Verily, verily, I say unto you, The Son can do nothing of himself, but what he seeth the Father do: for what things soever he doeth, these also doeth the Son likewise," (John 5:19). Things in and with creation that are done by God mentioned in his word and for his pleasure are numerous. After God creates such things, and that the Godhead has a hand in all parts of that creation, so equally, in all these outward works, they move and have their being by God's own will and pleasure. "For in him we live, and move, and have our being," (Acts 17:28) – *hold that thought for a moment.* He does all things of creation, in them, and through them, according to his eternal purpose, and after the counsel of his own will. "Declaring the end from the beginning, and from ancient times the things that are not yet done, saying, My counsel shall stand, and I will do all my pleasure," (Isa. 46:10). The "...LORD, hast done as it pleased thee," (Jonah 1:14). Even Eph. 1:11 says that God works "all things" after the counsel of his will. Even by his will Christ was crucified for the redemption of his people, (Acts 2:23 and 4:28). The work of man's redemption by Christ, and all that he did and suffered is attributed to the determinate counsel of God in the theater of the created order. "For to do whatsoever thy hand and thy counsel determined before to be done," (Acts 4:28). God's will and pleasure is the only inward moving cause of all his outward works, and that they are nothing but the execution of his eternal will which is settled in heaven, which is perpetual and unchangeable.

In the realm of Christian Theology there are certain theological subjects that stretch one's mind further than its capacity, and this verse is one of those subjects. From this verse, it is shown that God has created the earth, but more particular that it is established; this is a very important point to the psalmist, in fact to the Holy Spirit who set it down here. That the earth is *both* established and endures. These are important terms, *established* and *endure*. To be established, and to endure in its establishment, as it relates to the work of God's faithful covenant, and his settled and abiding word in heaven, are very important; both temporary and eternal realities are concerned here.

In the act of God's providence, he upholds all things in their being, to preserve their natures, powers and operations; without which they would cease to be. Nature surely seems to decay and die, and revive again, in almost as wonderful a manner, and as unintelligible to men, as it was first made. People speak of *chances*, often. What are the *chances* that such and such a thing came to be... but chance, which is a non-thing, cannot do anything in the world. Chance is merely the sum of a certain number of conditions. The word "chance", really, is a useless term, when a person says, *what are the chances that such and such will happen?* That's really a useless way of speaking. Oftentimes people mean the very opposite of it, that the chances are in fact very good all things considered, because many factors came into play which determined the outcome, as they are considered.

The same knowledge, wisdom and power which made the world, must govern it as well, and that is by God alone, never by chance. It is only a creating power that can preserve creation. And everything owes its being to that created power, they all owe reverence to him; atheists, deists, agnostics and Christians too owe reverence to the Creator for being created. For if something exists, then something exists necessarily (with *necessary being*) to uphold and work out the end and aim of all things for his glory. It is only God's creating wisdom that perfectly understands the natures of all things, that sees all, that can uphold nature, that can suspend or direct the influences of natural causes to work miracles by Moses, Christ or his apostles, or even that can govern hearts, change men's purposes, inspire wisdom and counsel, restrain or let loose their passions. God does all these things, but how? It is only the infinite mind of God that can take care of the entire world, the entire universe, in all places, and can give every creature its due portion, because they all exist in his mind. God adjusts the interests of states and kingdoms and can bring good out of the evil of afflictions, he can bring order out of confusion. But how?

The government of the world requires such wisdom and such power; no one has power like God does, and he can faithfully execute such power in the world. No being but God who made it and Christ who upholds it all by the power of his Spirit, can do any of this; they are all dependent on his preserving power. If the world is to be governed by someone, it must be and will be governed by the infinite God with infinite power and infinite wisdom who made it. But how is creation sustained?

Creation continues, and it continues because God upholds and preserves all of creation. Not only did he create it, and establish it, but it exists and is abiding, to bear witness to the word of God which is unchangeable, that speaks about God's power of creation. God has created all that exists out of nothing by the word of his power. In creating all things, he also upholds all things, or preserves all things, the world keeping one constant course. David approves of the righteous belief in the abiding nature of the world, at least for the time being as God has so laid out in Scripture, on God's constancy and faithfulness, his settled word, and faithful promises which are perpetual and unalterable. Christ holds the world together, and keeps it in its existence. The Bible is very clear on this (Col. 1:17; Acts 17:28, etc.) "...by him all things consist," (Col. 1:17). The providence of God's preserving power covers every area of the created order. Not only does God preserve the created order, but the manner in which he does this, the manner in which he preserves things in existence, is no different from him continuously creating them. This is where it is important to make a distinction, and *to put on your thinking caps.* It is very easy to believe that God made the apple tree but then, by his power, he continues to hold it together moment by moment, otherwise it would cease to exist.

God is the power behind the apple tree's consistency. His preserving power is why there are apple trees, or cars, or soda cans, elements on the periodic table, and other things which are upheld by his power, lest they cease to exist. God upholds his elect, and God upholds wicked sinners. This has *far* reaching connotations as we shall see, and why David used these words in this verse to describe his power in creation as established and abiding. The word of God, settled in heaven, teaches that God continually preserves creation *all the time*. This is fundamental to the Bible and easy to prove, and I've already given you a few verses. Two New Testament verses come immediately to mind; Colossians 1:17 and Acts 17:28. Colossians 1:17 states, "And he is before all things, and by him all things consist." The verb "consists" is an imperfect verb. That means it was initiated in the past but continues to be active from that time into the future with no ending point. That is an important tense to understand in Greek. God is still working, even now, to *uphold* creation, to continually work in it to cause it to abide or endure. This is one reason why Jesus said, "My Father worketh hitherto, and I work," (John 5:17). The "all things" of the Colossian verse is not "some things." In him *everything* consists, from mice to rocks to super novas – he continually holds their being in their respective places. There is nothing working out there in space on its own, and nothing working in the quantum realm on its own. There is no maverick molecule or autonomous atom running around outside of the consistency of the preserving power of God. I told you *to hold that thought*, now remember that thought, and consider Acts 17:28 which speaks poignantly. Paul states, "For in him we live, and move, and have our being." The climax and point Paul makes here is that creation, all of creation, which includes all men, is continually upheld by the power of these philosopher's "unknown God" who in fact *can* be known because he has expressed himself in his word. His word shows his faithfulness to all generations; they have merely failed in looking to this God for the truth. In this, all men have their being in God. That does not mean they *are* God, but it does mean that without God's sustaining power, men would not exist. They are continually upheld in their being in him all the time. It is his power of preservation that holds the fabric of cells, water, blood, veins, organs and the like to continue in their respective being, for every being every moment, of every second, of every hour of every day ... *etc*. Every breath is contained for every man woman and child by God's power, in his outward work of preserving creation. How?

Do created "things" (and things can be *anything*, but for this purpose "things" are going to be apple trees) do apple trees have power in and of themselves to exist? The answer to this is "no," they do not have *necessary* being. The next very important proposition comes into play: apples trees exist either by its own antecedent existence or by the power of a Creator. Either they exist on their own because they have some previous power to keep themselves going, or the Creator must continue to sustain them. The answer is that the Creator does this because apple trees have no necessary being. Consider, the past has no power to sustain that which is in the present or that which will be in the future. Time cannot sustain things, everything is simply moving through time. Nor can the things themselves sustain themselves, they have no power, apples trees have no power, so God must sustain things in each moment of time. If this is true, and no bible reading Christian would say otherwise, neither would the psalmist, then each successive moment must be the effect of God's creating power; moment by moment God preserves everything in its place and life. God, then, is continuously upholding the apple tree upon every moment of its existence. In upholding the apple tree's existence, God creates the thing itself in each successive moment with its aging being. And what he does each moment, preserves the creation of the apple tree. And each *moment* is in fact a *separate* moment. Life for the apple tree is not one moment, but a number of them, like frames in a movie reel; each frame is self-contained. All the frames put together make up one movie. God continually recreates the apple tree in each moment, in each frame, that it exists.

The apple tree's *existence* hinges on the reality that God continues to create it in that same manner, but with subtle changes as it matures. Its past existence does not hold the existence of the tree in its present state, it has no self-sustaining power to do it; in this way God must recreate the apple tree instantaneously moment to moment, with change *and* growth. Whatever exists right now is a new affect of God's continual creation and power to uphold all things. Like a movie film "in the can" in the old days. Movies "in the can" mean they have been finished and are ready to be distributed. The movie is one movie and should be treated as such. It is not a sequence of 18,000 movies, but the 18,000 frames make it one whole movie. The individual segments, or frames, give the movie its actual substance; each frame shows progression. Like the one movie, the one apple tree is one apple tree, but it's made up of successive moments which all combine together to make the one complete life of the tree – even if it grows, bears fruit, is chopped down, *etc*. God upholds the tree in all its stages throughout the time of its existence and recreates it moment by moment with growth and fruitfulness. He preserves the tree in every successive moment of the tree's existence. Like the individual frames make up the movie, so the individual successive moments, which have nothing to do with the previous moment, make up the whole life of the tree.

Can this be proved out in something people see and use everyday? Yes, it can. I like to illustrate this whole concept of God's continual creation of the substance of all things in upholding the world by the use of a mirror and light. Think of it this way – a woman stands in a room in front of a mirror, while the lights are on. Then she shuts the lights off and the image in the mirror can no longer be seen because the room is now pitch black. Turn the lights back on and her image again appears because of the light *bouncing* off her and reflecting in the mirror. While she is in the light, the mirror image appears in the mirror. But the light that is traveling from the lamp to the woman seems to be a continuous beam of light. But, it is not the same light bouncing off her as she stands there, and its new light recreating the image every time the new light particles bounces off her and reflect in the mirror. She can't perceive that happening, it just looks like one long image in the mirror, but it is happening. She can perceive the image disappearing when she turns out the light for the image no longer is there. Each particle of new light continues to preserve the image moment by moment when it's on. As energy travels from the led or bulb in the lamp, out into the "air" as light, it hits her image and then reflects her image off the visible mirror; it is only then that she sees her image.

Now if others joined her in looking at the mirror, it looks as though the image is continual. It looks like it is just *there* in the mirror. However, the particles of moving light are traveling at such a high rate of speed that the image *looks* that way, but is really being *replaced* by new light as it travels into the reflection. New particles of light continually bounce off the woman into the mirror to recreate her image every moment. Shut the light off. What is there now? Nothing. Since the light is off, there is no more reflection because the room is dark. As a matter of fact, everything in the room is "gone" because there is no light bouncing off of anything. Thus, no images are created, no one can see anything. Not one particle of light is reflecting in the mirror and creating the image any longer. The darkness proves that the light has a beginning and an ending. The particles of light bounce off the woman into the mirror and the new light which emanates from the lamp continually creates the image while the light is on. A human's eyes cannot see those particles because they are too small and seem as simply "the light" and not zillions of particles floating around through the room's space. However, while the lamp is off, those particles are not traveling or bouncing off anything anywhere in the room – that is why the room is dark, and that is why the image is gone, and nothing can be seen in darkness.

The same thing would happen to the universe if God stopped the continual use of his creating and preserving power on it; he is *the light*. Nothing else would exist because his "light of life" would cease, and all things in creation would cease. His power *gives* life. The reflection of the woman, while the light is out, does not "exist" so to speak, in the mirror. The universe, in turn, would not exist if God stopped his successive creation and preservation of it in each moment. This is why the psalmist said *the earth abideth*, because God continually creates it by his preserving power. Though mankind has years, months, weeks and days (even hours, minutes and seconds) where they divide time up, though it may seem one "day" to us, in reality, like the reflection in the mirror, the day is made up of a host of "moments." In each individual moment (however long a "moment" may be) God continues to "create" or "preserve" the universe by continual creation this way; *it abideth.* This stretches the Christian mind to consider the governing power of God in the whole world, which is so minute in this, consider, every single thing that God upholds and preserves and sustains every moment. Apple trees, stink bugs, tables, bibles, windows, asteroids, stars, fires, grasses, cats, fish, *everything.* What is *not* in his power? He does not forget anything he preserves and can sustain it all continually, for as long as he wishes. And he can, in the end, split the dimension that separates heaven and earth, to swallow the earth up into heaven, and recreate it instantaneously, as by fire as the apostle Peter says among others, and renew it at last, down to the last quantum sub-atomic particle, or whatever is smallest; he knows what that is.

The Lord Jesus Christ, the Word of Psalm 119, the One who upholds all things, and causes the earth to abide and endure, upholds *everything*, "who being the brightness of his glory and the express image of his person, and upholding all things by the word of his power, when he had by himself purged our sins, sat down at the right hand of the Majesty on high..." (Hebrews 1:3). The power of upholding the universe is through the spoken word. It is through the Christ who is the word. It is the same spoken word by which the Genesis account is narrated as the manner of creation. God spoke and things came into existence. God continues to speak, and, by the power of his word, all things are continually created and sustained as such moment to moment. Psalm 148:5, "Let them praise the name of the LORD: for he commanded, and they were created." Isa. 48:13, "Mine hand also hath laid the foundation of the earth, and my right hand hath spanned the heavens: when I call unto them, they stand up together."

The very fabrics of all souls are held together by the power of God's word. "O bless our God, ye people, and make the voice of his praise to be heard: Which holdeth our soul in life, and suffereth not our feet to be moved," (Psalm 66:8-9). It is a positive action that God continues to "hold" man's soul as living. Christians should be taken back by the sheer magnitude of this doctrine of God's outward works and continual creation and preservation of all things. Reformed Christians tend to think they have a grasp on God's sovereignty, but in reality, they barely scratch the surface of these ideas, or just spying the very tip of the iceberg. How practical is it to consider such government of the world as this? Christians often pawn off this idea to consider creation far more simply, but it has incredible ramifications for everyday life. Let me give you an illustration, Leviticus 14:34 makes a startling proclamation when God says,

"When ye be come into the land of Canaan, which I give to you for a possession, and I put the plague of leprosy in a house of the land of your possession..." God *places* the leprosy in the house. He puts it there. He is giving instructions to the priests on what to do when *he* does this. What does this say about cancer in a person's body, coronavirus, MLS, aids, headaches, acne, arthritis, stomach aches, and such things? Here is God upholding the fabric of the house. He is responsible for it, moment by moment. Suddenly, by the word of his power, he manipulates, changes, adapts, invokes, the molecules and atoms which make up "leprosy", to be created and present as leprosy in the house utilizing whatever elements may progress into leprosy, even any secondary causes. This is mind-bending that he governs the world in every way for all time for all things moment by moment. It is not enough that God simply *knows* everything, but thinking through such texts reminds men how much God keeps in mind and manipulates every second of every moment, for "thou hast established the earth, and it abideth," (Psalm 119:90).

Yes, this is something which transcends the particulars of the human mind, but at the same time, it also elevates it to a plane of praise and adoration for the Christian. God is in such control that for as long as he desires, the earth abides and endures. It is a testimony to his power. God is in control, even down to the very fabric of man's being from moment to moment, and takes careful notice of all things, because he is the faithful God who upholds all things by the word of his power.

God will never suffer his faithfulness to be stained or blotted, and therefore he will undoubtedly make good the word that is gone out of his mouth. That the continuance of the earth and everything created give witness to the eternity of God's word and work. Christians should know by considering the earth and all that God governs, that not one jot or tittle of the Lord's word shall be changed. The earth one day will be altered. Nature one day shall be altered. The heavens will one day be altered as by fire and renewed, because God said at such and such a time it will be done. But God's word and will shall never be altered, and by gazing on the minimal glory of the world, the truth of the word stands firm in the heart of the believer. Nature testifies of God's power and invisible qualities as Romans 1 says. God could easily bring men to utter destruction, as easily as he could make stones in the street be children of Abraham. Jesus was not being facetious when he said that. If God wanted to change stones into men he could altar reality and do it.

The Scripture reads this way of God's allowance of endurance, and the abiding of the earth, because there is no hope, no relief while men live on this earth but by God's power, his word, and his promises through his Christ. There is no other thing to place one's trust in. A tree? A job? A person at work? A concocted higher power? What will men place their trust in?

All things are upheld by God. God, as the divine King has established the heavens as his throne (Psa. 103:19) and the earth as his footstool and dominion (1 Chron. 16:30; Psa. 93:1; Isa. 45:18). All those things in creation merely give a context in which God's redemptive plan may be experienced by penitent sinners. As the divine King, his work is accomplished through wisdom and understanding (Prov. 3:19; Jer. 10:12; 51:15). This in itself leads to the immovability of what he has done and what he has promised in the Savior. God is intimately aware of everything in everyone's life because he upholds all of life moment by moment.

This means that the application of this truth of God's power establishing the earth and everything in it to abide is both horrifying and comforting. This is a horrifying doctrine for those who are not born again; *absolutely* horrifying.

God upholds every moment, every person in their fallen state in Adam, moment by moment. Jesus said of the betrayer, Judas, "it had been good for that man if he had not been born," (Matt. 26:24). It would have been better, knowing every moment, moment by moment, of Judas' wicked life, if such a wicked man was not born. All betrayers to Jesus Christ could be said of such. All rebels to God's holiness fall into this. It is horrifying to hear the Savior say this, that it would have been better for wicked men to not be born, than for God to continue to uphold them throughout their life, moment by moment, knowing all their sins, and then to damn them for their rebellion for all eternity and then uphold them continually for all eternity in eternal torment. Why? He knows their thoughts, he upholds them. He knows their actions, he upholds them. He knows why they get up in the morning, and they think the way they do, for themselves. He knows their sin, in every sin, in every moment, frame by frame so to speak, in every way not glorifying the Creator as they should. "And GOD saw that the wickedness of man was great in the earth, and that every imagination of the thoughts of his heart was only evil continually," (Gen. 6:5); he knows this about them; Gen. 6:5 takes on a *horrifying* turn in this doctrine. He sees because he preserves them moment by moment. He preserves all their rebellious actions, and all their wicked intents; whatever they want to do in whatever way they want to do it. He preserves them and knows them to their most sinful degree. They sin, but he upholds their constitution as a "person" while they rebel against him.

  And there will be a time when he no longer preserves their mortal bodies alive, and that when they come to judgment, they have no excuse before him, for they, immediately by sight, shall see the greatness of the Christ and his holiness, and his just judgment. They will know they have been preserved by his power to exist, and their rebellious natures must be rewarded by a just judgment. They were *law-less* in word and deed, and so their wage will be the second death. God knew this, and saw them in every moment of their whole life. In every thought, moment by moment, in every outward action, moment by moment. When they lied, lusted, killed, hated, were indifferent to his word and people, when they were loveless, when they were selfish, when they committed all kinds of atrocities against his holy law and nature, for the least sin is an infinite sin against his infinite nature, and they will be justly judged. And so, they will concur with the Christ, that justice must be done, and they will concur that hell will be just for them, though they will still hate him for it. This is horrifying for you who are not born again. If it is not horrifying, you have pushed God out of your thoughts as far as you can, hoping that ignorance will be bliss; but this is not the case because God has a perfect record, moment by moment of every vice and sin you have ever committed, and every intention, which was only wickedness, you have ever conceived.

It is a very horrifying thought that God has preserved you even to this day, for however long your life has been, to bring you to this point. Because you could have died at any moment, he could have stopped preserving life in your mortal body, and brought you instantly to the judgment an hour ago. What aneurism is being upheld and not bursting right now? What heart attack has not yet occurred, just a few more beats? What stroke can a man fend off? "...it is appointed unto men once to die, but after this the judgment," (Heb. 9:27). One's last breath here is their first breath there. But God is longsuffering, that you would come to this very moment, to consider this abiding truth about his abiding creation which shows his infinite power. He requires you to repent, and change your ways and follow him in his Son, to be redeemed by his cross; the preservation of creation shows forth his abiding power. His word tells you to live in the light of his countenance, rather than the rebellion of your wickedness. Atheists, and agnostics and deists and nominal Christians hate these kinds of words, as very *disagreeable*. That is equally horrifying for you who are left in that frame of mind, who find such words disagreeable, for that means God's Spirit has not yet changed you to see Christ's truth. You must bow the knee to the Christ, and call him Lord with all your heart, soul and mind, either now willingly, or at the judgment by being compelled by his glorious holiness, *which he will do to you*. Even the inanimate objects of the earth glorify the sovereignty and power of God, for the *earth abideth* as a testimony. Will you?

    This continuous creation and preservation of the earth is a comforting doctrine for those who are born again. God preserves things for you both in his outward working, and his inward working, as well as in his redemptive working for you as a believer. He does not do that for the good of the wicked. What does that mean for you when he orders everything for your good? "...all things work together for good to them that love God, to them who are the called according to his purpose," (Rom. 8:28). He never orders anything for your evil as an adopted child of the Father whom he's saved by grace. He orders everything for good and is intimately aware of everything frame by frame and moment by moment. What kind of attitude, then, should you have in his ordination of every moment of your life no matter what happens to you? When he continues and upholds you in your being. "O Lord, thy word is settled in heaven; thou hast established the earth, and it abideth," (Psalm 119:89–90) is a great comfort to the soul. When he makes provisions of things needful for your preservation. "The eyes of all wait upon thee, and thou givest them their meat in due season. Thou openest Thine hand, and satisfiest the desire of every living thing," (Psalm 145:15-16). He has created you, redeemed you, and made himself known to you; he does not do that for the rebels. He has, in his nature and essential attributes, communicated himself to you.

That God's external works all serve for this use and work in you for the effect that you may understand your dependence on him for everything, in everything, everywhere, even moment by moment. The psalmist having professed that he knows the Lord to be great and that he is the only true God above all gods, that is, who has all the essential properties of the true God, he proves it by and from his works, and shows the means by which he knows it. Is it not, "the heavens that declare the glory of God, and the firmament sheweth his handy work," to you (Psalm 19:1)? Is it not that, Rom. 1:20, "The visible things of God are seen from the creation of the world,

Chapter 3: God's Governing Providence Over the World

clearly being understood by the things which were made: Even his divine Power and God-head." So for you born again believers, the works of God's actual providence in governing and upholding the world, and in moving the heavens and the stars in order, show forth his infinite wisdom and celestial glory; that his promises in Christ are true to you; they testify to the word as true. Is it no wonder why Christ, time and time again references the world to help you understand his works? Does he not tell you to consider the ant, and the lilies of the field, the fish of the deep, the great animals of creation, and the sky, the trees, the mountains, things in daily life, all through Scripture? Why does he do that?

And yet, does it stop there for you? His overthrowing of his enemies and the persecutors of his church, as in the flood of Noah, and in the drowning of Pharaoh and his army show forth his abundant redeeming power. His giving of Christ his Son as your Redeemer profusely testifies that his infinite goodness and bounty is available to you and he desires to make it more known to you. God upheld you in your sin; when you were sinning against him, he still upheld you in that. He upheld you in your conversion, when you were created as a new creature. He upholds you by the power of his Spirit. When you sinned the last time, not long ago, he upheld you in that too. He wants you to place in your mind that he is intimately aware of everything you do, and everything you are, moment by moment, frame by frame; and that you live in service to him, as one forgiven and required to be holy. God took every sin that you had or ever will have, and punished the Lord Jesus Christ in his work of redemption showing forth his infinite justice, and his infinite mercy, pardoning penitent believers by Christ's satisfaction, and he knew what they all were, and what they are going to be in Christ, because every moment he upholds you in your being. What you did, what you do, what you will do, he is aware of it all, for every moment he upholds your being, and he is not constrained by time as you are. He is not surprised by your sin. Do you then see the implications of this and how far reaching it is in his wonderful providences to make good come out of the evil of affliction, or good come out of a frowning providence, or good simply be good for you? Does he not show you in his word, his faithfulness in freely giving and communicating to you his infinite mercy and free grace, moment by moment? By the power of the Spirit, the Scriptures testify constantly in our own consciences witnessing our daily sense and experience of this truth. That the continuance of the earth and everything created gives witness of the abiding eternality of God's faithful word in his redeeming power. The question becomes whether you are sensitive to its reality; praying for the ability to be sensitive to the Spirit takes on a whole new meaning in this, doesn't it?

    In our redemption and the application of it we see demonstrated, quite clearly, the Trinity of Persons in one God, who creates, preserves and saves in his inward will and outward work. And while we in these things, as in a mirror, behold the glory of God with open face (the veil of ignorance being removed) we are changed into the same image from glory to glory, and so come to have communion with God, and the fruition of him, (2 Cor. 3:18), in Christ Jesus and his abiding power of redemption, for God creates his people frame by frame to be made more like Christ. Of which he shall lose none that the Father has given him; the Father has not given him all men. More light means more of the image will be seen in the way of his glory as he continually sustains you. You see then, that creation has linked to it, all God's purposes, which in turn, sets before us the utmost end of all God's outward works, which is his glory in redeeming his people. The eternal blessedness of the elect, by the communion, vision and fruition of God in all his glorious attributes, as wisdom, power, goodness, mercy, justice, and the rest. The text of the Psalmist itself shows this truth to you clearly, all God's works proceed from his good will and pleasure to the good of his people. George Walker, a Westminster Divine, said, "For the good pleasure and will of God consists chiefly and principally in willing that his elect shall be brought to perfect communion of himself and of his glory for their eternal happiness."[12] That is why the Psalmist says what he does. Creation visibly testifies to his eternal word and gives a context to that word and a place where

---

[12] George Walker, *God Made Visible in His Works*, (London: G.M., 1641), 10.

you experience his redeeming hand; it abides by God's power and for his glory.

Whatever God wills according to his good pleasure, and is pleased to do so, even in upholding an apple tree, is necessarily aimed at his glory first, and the blessedness of his elect by seeing his glory in such things second; but what a happy consequence that is.

All God's outward works proceeding from God's good pleasure in this tend to this end. All things work together for good to them that love God ... and what? ... and are the called according to his purpose (Romans 8:28). All things, which include, your world, your life, your death, all things present for you, and all things to come. Sickness, prosperity, affliction, blessing, creation, down to the very apples you pick off the apple tree to eat, show forth his glory, for your good, and demonstrate his faithfulness in creation; he does not do that for those who are not born again. Such things give testimony, they bear witness, to his faithful word. They give testimony to his power. They give testimony to you where you see the reality of the word of God working out in your daily life moment by moment, so that you can trust him more; for his word is settled in heaven, and his promises are perpetual and unalterable to his people. All things are Christ's, and Christ is God's, (Col. 1:16), and all such things are given to you his people as gifts. All things visible and invisible were created by Christ, for him, that they might serve him for the salvation of his elect, and for this end and purpose angels, principalities and powers are said to be made subject to Christ, (1 Peter 3:22).

What is your response, then, to your Creator, and his abiding faithfulness to continue your existence in the world? Are you faithfully subject to him? Continuous creation and preservation are hinges in the psalm, showing the abiding and enduring nature of God's settled word and unchangeable promises to you. And why is this testimony so important to the psalmist? For God's settled word. For his faithfulness. For the abiding earth that is upheld by God's power. He says this next, "They continue this day according to thine ordinances: for all are thy servants," (Psalm 119:91), which we will consider in the next chapter.

Chapter 4: All Things Serve God at God's Pleasure

"They continue this day according to thine ordinances: for all are thy servants," (Psalm 119:91).

God's sovereign decrees are *universal* and *comprehensive*. His decree includes *whatsoever comes to pass* in the world, whether it is in the physical world, as it pertains to creation, or in the moral realm, whether it is good or evil; it pertains to the spiritual realm as well as the physical.

God's decrees include everything; God orders, by his will, all things, though many times they may not be known or prophetically revealed; however, there *are* many decrees revealed in his word, such as, the good actions of men, Eph. 2:10 "For we are his workmanship, created in Christ Jesus unto good works, which God hath before ordained that we should walk in them," (Eph. 2:10). The wicked acts of men, Acts 2:23, "Him, being delivered by the determinate counsel and foreknowledge of God, ye have taken, and by wicked hands have crucified and slain," (Acts 2:23). All events are under his governance, even things that occur in the world, like some national and country-wide political direction, prosperity or even famine. "But as for you, ye thought evil against me; but God meant it unto good, to bring to pass, as it is this day, to save much people alive," (Gen. 50:20). The means of those events as well as the end of those events are ordained by God ... as it is in this verse of Psalm 119, they are his *servants*.

What does it mean when it says "they continue this day"? It concerns creation, everything God has made as it pertains to "thou hast established the earth, and it abideth," (Psalm 119:90). The psalmist lives on the earth; it continues because God has created it and upholds it, sustaining it moment by moment, frame by frame in its existence by infinite power. Such creating power not only created the earth and all its inhabitants, but has created in such a way as that all of creation "stands" or "endures" because God providentially watches over every part of his creation, and governs everything in every corner, in every hidden cave, into the very depths of the human heart. Men tend to gloss over this, that God's general providence is generally considered in a *general* way: he upholds things, in fact, he upholds *all of* creation. He knows the exact measure of every grain of sand on the beach in CA to every tip or point of each leaf of every tree in TN. He knows how those computations change as the wind blows, or a foot disturbs the sand on the beach. Everything is under his providence, and there is not a bird that falls from the nest, or dies, without *your heavenly Father's watchful eye over it*; he has an eye to everything. Such things continue to exist, as they are upheld by God's continuous act of creating them, upholding them, and beholding them. They exist because of God's divine decrees, the judgments of his will as they concern everything. He speaks his decrees that set even minuscule things down like the sand of the seashore. "...which have placed the sand for the bound of the sea by a perpetual decree, that it cannot pass it," (Jer. 5:22). Little things he governs. Or he has decreed the movements of the heavenly bodies, like the stars and sun and planets and such. God "commandeth the sun, ... and sealeth up the stars," (Job. 9:7).

God directs all things after the counsel of his will. Why do such things occur even as it pertains to creation? "...for all are thy servants." All things serve him, all things are for his glory first and foremost. God's laws are fixed for the government of all creatures and things, and God's power of providence acts in relation to execution of the laws of their creation. Providence itself is a servant to God's eternal counsel and purpose in all things. In fact, all things are in *service* to him. God has established "all things for ever and ever: he hath made a decree which shall not pass," (Psalm 148:6). Is this *some* things ... or *all* things? Do Christian believers believe, really, *all* things are his servants? Do they live that way before him? The psalmist testified to this. By his decrees and judgments, plants grow, animals live and die, and they live according to the laws that apply to them, as God has so ordered. In some measure, from this verse, it is seen that it is a forced, or coerced government for those things, as things occur according to their nature and kind *by his will*. The sun rises, because that is what

Chapter 4: All Things Serve God at God's Pleasure

the sun does. That is the way God has set it. Animals build houses for their young, and birds create nests because they are programmed that way. That is the way God has set them. Rocks sit in place, unless the earth shakes and moves them because gravity causes them to do so. But they are all sustained by God, and ordered according to his will. It is a set service that God has put in place for irrational creatures. All these things keep their station, because they exist to serve the living God.

What of rational creatures, of men, and angels, and devils? What does the word say but that, "all are thy servants."

Doctrine: All created things serve God at God's pleasure. "In the beginning God created the heaven and the earth," (Gen. 1:1). From the very beginning, God is depicted as determining all things. It is interesting to me that the most despised doctrine in the history of the Christian church by professing Christians is set down immediately, and assumed to be true in the first verses of the Bible. God is *sovereign*, as he *is* Supreme power and even is *Supreme freedom* to do whatsoever he pleases with all things, for all are his servants. No one counsels God as to how he should be, what he should do or how he should act; but the greater portion of Christianity *hates* that he is this way. They want a voice. Sovereignty is fundamentally the supremacy of God, the kingship of God, and the godhood of God in action over and against their voice. The *sovereignty* of the God of Scripture is absolute, irresistible, and infinite in power.

It is stated this way from the outset for the psalmist, that in the beginning God created everything, and all are his servants, everything created serves him in some capacity as he ordains, because he is sovereign.

God is called the Most High God (the *sovereign God*), because all things are *beneath* him and serve *him*. He is the great King, he is the most High God, Genesis 14:18–20 says, "Then Melchizedek king of Salem brought out bread and wine; he was the priest of God Most High. And he blessed him and said: "Blessed be Abram of God Most High, Possessor of heaven and earth; And blessed be God Most High, Who has delivered your enemies into your hand." And he gave him a tithe of all." Oversimplifying it, *El Elyon* in Hebrew means *God Most High*. The word "most high" is often used of the Davidic king exalted above all other monarchs; and of the spiritual David, the Righteous Branch that will come as God Most high with the sure mercies of David, with the eternal covenant of the Trinity to bless men. Everywhere in Scripture God is seen as supreme, high and lofty and lifted up, whether in covenant or creation. God is the sovereign God who is above all "gods." Melchizedek says it three times in that chapter. Interestingly, he uses the triplet idea to emphasize the nature of God; and that is no mistake from his lips. He is a thoughtful and good priest of God, who knows his God as the high and lofty one, the Father, the Son and the Spirit. This is because all are his servants, including Melchizedek.

Chapter 4: All Things Serve God at God's Pleasure

One of the most devestating acts of God in the beginning times of the world, was the flood. God created men, then, in his decree, he had planned to wipe wicked men from the face of the earth, and so God sovereignly enacted the flood, or the destruction of all mankind which he had made. The psalms are filled with images of God sitting enthroned over the flood directing its course, because all are his servants... But this, then enacts another dimension to this, in that, all things serve at God's pleasure. All things serve God, because all are his servants, and all serve him at his pleasure in the way he so determines. All things are in service to God at God's pleasure. God can create and destroy as he sees fit. God sets the time of people's lives. "And the LORD said, My spirit shall not always strive with man, for that he also is flesh: yet his days shall be an hundred and twenty years," (Gen. 6:3). Everyone has one life to live. In this case God said that there would be 120 years before the ark was completed and the world destroyed. Once Noah and his family climbed aboard the ark, the world would be extinguished due to their wickedness and iniquity; God determined that he would destroy it. Everyone has one life, but God determines its length and use in service to his glory. A life might be one day, or three days. A life might be 120 years, or 65 years, or 20 years. Genesis 6:17 says, "And behold, I Myself am bringing floodwaters on the earth, to destroy from under heaven all flesh in which is the breath of life; everything that is on the earth shall die." *All things* serve the God of heaven, and he determines all things for his pleasure. God brought the flood, because the waters serve him like an army, and after the flood had come, and after a certain number of days, the waters receded, because *they* serve him at his pleasure. Genesis 8:1 says, "Then God remembered Noah, and every living thing, and all the animals that were with him in the ark. And God made a wind to pass over the earth, and the waters subsided." The waters and the wind serve him, at his pleasure, because *all* are his servants. The waters and the wind have no qualms at destroying men's lives, or bringing life, to do whatever serves God as God's will, his pleasure, determines. In contrast to the counter culture of our day, even the use of language and ideas are all in service to God. God confused human language and dispersed the nations in Genesis 11:7, "Come, let Us go down and there confuse their language, that they may not understand one another's speech." This is a particularly amazing verse. It is closely related to the doctrine of God's continuous creation of all things, including the learning capacities of men and what he may plant in a moment, in their minds, or change, or add. These builders desired to do the opposite of what God had commanded. They did not want to fulfill the cultural mandate to go forth and multiply. They thought they were in service to themselves; they were greatly mistaken. God had commanded that they go across all the earth and multiply. Instead, they gathered together in one place and wanted to reach up to the heavens by building a tower in order to increase their fame. The human race would not, then, fulfill the cultural mandate as God set down, to have dominion over the earth. So God confused their language. They all spoke a specific language, but God changed it. The minds of men are in service to God. Not only did God *remove* the ability to understand their own language (think that through), but implanted, in their mind, the *ability* to communicate with a new language (think that through and tell me where man's "free will" begins and ends in such a sovereign act!). Men serve God, because all things serve God at his pleasure, without violating their will.

Time is in service to God. God commanded and issued time itself, which means that God has the ability to control the path of time and its outcome to bring those things to pass. To Abraham he said, Genesis 15:5 says, "Then He brought him outside and said, "Look now toward heaven, and count the stars if you are able to number them." And He said to him, "So shall your descendants be." Time serves God, and in the course of time prophecies come and are fulfilled, because time is decreed and set by God.

The land is in service to God. God promised the land of Canaan to his people which shows, he commands the boundaries of the land, Genesis 12:1, "Now the LORD had said to Abram: "Get out of your country, From your family And from your father's house, To a land that I will show you." It is his land to do with what he wills; he owns the world, the universe in its entirety. Genesis 17:8, "Also I give to you and your descendants after you the land in which you are a stranger, all the land of Canaan, as an everlasting possession; and I will be their God." God will give the land to whomever he wants because the land serves him, at his pleasure; he has set the bounds of where men live, and where men die.

All kinds of powers serve God at his pleasure. God sets up people in political power. Genesis 41:38 says, "And Pharaoh said to his servants, "Can we find such a one as this, a man in whom is the Spirit of God?" God rules, Pharaoh bows to that rule. And Joseph says of this act, Genesis 50:20, "But as for you, you meant evil against me; but God meant it for good, in order to bring it about as it is this day, to save many people alive," Pharaoh said it, but God determined it. The brothers sold Joseph into slavery; but out of that evil God uses secular and political power to place him highest in the land only second to Pharaoh. Because political power is in God's hands to serve him. (Hold *Joseph* in your mind for a moment).

The dreams of men serve God at God's pleasure. God summons and controls the very dreams dreamt at the time men sleep. A vision with Abram (Gen. 15:1); a dream of a ladder with Jacob (Gen. 28:12); Laban in his dream (Gen. 31:34). In Genesis 40:8 it says, "And they said to him, "We each have had a dream, and there is no interpreter of it." So Joseph said to them, "Do not interpretations belong to God? Tell them to me, please." Dreams are in service to God at his pleasure.

Heavenly bodies, meteors and comets and things that fall from the sky, serve God and are at God's pleasure, at just the right time he so desires it. God destroyed Sodom, by, a fiery meteor from the heavens, with a destructive power of thousands of nuclear bombs. Genesis 19:24–25, "Then the LORD rained brimstone and fire on Sodom and Gomorrah, from the LORD out of the heavens. So he overthrew those cities, all the plain, all the inhabitants of the cities, and what grew on the ground." God destroyed the Sodomites by a sulfuric meteor. Such a meteor, which impacted in the religion can be seen as completely obliterating everything, even by archeological standards today. Meteors and comets and heavenly bodies like the sun and moon, serve God at his pleasure; he can call them down at any moment for his purposes.

Sickness and disease and famine and pestilence serve God at his pleasure. God designates the physical infirmities men bear including leprosy, cancer and any disease, like covid. Genesis 32:25 states, "Now when he saw that he did not prevail against him, he touched the socket of his hip; and the socket of Jacob's hip was out of joint as he wrestled with him." Jacob's hip was never the same. It remained maimed for the rest of his life because *God* decided to do that.

Infirmity is at God's will. "When ye be come into the land of Canaan, which I give to you for a possession, and I put the plague of leprosy in a house of the land of your possession;" (Lev. 14:34). He controls leprosy. "The LORD shall make the pestilence cleave unto thee, until he have consumed thee from off the land, whither thou goest to possess it," (Deut. 28:21). The *coronavirus* serves God at God's pleasure. Vaccines may be a help, but are not the first answer. "Cursed be the man that trusteth in man, and maketh flesh his arm, and whose heart departeth from the LORD," (Jer. 17:5). The first answer to such as God has laid out is repentance; which the church today has not done, which is why the virus is still around, and now the delta strain is becoming a problem. Such diseases serve at God's pleasure. Such quick mutations of disease serve him at his pleasure.

Nations serve God at God's pleasure. "For thus saith the LORD of hosts, the God of Israel; I have put a yoke of iron upon the neck of all these nations, that they may serve Nebuchadnezzar king of Babylon; and they shall serve him: and I have given him the beasts of the field also," (Jer. 28:14). A nation's economy serves God, at God's pleasure and judgment, right down to the beasts. He brings famines and calamities if he desires, if the people are stiff-necked; or prosperity if it suits the cause. "And your strength shall be spent in vain: for your land shall not yield her increase, neither shall the trees of the land yield their fruits. And if ye walk contrary unto me, and will not hearken unto me; I will bring seven times more plagues upon you according to your sins,"

(Lev. 26:20-21). Whole nations bow and serve God at his pleasure, even if they are unaware that they do so.

Sin serves God at God's pleasure. Genesis 20:6 says, "And God said to him in a dream, "Yes, I know that you did this in the integrity of your heart. For I also withheld you from sinning against Me; therefore I did not let you touch her." In this case, God sovereignly held back Abimelech from touching Sarah and sinning. God did that, for sin or restraining sin will serve to God's glory. In this, *the devil* serves God at God's pleasure, as do all wicked spirits, unclean spirits or fallen angels. And the LORD said, Who shall entice Ahab king of Israel, that he may go up and fall at Ramoth Gilead? And one spake saying after this manner, and another saying after that manner. Then there came out a spirit, and stood before the LORD, and said, I will entice him. And the LORD said unto him, Wherewith? And he said, I will go out, and be a lying spirit in the mouth of all his prophets. And the LORD said, Thou shalt entice him, and thou shalt also prevail: go out, and do even so," (2 Chron. 18:19-21). The devils serve God at God's pleasure. They can do nothing without his permission. "So the devils besought him, saying, If thou cast us out, suffer us to go away into the herd of swine. And he said unto them, Go," (Matt. 8:31-32). They plead to the Christ for his approval. "And the LORD said unto Satan, Behold, all that he hath is in thy power; only upon himself put not forth thine hand. So Satan went forth from the presence of the LORD", (Job 1:12). They all serve God's will at his sovereign pleasure.

Wicked men serve God at God's pleasure. "The LORD hath made all things for himself: yea, even the wicked for the day of evil," (Prov. 16:4). There are a great many professing Christians that do not like that God is that much of a God; they find it acceptable that *devils* are at his pleasure, but don't like the idea that wicked *men* are as well. They would rather not have God so powerful. They would rather have a tiny God, a manageable God to their own liking. "And truly the Son of man goeth, as it was determined: but woe unto that man by whom he is betrayed!" (Luke 22:22). Even to the death of the Savior, wicked men do what God ordains of them, which in this case, was to crucify the Christ "Him, being delivered by the determinate counsel and foreknowledge of God, ye have taken, and by wicked hands have crucified and slain," (Acts 2:23). "For to do whatsoever thy hand and thy counsel determined before to be done," (Acts 4:28).

I told you to keep in mind Joseph. He was made second in command to Pharaoh, how? The evils of men are ordered by the wise providence of God to his good purposes, because all are his servants. Joseph's brother's evil, the evil of the traders in buying him, the evil of a false accusation of Potiphar's wife and his jailing; God sent Joseph for good, for the preservation of God's people in Jacob's family. In this way, we look at the providence of God in ruling the actions of wicked men for Joseph's good, for the people's safety, because all are his servants. What does it mean to serve God at God's pleasure? "There are many devices in a man's heart; nevertheless the counsel of the LORD, that shall stand," (Prov. 19:21).

The 1647 Westminster Confession of Faith in 3:1 says, "God from all eternity did, by the most wise and holy counsel of his own will, freely and unchangeably ordain whatsoever comes to pass; yet so as thereby neither is God the author of sin, nor is violence offered to the will of the creatures, nor is the liberty or contingency of second causes taken away, but rather established." Why is this? "For of him, and through him, and to him, are all things: to whom be glory for ever. Amen," (Rom. 11:36). *Some* things? No, they continue this day according to thine ordinances: for *all* are thy servants.

All Christians, should, then, serve God's Christ at Christ's pleasure, and for his glory, without coercion. It is one thing to be created and forced to be what a thing is, whether a rock, or a tree, or a devil or a wicked man in sin, and do what those things do. Birds make nests. Rocks sit where they are due to gravity. Devils and wicked men rebel against God. But, wicked men and devils act wickedly being chained in darkness and sin, and yet God's uses *all* these things for his glory, for *all serve him*, they are coerced according to their nature. Even if they do not know it, or even if they do not acknowledge it, they serve his glory. But in Christ, the godly man is made to know God, and then is beckoned to do all they do in godly service to Christ, at Christ's pleasure, for Christ's glory, and yet for their good, without coercion. They are instructed as to what they ought to do, and then they must, utilizing the Spirit of Truth that prompts them, do what he says. He is the King to be served, with humility and zeal for his glory. They should render all service to Christ for Christ's pleasure. They should render all service to Christ for Christ's glory. They should render all service to Christ for their own good too. For all are thy servants, especially those who profess to serve him.

All things serve Christ at Christ's pleasure, and *that includes you*. What do we see in such a statement of the psalmist? All things serve the great King, they are all in subjection to him. All these things on earth that abide, that are ordered for the glory of God's power, concern you as well. It presses you to really consider the question, who do you serve? God, blessed forever, has an absolute power and right of dominion over all his creatures, to dispose and determine them as seems good to him, and that includes everything in your life. Every single thing. Do you see it that way? There can be but one infinite King; for such a being fills heaven and earth; and so there is no place or room for another of equal power or glory; he has not created you with that title, or power, or position. You are a servant. There can be but one omnipotent King; for he that is such, has all others under his feet, for they serve him, at his pleasure, according to his will. There can be but one Supreme

King, who has all other beings and things, rational or irrational, serve at his pleasure. It is true that power may reside in many people, as in presidential cabinets, monarchies and commonwealths, countries and such. But, there can be but one *First Cause*, from which all beings derive their origin; "of whom, and for whom, are all things."

Let's take a moment to briefly apply the idea of service to the pleasure of King Jesus to our own Christian walk and life. The Scriptures everywhere attest to God's absolute dominion of you in everything, even things you forget to take notice of. You often forget that God numbers all your hairs. You did not think about that yesterday. You forget that he has a special eye to the marrow of your bones. You were not considering that this past week, how the inside of your bones worked. You give no mind to the blood, arteries and veins inside your body day by day. You don't think about oxygen levels in your home. You don't consider whether the seats you sit on will hold you up or not, generally speaking. You might say, *what do things like that have to do with anything, they are just things that continue to occur day by day?* Such things continue this day according to Christ's ordinances: for all are his servants. He commands hairs, and arteries, and oxygen, and gravity. You might say, "prove it! Does Scripture bear that out in relation to me?" Assuredly it does. "But the very hairs of your head are all numbered," (Matt. 10:30). Jesus desires you to take notice of things he has instructed you on, including your hairs. *Marrow?* you say? Of course, the marrow of your bones. "Be not wise in thine own eyes: fear the LORD, and depart from evil. It shall be health to thy navel, and marrow to thy bones," (Prov. 3:7-8). Even your blood has a position of notice to God, "...the voice of thy brother's blood crieth unto me from the ground," (Gen. 4:10), when Abel's was spilt. And what of your breath, and breathing, the very act of breathing day in and day out, "Thou hidest thy face, they are troubled: thou takest away their breath, they die, and return to their dust," (Psalm 104:29). God orders *breaths*; even *breaths* serve him at his pleasure, day by day. "They continue this day according to thine ordinances: for all are thy servants," (Psalm 119:91), including gravity. "...he maketh his sun to rise on the evil and on the good, and sendeth rain on the just and on the unjust," (Matt. 5:45). Gravity is very much involved in sunrises and rain showers; they serve God at God's pleasure. Christ calls things into being, upholds them by the power of his word, and works all things for his own glory in your life. Psalm 135:5-6, "For I know that the LORD is great, and our Lord is above all gods. Whatever the LORD pleases he does, in heaven and in earth, in the seas and in all deep places." Is that Ok? Are you *okay* with the Lord doing whatever he does, whatever is his pleasure? The psalmist was; he was happy that all things are servants of the most high God. God's pleasure in his judgments, in this sense, is often very appalling to carnal man. Carnal men have no desire to be ruled by anything other than their own wills. They will never think of themselves as beings that can be disposed of by God's good pleasure if Christ desires. What a frightful phrase that is, "disposed of". They want to be masters of their own destiny. They do not like such language as, "God can dispose of me in any way he sees fit at any time according to his pleasure." They do not like such language that God has made all things for himself, even the wicked for the day of evil. But men's wills are *no* match for the will of the Creator and Sustainer of their being. Even with Pharaoh, Exodus 10:20, "But the LORD hardened Pharaoh's heart, and he did not let the children of Israel go." God so set the circumstances around Pharaoh that the only choice Pharaoh would make was according to God's pleasure – and so he was further hardened. Exodus 5:2, "And Pharaoh said, "Who is the LORD, that I should obey his voice to let Israel go? I do not know the LORD, nor will I let Israel go." God so ordered things around Pharaoh that he had no other choice than to choose to do what God decreed to ultimately come to pass. God utilized Pharaohs' rebellion to demonstrate his own glory; for Pharaoh serves at God's pleasure in this. He does the same with you, circumstance after circumstance, to see how you, as a servant, *serve* him at *his* pleasure when he brings all kinds of events into your life. Will you be patient? Humble? Loving? Kind? Faithful? Cynical? Complaining? Rough? Unloving?

You might give an objection. "If God is this sovereign, then man is not really free, man has no responsibility. We are all just puppets on a string, and the Bible is simply the record of a play already written and forced by the hand of God, where all things are his servants." But such an objection misses the idea that all things serve God's will and that God's judgments not only deal with the *end itself*, but also the *means* to the end, *as well as* the end. Answer this question honestly, *Do you feel like a puppet?* I've never spoken to one person who has ever said they feel like a puppet. Yet, the clothes that you have on today are exactly what God so ordered. But when you got dressed did you feel like you were being manipulated, someone pulling on your strings? God's judgments comprise all secondary causes. God ordains the means as well as the end, all his means are his servants, and they all serve at his pleasure. But the reason people give that kind of excuse to believing that all things serve God, at God's pleasure, is because God is *scary* in this way. Think about Pharaoh, Romans 9:17, "For the Scripture says to Pharaoh, "For this very purpose I have raised you up, that I may show My power in you, and that My name may be declared in all the earth." Millions of people in history have miscarried their souls on not believing the Christ of Scripture; they speak like Pharaoh, "I know not the Lord". It's scary to think that God sees even those who miscarry into hell as those that serve him at his pleasure. God says, Psalm 46:10, "Be still, and know that I am God." Literally, the Hebrew is, *shut your mouth*. "We don't say shut up in this house," a mother may say. God says shut up, be

Chapter 4: All Things Serve God at God's Pleasure

disheartened to silence, literally, and "know I am God," for all things *serve me* at my pleasure. If we find fault with God's government, we virtually suppose ourselves fit to be God's counselors. Are *you* his counselor? We know better than he does when we complain about circumstances or simply don't like what he has ordained for us. But God says, Job 41:11, "Whatsoever is under the whole heaven is mine." *All things* serve at his pleasure.[13]

As Christ is God, all things are his own, and he has a right to dispose of them according to his own pleasure. All things are his, for all are his servants, and serve at his pleasure, his glory and honor and power. But there is a sweet side to this; it's not all fire and brimstone. All things in service to Christ, should be sweet for you as a Christian. God's power in this is only sweet as a result of Jesus Christ. It is impossible for us to look at all things in God's service, with comfort of any

---

[13] Free will, in this, as the contemporary church believes today, is a *myth*. Adam had a changeable will that had not sinned when he was first created. In this he was *perfect*, but *changeable*. He was the only one (along with Eve) that could go *either way. Shall I choose good, or shall I choose evil? Shall I choose to heed God's commands, or shall I disobey God's commands?* Then, after the fall, men become "free moral agents." This is a fancy way of saying, *they do what their hearts desire, freely*. And they do. The problem is that they are not neutral, and cannot, like Adam, go either way. They freely choose evil, and do nothing but evil. Read Genesis 6:5 again. Men are wicked, evil, fallen and dead in sin. They *only* choose to do evil. If God changes their heart, (John 3:3-5), and regenerates them (saves them), then they have the ability, again, to choose to do good or evil. But God's finger is on all they do, and he orders circumstances that they would accomplish his will in his way, even when he orders that sin will be used sinlessly.

kind without Christ the Mediator, who shows us that we who believe in God by faith serve him with a special service that is not merely *coerced*. Comfort is where this leads to. God is in control and all things serve him at his pleasure. There is nothing outside of his power. Piling up of bills; too many expenses, not enough money. Difficult work situations, or the lack thereof. School situations, studies, tests, hard classes. Diseases of any kind, surgeries and such. Old age and the loss of mobility; all health issues. Even prosperity and times of ease. Pick *anything*, and that little word is so condemning against all thoughts contrary to this truth. What word, but the word "all." *All* are your servants, *all* things serve at his pleasure. The word *all* is a universal term. When the Christian with cancer is undergoing treatment, *all is all*, cancer is part of *all*. When finances for the Christian seem bleak, *all is all*. When a loved one dies, *all is all*. When wars break out, *all is all*. When time seems to fly by so quickly and moments and events and opportunities and growth in grace are lost to time, *all is all*. When one can no longer run, because their legs are now crippled, *all is all*. When one's body does not work as it used to in youth, *all is all*. When one person has more wealth than another, *all is all*. God's godhood, in some ways and at some level, ought to have a dimension of being exceedingly comforting to us, though, as much as being *scary* to us. Maybe God is scary to you in some respects, and ought to be in other respects. Your house, your job, your finances, your intellect, your degree of talent, the boundaries of your home and where you live, your soul, everything serves God at God's pleasure whether you acknowledge this or not; but for his children he desires you to acknowledge it by the way you think, feel and act. He doesn't look to gain *a little* glory from you, but rather he desires you to acknowledge him in *all* his glory in every area of your life that he has decreed in his settled word in heaven; and to serve him accordingly.

But it is impossible to think sweetly of God's power in this way, and his governing without *Christ's mediation.* It can only be a matter of terror and amazement to sinners without Christ to hear such things. They try to suppress the truth of this in their thoughts. Many Christians even try putting such ideas out of their thoughts. Sovereignty and providence in this psalm are not the popular view. But nothing about God, or what is pleasing to God, can be sweet to you without Jesus, in and through Christ. Nothing in God is comfortable to men or for their eternal good, but as it comes to them through Christ. Imperfect men and women who do not have the blood of the Savior covering them are *not* pleasing to God, though they serve at his pleasure in whatever way he will use them for his glory. God sees them as, "children of wrath," fallen in Adam. And there they meet with him, at the judgment, in Adam's sin, and aggravated in their situation by their own naughtiness. Or they will find Christ here while they live, for their eternal good, in eternal salvation if they believe what God says and the Spirit spiritually persuades them to the truth. And the concept of all things serving God becomes sweeter by seeing this service though the work of Christ. That it is all for good.

We are dependent on God in the great matter of the eternal salvation of our souls, and those who desire to serve at God's good pleasure, in all the ways that word "good" might be thought of in Jesus Christ, serve God acceptably with reverence and godly fear. "Present your bodies a living sacrifice, holy, acceptable unto God, which is your reasonable service," (Rom. 12:1). For the Christian, Christ is the *loveliest* thought that can be conceived, and they are happy to serve him at his pleasure. They think, with the spouse, in Song of Solomon 5:16, "Yes, he is altogether lovely," even when we consider that all things serve him, and all things are for him, to his glory; whatever befalls us. God saves and blesses his people in Christ, and that abundantly. You have to look at your service to God through Christ and his will, then you will see it is very sweet, because in that you bring Christ to everything you do for his glory, not for your own glory. This is what the Psalmist does, which is why, in just a few verses he will revel in God's rescue from affliction, he will revel in eternal election and the power of God's salvation. "I am yours, save me."

God expects you as his people to serve him daily, knowing full well that all are his servants, and serve at his pleasure; which includes your acknowledgement of this. God is in control, at any moment God could require our lives. He has set a day when our earthly breath will cease. We serve at his pleasure, for his pleasure, all our breaths are ordered by him. But all this is a very good thing, from our perspective. God orders such things for us and for our good, and we are then happy *in him*, looking forward to that entrance that shall be ministered unto us abundantly into the everlasting kingdom. Imagine if you were placed in control of your life? What would you first do if God said – *for 5 minutes I will give you complete sovereign control over your own life to affect any change that will afterwards remain permanent?* What would you do? Have the perfect body? Become instantly rich and debt free, greater than the accolades of Solomon in all his glory? Be free from any disease or ailment? Do you see how quickly such a thing would become *a genie in a bottle* of sorts? You would not be thinking first about *how God might be glorified in those acts, or how your sanctification in affliction may best glorify him because you serve at his pleasure.* You wouldn't choose to enter into the worst suffering for Christ's glory, you would not choose to enter into Christ's school of affliction for his glory; *that* would not be your wish. Your thoughts would be to deliver you from temporary suffering, or make this life better in some way. Not to exceed in holiness.

  We would have carnal thoughts if even a limited amount of power were placed in our hands. That's why we often like stories about genies in bottles, and three wishes; and *what would we wish for?* Would we wish for more *holiness,* would that be one of your wishes? Would we wish for more *heavenly mindedness?* James 4:15 is correct, instead you ought to say, "If the Lord wills, we shall live and do this or that," for all are his servants, and they all serve him at his pleasure. But we do not need three wishes or a genie in a bottle to know this. Romans 8:31 states, "What then shall we say to these things? If God is for us, who can be against us?" If you are a Christian, God is for you; in this way everything is sweet. School tests, employment difficulties, marriage problems, dry personal devotions, the mundane of everyday life, difficulty in daily living, – if God is for his people, then there is a treasury of blessings waiting to be poured out on his people at the right time and the right place, for they *all* serve at his pleasure, and you must merely tap into those things and use them in wisdom, use God's ordained means of grace and do not neglect them. But we are impatient, and we often break that least of commandments, "do not covet," for we are not very content, and often hurried and anxious; yet, *be anxious for nothing,* your Savior and King tells you. Our plan is often thought of as a better plan than God's plan; *I would be better if I had such and such, or could do such and such, or knew such and such.* We forget that we serve him, and we often find ourselves kicking against the goads. Or, even worse, becoming like the Stoic, and we go through life by simply biting our upper lip and enduring it; until we can't bite our lip anymore and we start lashing out, because we have been worn down by life; that is not abundant life. "...count it all joy when ye fall into divers temptations; knowing this, that the trying of your faith worketh patience. But let patience have her perfect work, that ye may be perfect and entire, wanting nothing," (James 1:2-4). Are you *bitter*, like Naomi? "Call me Mara," because she was pressed by God in the circumstances surrounding sin? Or are you virtuous and obedient and industrious as a servant of the most high as Ruth was?[14] How could we have any excuses to serve God at God's pleasure if God has so ordered all things in service to him for our good and his glory? The Almighty God of the universe has taken notice of us. And he saved us to give us everything in Christ for our good. And all things serve him, at his pleasure; and you must be on board with that if you desire to follow him; to deny self, and pick up your cross. And the psalmist tells us why he is so theologically well instructed in this, because the law was his delight, which rescued him from affliction, and this we will consider in the next chapter.

---

[14] See my work, *Practical Observations on the Book of Ruth*, for a detailed explanation of Naomi's difficulties.

Chapter 5: Immoderate Sorrows of the Sinking Soul Crushed by Delight in the Word

"Unless thy law had been my delights, I should then have perished in mine affliction," (Psalm 119:92).

The word "law" is sometimes used just of the Moral Law, (James 2:10); sometimes it is used for *all* that Moses wrote down (moral, ceremonial, and judicial law), (Gal. 3:33; Luke 24:44); sometimes it is used for the whole doctrine of God contained in the Scriptures of the Old Testament, and sometimes for *all* of Scripture. "But this people who knoweth not the law are cursed," (John 7:49).

The word "law" in this verse (v. 92), in the time of the psalmist, means all of Scripture written as far as the psalmist knew it. For the Christian today, this interpretation would include, then, *all* the Bible. "Unless thy law," [that is, *God's word*], had been my delights, I should have perished in mine affliction." The word "delights" is *sha'shua*, a plural word, intensive, meaning *enjoyments*, that which one takes pleasure in. If it were not his delights or enjoyments, he would have perished, literally, in his misery because he would have been indifferent to the word of God, or neglected the will of

Chapter 5: Immoderate Sorrows

God. His misery would have been overwhelming. Nothing would have decreased his worldly sorrow. There are many afflictions that the saints must endure. But, the word of God is the saints' delight and enjoyment to rescue them out of all afflictions, because it is so unbounded in its scope. It covers everything for life and godliness. Even the *ten commandments* do so as they are particularly considered covering all of the Christian walk.[15] The law of God or the word of God is the solution and answer against all misery, all perceived misery, all immoderate misery as well as justified affliction. It is true that God's people are exposed to many afflictions in God's good providence. How will they think about them? How do people perceive misery? The psalmist, in his situation, saw his as *misery*; this is a word more powerful than merely using a term like affliction or difficulty. It holds in it the connotations of something immoderately thought about, which is so overwhelming that they feel as though, their *perception* is so, that they will drown under it; that without relaxing in some way from it, they would be so overwhelmed that it would manage them instead of them managing it. David said elsewhere, "Save me, O God; for the waters are come in unto my soul. I sink in deep mire, where there is no standing: I am come into deep waters, where the floods overflow me," (Psalm 69:1-2). This is much the same idea. David had many troubles of all kinds and extents,

---

[15] See my work, *The Ten Commandments in the Life of the Christian*, for a detailed study of that topic.

but his reliance on the word, his delight in the word overcame any trouble by dispelling misery, so that he would not have an immoderate disposition. What does this word mean, *immoderate*, but excessive, extreme, intemperate, over-the-top, even uncontrolled? David had sorrows; Job had sorrows; Jesus had sorrows, in fact, he was *a man of sorrows*, (Isa. 53:3). But the word of God is so sustaining that immoderate sorrow will not overtake those who trust in what God says, even when they encounter worldly or spiritual miseries. God's intention in his word and through his word is to teach his children to know him and to trust in him, and to know themselves in light of the word, and to walk accordingly. Not merely to know God, as many professing Christians do, as heathen do, and *the devil* does; but to know and trust him, and *take him at his word*. And sometimes God will bring his saints right up to the very gates of hell itself, and to overwhelming afflictions, that they would learn not to trust in their own ways and thoughts, but have delight in God's ways and thoughts. What shall they do to throw off all anxiety? Shall they lie in a hammock in the backyard? Shall they take a vacation? Will a vacation *dispel* misery? Where shall they find such delight? The psalmist shows the Christian where they are to go to cast off any excessive sorrow they may have in their sinking soul.

    Doctrine: immoderate sorrows of the saint's sinking soul are crushed by delight in the word. What is *immoderate sorrow*? Immoderate sorrow is a kind of *murder* on the soul, it is, in fact, a sin against the sixth command.[16] The soul is wearied and weakened by excessive sorrow; it is made inoperable by it, it is in fact made *useless*. Instead of praying, there is complaint, and instead of believing God, there is murmuring. There is too much of the flesh in that. Andrew Gray said, "Is there not too much of the flesh in your immoderate sorrow? O remember! Satan loves to fish in muddied waters."[17] The Christian's life turns muddied by immoderate sorrow.

Immoderate sorrow can be classified as *worldly sorrow*. It is a sorrow that is housed in the fall, and in the curse, and after the *manner* of the world, which arises from some *love* of the *world*, some pleasure of the world, more than delight in God's word. When some trouble or affliction spoils the Christian spirit with discontentment, and makes it inwardly bitter against God's providence, then misery in this light, is full of sin, where the Christian ought to be humbled instead of annoyed. Such sorrow is to enlarge and swell up with a secret discontentment, to have hard thoughts of God, as if God had wronged the Christian in some way. It houses in it the attitude of Jonah, "Yea, I do well to be angry even unto death," (Jonah 4:9) when God killed the gourd giving him shade in the heat by the worm that gnawed it out. A vile temper coming up out of a bitter root; a very

---

[16] "Thou shalt not kill." (Exod. 20:13), also pertains to the soul, which includes soul-murder.
[17] Andrew Gray, eBook, *A Door Opening to Everlasting Life*, (Coconut Creek, FL: Puritan Publications, 2013) Objections, Treatise 2.

proud heart, one thrown wholly out of order, in confusion. Was this how Jonah *always* was? Or was he thrown off track here in an over-heated passion, in immoderate sorrow?

Immoderate sorrow is really substituting a delight in the word of God, with a delight on carnal things instead. When Jacob saw Joseph's coat of many colors covered in blood (thinking his son was dead), he was immoderately sorrowful. First, "And Jacob rent his clothes, and put sackcloth upon his loins, and mourned for his son many days," (Gen. 37:34); and that would not have been so bad...but listen to the next verse. "And all his sons and all his daughters rose up to comfort him; but he refused to be comforted; and he said, For I will go down into the grave unto my son mourning. Thus his father wept for him," (Gen. 37:35). William Bates said, Jacob, "abandoned himself to desperate sorrow, and continued mourning...this immoderate sorrow is a heathenish passion, suitable to their ignorance of the future happy state, but very unbecoming the complete assurance the gospel affords us."[18]

Let's consider a definition: *immoderate sorrow is an excessive affection on the temporary things of the world.* God deals with his children as a Father deals with his child. If the father sees his child corrected, he lessens the corrections. If the father sees his child stubborn, he will increase them. What misery is bound up in such

---

[18] William Bates, *The Whole Works of William Bates*, vol. 3, (Carlisle, PA: Soli Deo Gloria, 1990) 253.

immoderate sorrow? If the Christian murmurs against God, and they are immoderate in their sorrows, in their speech, in their life, it is the way to have them increased, not lessened.

How are people *immoderate* with sorrow? When a Christian loses his comfort in Christ because of excessive sorrow, his disposition becomes uncontrolled; his flesh takes over. When it affects personal and family devotions, there the household goes awry. When it affects church worship, there the church goes awry; it can become infectious. When it affects the witness one has in the world for God, it makes the Christian incapable and inadequate to act in the manner befitting a servant of Christ. He cripples his walk and becomes useless to the Kingdom; what do we hear of Jacob from the time of his sorrowing until the time of Joseph's revealing of himself, but *nothing*. It will affect the way the Christian hears God. Exodus 6:9, "Moses spake unto the children of Israel, but they hearkened not unto him, for anguish of spirit..." The people were so grieved at their bondage, "cruel bondage," that Moses, was cast off; they did not take solace in the word. If miseries of any kind climb up and into the heart, as to sit and settle there and steal away and interrupt hearing God's word, that is immoderate sorrow; a person is never changed by the word because it makes no impression on them because something else is ruling their heart. If a person will not be comforted by the word, or cannot be, sin is reigning, passion is reigning instead of patience.

When a Christian is interrupted in their private devotions, or is kept off of their private devotions because of worldly miseries, that is immoderate sorrow. Asaph said, "I remembered God, and was troubled: I complained, and my spirit was overwhelmed. Thou holdest mine eyes waking: I am so troubled that I cannot speak," (Psalm 77:3-4). What is this when a Christian cannot pray because of some worldly misery occurring, or cannot pray well, or is distracted in their spiritual disciplines? Cannot pray well, distracted in prayer, weak in prayer, negligent in prayer; and this may not be for a month or a week, but could be for years?

When a Christian cannot gain comfort from Jesus Christ, and all the mercies which are new every morning for the Christian are swallowed up, that is an immoderate sorrow that they have fallen into. "And Ahab came into his house heavy and displeased because of the word which Naboth the Jezreelite had spoken to him: for he had said, I will not give thee the inheritance of my fathers. And he laid him down upon his bed, and turned away his face, and would eat no bread," (1 Kings 21:4). He could not have what he wanted when he wanted it. And what did Ahab have but a kingdom, and yet, he was immoderately sorrowful over a vineyard he could not have. Sometimes Christians are *dejected in soul* over things of the world, and circumstances they wish they could be sovereign in, though they have much, because they *want* more. They are pressed in the winepress and instead of coming out sweet, they come out sour.

When misery presses the Christian to sin, that is immoderate sorrow. They act like Judas when they sin. "Then Judas, which had betrayed him, when he saw that he was condemned, repented himself, and brought again the thirty pieces of silver to the chief priests and elders, saying, I have sinned in that I have betrayed the innocent blood. And they said, What is that to us? see thou to that. And he cast down the pieces of silver in the temple, and departed, and went and hanged himself," (Matt. 27:3-5). He did not really repent. Instead, his immoderate sorrow turned to a worldly and devilish act of suicide. His immoderate sorrow, a false worldly sorrow, turned to a heinous act of sin. Immoderate worldly sorrow always turns to sin if left unchecked.

When a Christian cannot comfort another Christian because of the grief of their own troubles, they are immoderate; they are selfish in their talk. Life is all about them, all about their problems, all about their needs, their wants, "me, me, me," and they do not first look the welfare of others, where they are commanded to esteem others better than themselves. "Wherefore comfort one another," (1 Thess. 4:18), but they cannot do it. They are so preoccupied by their own immoderate thoughts of the world, that they sin in stealing from others the comfort they ought to bestow to them. This is where they practically think, for selfish reasons that their miseries are greater than all others. Lamentations

1:12, "come and see if there be any sorrow, any affliction like unto mine wherewith the Lord hath afflicted me." The objection comes, "You don't know how harshly I am being dealt this hand of cards, unless you are in my shoes," they say. In other words, *you haven't gone through what I have gone through, so don't lecture me about life, such and such.* Consider in this that immoderate sorrow is excessive, worldly sorrow.

Immoderate sorrow progresses sin and produces sin. When Christians have an immoderate affection to the world (or the things in the world), where they grieve over such, or are affected by such overwhelmingly as misery, they love the world too much. *I wish I had his money. I wish I had his life. I wish I had his things. I wish, I wish, I wish, me, me, me; I wish God were like a genie, a cosmic bell hop to do what I want him to do.* Christopher Love said, "Genesis 37:35 When Jacob supposed that his Joseph was slain, he so exceedingly mourned for him, that though all his sons and daughters rose up to comfort him, yet he refused to be comforted, and said. "I will go down into the grave unto my son mourning," (Genesis 37:35). And why did Jacob so mourn for him, but because he loved him, more than all the rest? It was his immoderate love to him that made him sorrow so immoderately, if your hearts are glued to the things of the world, you cannot part with them but with a great deal of vexation and sorrow."[19] Immoderate sorrow breaks the tenth commandment, as well as the sixth, *Thou shalt not covet*. It comes from a discontent murmuring of the hand of God's providence on their life; they *want* other things.

Immoderate sorrow shows the Christian's ignorance of God, and his ways. Such professing Christians are ignorant of the reality of spiritual things, and they act in a fleshly manner in carnal things. They are degenerated into distraction, because they do not pick up the remedies of the means of grace, and instead, wallow in their sorrow, which is sin. It is an irregularity and oddness from the rules of Christianity, because it argues immoderate despair and a lack of any hope; woe is me, and this providence on me.

There are warnings against having immoderate sorrow of this kind in Scripture. The opposite is, "...godly sorrow worketh repentance never to be repented of; but worldly sorrow causeth death," (2 Corinthians 7:10). There is a worldly sorrow and a fleshly sorrow different from a godly sorrow. Godly sorrow works a right spirit up before God, and causes the Christian to take hold of the means of grace. Fleshly sorrow works further misery, where people even feel justified in exercising themselves in it. Solomon says, "a sorrowful spirit drieth up the bones," (Proverbs 17:22). David says, "My life is spent with grief, and my years with sighing, my bones are consumed," (Psalm 31:10). Is the joy of the Lord one's

---

[19] Christopher Love, *A Christian's Directory*, eBook, (Coconut Creek, FL: Puritan Publications, 2012) 22.

strength or not? What does the Christian lack that he must run after the world for or be so attached to it? What makes him run to the world and fall in such love with temporary things, worldly things, that would cause his love for Christ to be eclipsed by such carnal thoughts? It will embitter Christians to be taken up with those thoughts, as Haman was taken up with the idea of being out done by Mordecai, as Esther 5 says, "yet all this availed him nothing so long as he saw Mordecai sitting at the king's gate," (Esther 5:13). It just stuck there, was a pricking under his skin; an *annoyance*. Will a Christian throw away all comfort, all mercies, all grace, to be embittered in soul by the world in their misery? Will they see it as acceptable to do it even for a time, and feel justified in it when they do it? Haman complains of losing prominence, that causes his immoderate sorrow, but does he, or any worldly person, complain of losing holiness? They should be more occupied in those thoughts. Christians will complain of miseries and afflictions, but often do not complain of their sins and their lack of holiness. Where will they find a remedy in this immoderate sorrow that is attached to worldly thoughts and ideas?

Consider, divine comfort for all afflictions comes through the word of God. As the Christian's heart exercises itself in the promises of God, the promises work on the heart. David says, "Unless thy law had been my delights, I should then have perished in mine affliction." It is interesting for the word not to be merely delight, but translated delights. An intensive abundance of delights in the word. Faith sucks virtue from Jesus Christ, and that virtue is a comfort and quickening power found only in the word, by the spiritual persuasion of the Spirit of Truth. Psalm 119:81, "My soul fainteth for thy salvation, but I hope in thy word." Faith looking to Christ who is the word, will cause the Christian to gather up strength and hope in him. "Having therefore these promises, dearly beloved, let us cleanse ourselves from all filthiness of the flesh and spirit, perfecting holiness in the fear of God," (2 Cor. 7:1).

Worldly immoderate, discontenting dispositions are to be cleansed by the word; if they are believed. Christ sends the Spirit, and the Spirit by the word, through faith, transports the soul into the immovable support of his decrees, promises and word. What? Did you think the Spirit zaps the Christian while he is slothful and sluggish and is pitying their own nature in immoderate sorrow? No, he does not do that, which is why when Jacob was immoderate in his worldly sorrow and clung more to the world in an over-love of *his Joseph*, he was not helped by the Spirit. The Spirit did not zap him out of it. How long, how many *years* was he in it and how miserable was his house while he was so? It affected everything. Joseph was in Egypt many years and Jacob had no respite until he heard the news that Joseph was alive; Christians tend to think that such events are momentary, and will only last a short time, but for godly Jacob, it was for *decades*. It is by

Christ's grace, on the actions of the Christian's faith in him and apart from the world, for, "Unless thy law had been my delights, I should then have perished in mine afflictions."

I pose a question in this though, something to take and ponder, "Would the costliness of the word of God and the quality of true faith ever be known, unless God brought the Christian into afflictions? Are not afflictions often, if not always, the school of Christ? That is a very dangerous idea to ponder, because once the Christian realizes that the value and exercise of faith in testing occurs in the midst of affliction, they begin to sweat, "what will God bring them to be tested in?" What will he do to try them and test them in that way? How will he make to them the virtue of Christ sweet, and the comforts of another world their hope in affliction?

Christians want a *life of ease*, and they sin against Christ by questioning his sovereignty in their immoderate sorrow of the world when they don't get ease. There are no afflictions, no miseries, that can fall on a Christian but they have many promises of God's unchangeable word to settle themselves upon. They have grand comforts to support them in everything. This was the place the psalmist rested, otherwise, he would have perished in his affliction. The world indeed is a heavy weight, too burdensome for sinners to bear on their own shoulders. Has not Jesus Christ promised to always be with them? Does he not give gracious assistance, that he will never fail them? Are the afflictions of this world, are all the frowning providences, not worthy of the excellence that shall be revealed in him in another world? Where then is the Christian's strength but in the voice of the Shepherd to their soul? It is no wonder that in the word of God, the words of Christ's mouth to the soul, enables the Christian to accomplish all duties before God even amidst afflictions, that would have produced worldly and immoderate sorrow. "...his lips like lilies, dropping sweet smelling myrrh," (Song 5:13). "His mouth is most sweet: yea, he is altogether lovely," (Song 5:16). "Let him kiss me with the kisses of his mouth," (Song 1:2). The words of the mouth of the One altogether lovely are sweet, most sweet, like the sweet smell of the most fragrant flowers.

But do Christians, think this way to perform well and godly and holy in afflictions? This is the same thing as saying, do Christians know the Shepherd's voice in the word when afflictions come? "I am the good shepherd, and know my sheep, and am known of mine," (John 10:14); not known about, but known. There is the sweetness of intimacy in this, because they hear his voice *directing* their lives.

Jesus Christ, is the believer's Surety, and in his place, has fulfilled "all" for the believer, and all the promises of God tend to that end, all through the bible. God will accept Christ's perfect work and merit, as a cover for the Christian's imperfections, while he is tested and tried ... and even failing. But the Christian looks to the word of God to find that comfort in this. Will he delight in the word? If a wounded sinner would just take time to meditate on these things, the promises of God would fill him full of joy and comfort. *Unless thy law had been my delights.* The word is a delight to the psalmist, otherwise he would have perished; this is because the world is perishing, and immoderate sorrow cannot help.

Immoderate sorrow brings the Christian to a perishing misery and a worldly affliction. The word "perish" in this text, certainly means destroyed, and perish, and exterminated. But I saved this for this point, to say, that it also means and has ideas surrounding *going astray.* "Unless thy law had been my delights, I should then have perished in mine affliction." Unless the word of God guided me in just the right way, I would have been led astray by such immoderate sorrow in all my miseries that I would have been vulnerable, and aimless, and helpless and abandoned to the world. I would have been bleating like a wandering sheep in the wilderness of the world ready to be eaten by the mouth of the lion and crushed under the paw of the bear. The psalmist says he would have gone astray. Going astray is to perish, as it relates to the word of God. To miss Christ's voice calling to the soul to come back, to consider his love, to take his hand, to walk with him, to abide in the vine, to remain in his comfort, to use his means of grace. To be without the word in affliction is to perish. It is to be misguided. It is to be worldly. If the spiritual means of Christ are lost to an excessive overwhelming dissatisfaction to God's ordained direction in life, what is left but to listen to and pander over to the world in sin. And what good will that do any Christian?

As a born again believer, you can expel all immoderate sorrow by the power of the Spirit using the word of God. The sword of the Spirit *is the word of God*. Immoderate sorrows of your sinking soul are crushed by delight in the word. How well do you wield the word as a sword to cut down misery? When you are well-versed in the word, and you have made the rule of your life, to be guided and governed by it in all things, it will comfort you and guide you and dispel all immoderate affections and sorrows. The word of God is Christ, and Christ answers all temptations, for he is the remedy against any worldly friends, and all their reasonings for life. It will keep you from sinning. It will keep you from all kinds of devilish mischief. It serves to direct you in all conditions how to carry yourself in life and godliness, which is why Jonathan Edwards said you must have a right attitude when you do anything for God in this, "Whatever is done or suffered, yet if the heart is withheld from God, there is nothing really given to him."[20] And this is often the reason that sorrows continue for years for people like the Jacobs of the church. "Thy word is a lamp unto my feet, and a light unto my path...it giveth understanding to the simple," (Psalm 119:105, 130). Who

---

[20] Jonathan Edwards, *Charity and Its Fruits*, (Carlisle, PA: The Banner of Truth Trust, 2005) 57.

said that but our psalmist not but a few verses from now? Not a light at a distance, but a light for *each* individual step. You, as a Christian, *must* (emphasize *must*) not be about generalities in the word, but the fundamentals of those specific that will guide you for each step you take. Do not be sidetracked with quarrels and controversies of a second hand nature, as keyboard theologians often do all over the internet today. Be militant in your understanding of those fundamentals of religion that will ward off worldliness of all kinds, for if you are well versed in those, the word will guide you in all basic steps. It comforts you with its most gracious and most sweet promises if you know them. David said, "In the multitude of my thoughts within me thy comforts delight my soul," (Psalm 94:19). Does this sound familiar? When David was cast down with troubles and miseries on every side, so that he did not know what he should do, the word directed him into the sweet comfort of God's deliverance. Again, "Unless thy law had been my delight, I should then have perished in mine affliction," (Psalm 119:92). It drove him to the word, to the God of the word, to the Christ of the word which he believed in God's promises by faith, the sure mercies of David, to the covenant of the spiritual David, the Christ, "Yea, though I walk through the valley of the shadow of death, I will fear no evil: for thou art with me; thy rod and thy staff they comfort me," (Psalm 23:4). God with him? *Thou art with me*, speaks of the incarnation of the Christ to come; God *near* him. The rod and staff for

Chapter 5: Immoderate Sorrows

you are the word of God, especially the promises that are as a staff to lean on and trust, and the rod to break off the remnants of remaining sin.

Labor to have the word of God dwell in you richly (Col. 3:16), to be well-skilled and versed in it, that you may have it ready on all occasions to make use of it. Otherwise, by your indifference to that task, you show yourself to be just like people of the world, who go through life without the word, without its effectiveness in their life, and they are very afflicted. It is necessary for you to have comfort; Christ *the comforter* sends the *Comforter*; the Spirit who will teach you if you but open up the book. Without the word of God in use and exercised about you, all your graces wither; you will be like the frog in the pot of water being heated up slowly, and not even know such graces are withering. Thomas Manton said, "Faith is lean unless it be fed with meditation on the promises."[21] He quotes Psalm 119:92 as a proof to that. The more we study the height, and breadth, and depth of God's love in Christ, (Eph. 3:18-19), the more our hearts are brought into conformity to the Christ, melted and quickened to obedience.

You will never discern or be sensible of the work and power of Christ in your soul during times of affliction until you ponder them, and go over them again and again. Not but in a couple of verses, David says "I have more understanding than all my teachers, for thy

---

[21] Thomas Manton, *The Complete Works of Thomas Manton*, Volume 6 (London: James Nisbet & Co., 1872), 141.

testimonies are my meditation," (Psalm 119:99). Preachers can sermonize, and you can hear, but the thing that places the word of God in our hearts is *pondering* and daily *meditation*. And if you leave the service or church without any change, if you do not consider the sermons each day through the week, and work them into your soul, it is because the word has made no impression on you; and you will lose them; they will never take root. When times of afflictions arise, you will give yourself to your own thoughts, and you will give yourself to the world's way of dealing with problems which is by winging it. You will find life a wet blanket, and you will become a killjoy to yourself. What good is immoderate sorrow to you? Will it make your life better or worse? What is the foolishness of struggling and contending with God?

To have that kind of worldly sorrow about you, that discontentedness, that placing your affections on things that are temporary in hopes that they will alleviate you more than the word of God, is to be comfortless in all your troubles. You misuse Christ, and his words to you, by going astray in a course that way. John 14:1, "Let not your hearts be troubled; ye believe in God, believe also in me." He tells you outright, be anxious for nothing, and do not let your hearts be troubled. Immoderate sorrow in afflictions is not becoming of a servant of Jesus Christ. Your delights must not be from the world, there must be no delights arising from the pleasures merely of temporary sense, but out of the word of God.

How do we comfort ourselves in our sorrows and heartaches? God's comforts are gospel comforts, they are found there in the midst of promised tribulation in the world. We have the word which will make us trust God, and more confidently expect the wonderous performances of his promises in our life. His promises are both good and sure, for his word is unchangeable, and settled, forever in heaven, as we saw in the first part of this section of the psalm.

Do you weep in afflictions, in times of seemingly great difficulties and miseries? Scripture records, "But one of the elders said to me, "Do not weep. Behold, the Lion of the tribe of Judah, the Root of David, has prevailed to open the scroll and to loose its seven seals,"" (Rev 5:5). One of the elders informs John that there is hope. John is instructed *not* to weep; though there may be times of weeping and mourning. *He is not to have immoderate sorrow based on limited information.* He is not to weep because there is the Lion of the Tribe of Judah who is able to open the scroll, he is told. Only he who is holy as God is holy, to come to take the document out of the Father's hand, One born of the seed of the woman, in the lineage of David, the promised Messiah, can open the scroll, who is a near kinsman to his people. The One is the Lion, literally, of the race of the praised. He is called the Lion of the tribe of Judah, as Genesis describes what Jacob said in blessing his tribe before he died, his last faithful work after so many years of immoderate sorrow; Gen. 40:9, "Judah is a lion's whelp; from the prey, my son, thou art gone up: he stooped down, he couched as a lion, and as an old lion; who shall rouse him up?" Strength is ascribed to the Messiah from the lineage of David, and is heralded as a Lion. David's insignia or flag standard, according to the Jews, was a lion. Here we find the Messiah, Christ, who prevails. He has conquered. He has reigned victorious in all his work, meriting the favor of God for his people. This is the beloved Son in whom God is well pleased. He is the root of David. "Then it will come about in that day that the nations will resort to the root of Jesse, who will stand as a signal for the peoples; and His resting place will be glorious," (Isa. 11:10). The mercies of David were the mercies of the everlasting Covenant made through Christ. The *sure mercies* of David are found in the word which leads, not astray, but to comfort. The root or stability of the church is in and from him, founded and set on him, planted in him. Do you have time to have immoderate sorrow connected to the things of the world? Your time here is short and uncertain. Thomas Boston said, considering time, "would be an excellent antidote against immoderate sorrow; for we are here but as actors in a play, where it is no great matter whether one be the king or the peasant; for in a little time the fable is ended, and each appears in the station he really is."[22]

---

[22] Thomas Boston, *The Whole Works of the Late Reverend Thomas Boston*, vol. 5, (Wheaton: Richard Owen Roberts Publishers, 1980) 268.

Chapter 5: Immoderate Sorrows

The negative part to this verse is to fall into immoderate sorrow instead of the comfort of Christ, the praised Lion who is able to comfort. When afflictions come people must turn the right way, Jer. 5:3, "I have smitten them, but they have not grieved." God is saying through the prophet, that they are not reacting in the right way. They should be grieving with a godly repentance, but they are acting in a worldly manner. When people are set in afflictions, difficulties, miseries, when you are afflicted, when you are starting down the path of being discontent, do not be senseless and unaffected to what God is doing with you.

Don't misunderstand, truly, as an afflicted Christian you may, in humility and submission, pray with fervency and zealousness that God would remove afflictions; but how will you pray? Thy will be done; for there is no sin in asking for a removal of miseries. But when affliction pushes you above your strength, when it disables you to do your duty, or when it gives some kind of help to further temptations, then sorrow becomes sinful and excessive; it is immoderate sorrow. It will cause you to despise all other mercies. You will find little enjoyment in the Christian walk. It clouds everything. It causes you to be ungrateful to God. It is a provoking thing to him and hurts both you and the church. Sorrow is not sinful; Jesus was a man of sorrows and acquainted with grief. But immoderate sorrow is of the devil and it is worldly. "Love not the world, neither the things that are in the world. If any man love the world, the love of the Father is not in him," (1 John 2:15).

Immoderate sorrow renders you unfit for service; God will not use you and not open doors that ought to swing open but remain closed; for, if you cannot fend for yourself in acting in a manner befitting Christ's work of grace in your life, how will you be a help to others, or how will you be useful in the Kingdom? You will be like immoderate Jacob. Worldly sorrow works *death* in you, (2 Cor. 7:10), that is, sorrow after the manner of worldly men; sorrow in a carnal, natural way, which is not lightened and helped by any spiritual reasonings and any Scriptural thoughts. John Flavel said, "Whatever God does with us, or ours, still we should maintain good thoughts of him. A gracious heart cleaves nearer and nearer to God in affliction, and can justify God in his severe strokes, acknowledging them to be all just and holy, Psalm 119:75, "I know also that thy judgments are right, and that thou in faithfulness hast afflicted me."[23]

Remember that the lack of comfort in a time of affliction, is an aggravation of sin. You must look to the word of God and Christ to have such alleviated. Because all immoderate sorrows of the saint's sinking soul are utterly crushed when they delight in the word, which causes them to delight in the Christ. And when you use his word well, you can say with the psalmist, ""I will never forget thy precepts: for with them thou hast

---

[23] John Flavel, *A Token for Mourners*, (Boston: Re-printed by S. Kneeland, and T. Green, 1730), 31.

quickened me," (Psalm 119:93), which is the next verse and we will consider in the next chapter.

Chapter 6: Christian Resolve Set in Remembering the Word

"I will never forget thy precepts: for with them thou hast quickened me," (Psalm 119:93).

To forget or ignore something, שָׁכַח *shakach*, is a fault of the mind, *and* the heart. It is to neglect something, or that something that once was in the mind has now started to wither, that is not in the heart, or that the heart is indifferent to. Forget: To treat with thoughtless inattention. Wither: To lose force or life, and become diminished. The psalmist will not forget, or cause to wither, or give thoughtless attention to, or have the force of it lost, or allow it to become diminished. What will not be diminished? God's *precepts*. פִּקּוּד *piqquwd*. People of the world do not consider his *precepts*, so they can never be diminished if they were never brought up to a point where they were spiritually considered. Worldly people may in fact know a great deal about God's word, but never know its spiritual power, and in this way, it cannot be diminished if they never knew it; if a person does not have an experimental relationship with the word, there is never any diminishment in it, because it is, has not, first been remembered, or empowered in their life.

Chapter 6: Christian Resolve in Remembering the Word

These *precepts, statutes, etc.*, have given the psalmist life, quickened him, preserved his life, made him *alive*, חִיִּיתָנִי. *Made* him *alive?* What does that mean? Was he not *alive* before? It is assumed *by the verse* that he was not alive before, and this speaks to spiritual things, and he was made alive by the word of God. He was not only quickened, but preserved in it. He was made alive and kept alive, to continue in spiritual life. This verse itself is set down as a kind of resolute thanksgiving; a kind of prayer and a kind of vow rolled into one. As the law of the Lord had made him alive, (which was the means of grace to quicken his soul), so he says that he will never forget it. Yet he, at the same time, reproves himself how necessary it is to cherish in the heart (not merely with the mouth, for that would make him a hypocrite) to remember, and not to forget, God's word. He is speaking to God here. He had experienced, through the word, its life-giving power. And yet David knew how easily the flesh desires to slumber, which leads to sleep, which leads to forgetfulness. He knew that God had not allowed him to perish in his miseries, or in his humiliation, or in his affliction. Instead, he is brought to remember God's word. His words are a stirring up of himself to do so; to be resolved by vow to never forget what God says.

Doctrine: Christians are to be resolved never to forget God's word, for in it is found salvation and a blessed life. Why will the psalmist "never forget thy precepts?" For, "with them thou hast quickened me."

Such a soul thinks, "I shall never forget such a sermon," "I will never forget such a prayer," "I will never forget such a scriptural passage," "I will never forget such a time of application of the word to my soul," why? "Because in those things, there, *I met with God.* God quickened me in those words, encouraged me, threatened me, promised me, helped me, enlivened me, *etc., so I remember."* And it is, according to the psalmist, as Matthew Henry said, "The best evidence of our love to the word of God is never to forget it."[24]

Christians ought to be resolved never to forget God's word, especially as it relates to remembrance. To be resolved is a fixed determination of the will about anything, either to do it, or not to do it, with an appropriate reflection to judge and conclude the action to be necessary, or proper to be done, or not to be done, as befitting the glory of God. This means that Christians must consider what *ought* to be considered. *Will such things* (whatever is being considered) *be a hindrance to my walk, or a help to it as it pertains to the Savior's glory?* Being resolved as a Christian, sets forth a reflection of the mind about the thing to be resolved on; should it be done, why so, how so, when so, and will Christ be glorified in it? To reflect and think will bring in a clarity of judgment on the thing, after the Christian has pondered about it, to remember what God has said about it. For the Christian,

---

[24] Matthew Henry, *Matthew Henry's Commentary on the Whole Bible: Complete and Unabridged in One Volume* (Peabody: Hendrickson, 1994), 922.

being resolved is a system and structure, a plan, to all holy actions. It is a strategy put into motion, "I will never forget." Why won't Christians forget? Because they take these thoughts and put them into remembrance. This is a forceful action, of continued repetition. They have been put there because not only should they be remembered, but because the psalmist, and the Christian, have been profoundly affected by them, so they take time to categorize them and study them and remember them.

Why are they to be resolved in this? Why use such language as "I will never forget..."? The Christian knows and has sensibly experienced that the birth of his life and the preservation of his life, is by the word of Christ; what do people do with things that are valuable to them? It is there the psalmist finds the first fruits of life, in being born again, and a continuation of his life by the power of the Spirit of Christ in grace; to further grace is to cultivate the word in one's life. He must have the one in order to have the other, and he knows this. To have life is to have the word, and to have the word is to have life, that is, to be discernably sensible of its effects by the power of the Spirit in the heart, mind and soul because they were captives to the kingdom of darkness, and they were rescued from the horrors of hell. And what is this, but really, to love the Lord thy God by God's means? David does not simply say, "thank you for my life" and be on his way. But in order to have life, quickening life, Spirit-filled power, he regarded God's word as a quickening source of power. And so he wanted to have a mind filled with this life-giving power, and a heart set to obedience as such, and a right spirit within him. And why does he place so much time and effort on this idea of God's word, not to forget it, and as he said, to hide it in his heart, and such?

The whole psalm deals with this settled word in heaven. Because as Christ said in John 14:21, "He that hath my commandments, and keepeth them," implies knowing them; *remembering* them. How can a Christian *have* them before they are able to keep them? And how can they do them if they do not keep them? And what if the Christian does not keep them? And why would the Christian not keep them if they have given him life? Christ is vitally connected to such things and they are eminently important for the Christian to remember. If the Christian forgets or neglects the word which brings life-quickening grace they will be impaired and grace will decay and decline. Reformed Christians must be rebuked - a point here is to be corrected for them; when God decrees an end to any *thing*, a goal to *anything*, it will come to pass, they think. True, when God's decrees are considered, they must always be considered as a theological idea, they will come to pass. God's decrees belong to the theoretical realm; they are true, but they are theologically true when they are thought about: God decrees someone will be saved, and so, they will be saved (like Jacob in Romans 9). God says about his decree, "Calling a ravenous bird from the east, the man that executeth my counsel from a far country: yea, I have spoken it, I will also bring it to pass; I have purposed it, I will also do it," (Isa. 46:11). What God decrees will come to pass, by way of theory. What will tomorrow be like, well, the Reformed Christian rests in the truth that it is ordained of God by his decree – what will be will be. Does God want them to think about such things in that way? No, the Christian is to be far more spiritually practical than that. The psalmist is not considering what the misguided reformed Christian considers when they set theory before practice. When God's word is considered as it pertains to holiness, one cannot merely say, "Whatever God decrees, I will be that holy." How one walks, or doesn't walk is not set in theory, but practice. The psalmist knew that; it was very personal. That is why, before, he begins with the settled word, works his way through creation, and the sustaining of creation in providence, moves to God's help of him in affliction and the sin of immoderate sorrow, and now is resolved to do something. It is not merely set in theory.

The Reformed Christian often does not consider practice, and uses that as an excuse to do nothing because, (glibly) "God has ordained all things, and what will be will be." That is not the path of a blessed life. It is right to say, that if the Christian forgets or neglects the word which brings life, and quickens him, quickening grace will be impaired and it will decay and it will decline. We call this, spiritual declension. A descent, a decline, a deterioration, a deviation from the highway of holiness. They look at their life last year and they look at their life this year and they see little to no difference. That is spiritual declension because the quickening word quickens. It doesn't not quicken unless it is forgotten, or if it is withering. This is not necessarily by the outward practice of wickedness or sin that something is impaired; it may not be a David and Bathsheba sin, it may not be Achan's wedge of gold. Spiritual declension, spiritual decline simply points from the beginning of what has occurred "it has quickened the Christian to new life," even made him a whole new creation, and yet, in spiritual duties, in some way or fashion, he declines in them, and neglects them, and does not remember them as he should. This is always by neglect of the word in some way. Why so? The word of God is the means that should nurture and feed the Christian soul. "...desire the sincere milk of the word, that ye may grow thereby," (1 Peter 2:2). It is the tool by which Christ, through the Spirit, quickens them. And if the Christian does not have time for the word, and does not remember it, and its *quickening* power is not experienced, they will decline; and holiness will turn cold.

What is *quickening*? The idea of quickening in the Bible is either for 1) regeneration, or 2) excitement to grace; both are something God does to the soul by *effect*, but never without *means*. Eph. 2:5, "And you that were dead in trespasses and sins hath he quickened;" God infused life to David who was dead and was made alive by the precepts of the word. Men who are dead are quickened to life by the word. Men who are spiritual corpses are made alive by the virtuous power of Jesus in the word. Lazarus was dead in the tomb, so much so that *he stinketh*. But dead corpses in Christ's hands can be made alive when he says, the word, *Lazarus come forth!* David references this quickening word, and then applies it, experientially to himself. The second idea of "quickening" is for being further excited in grace. God quickens dead souls to life and then works in those souls to excite them to gracious ends. They are not puppets to gracious ends. They are not merely declared quickened in excited grace as they are declared justified in Christ. Many Reformed Christians turn *Antinomian* in this. They think that as they are justified, declared such, so they are sanctified in the same way, and that it is inherent in them by God's declaration of them being *holy*. No, God motions the soul by the Spirit *to work to holy ends*, and the soul *must* move. To be quickened is the opposite to being dead in holy works; or negligent, or slothful, lazy, indifferent, etc., whatever word one wants to use.

Quickening in remembering God's word is opposite to being negligent, or having some hindrance to the motions of the Spirit (being *sensitive* to the Spirit). Spiritual laziness is to be "stirred up" to act. Isa. 64:7, "There is none that stirreth up himself to take hold on thee." What a sad commentary! Christians are to stir themselves up, to *take hold* of God. "But I'm waiting for the Sovereign God to work out his decree in my life by zapping me." That won't work. If they do not stir themselves up, which in and of itself is a really interesting thought, that stirring to remembrance take place, if this does not occur it is to grow careless, the opposite of watching and taking heed. When Christians become slothful, lazy, careless, negligent, busied with the world, instead of busied against it, they decline in their soul, and the effects of grace begin to wither; and they then act as *the world*, instead of being instructed by *the word*. Lift weights for a year, then stop and see what happens to the body. It weakens, and becomes faint. Do that for a prolonged time, and then work out again, and most of what was gained is found to have been lost, and ground must be made up all over again, just to get back to the place where one *was* once. Christians will grow weak, and they will faint, if their spiritual duties are cold, for a lack of exercise.

How does God quicken his people, but by his Spirit-empowered precepts? Where will they find comfort? Where will they find the Spirit working Christ in them? Where will they find revival? Christians are praying for revival without using the constituted means that God has given them to enact it. One might object and say, "That has to be done by the sovereignty of the Spirit." It is never by zapping, but the Spirit uses the means of grace as the means of grace are used. In spiritual declension, in decline, in deviancy, Christians are indifferent to them; they are not used, they are not stirred, they are lazy with them. Revival does not come when people are *sleeping* in their beds at night; no revival has ever come that way while people were sleeping. Revivals have always occurred by the preaching of the word and prayer and fresh stores of grace given in God's constituted means. Where will Christians find fresh stores of grace? Will they find it when they are faint, and weak, and defeated to some measure in all kinds of miseries and afflictions by just wondering what God will do? The Reformed Christian wants to pick and choose verses they like at that point, "...quicken us, and we will call upon thy name," (Psalm 80:18). "Wilt thou not revive us again: that thy people may rejoice in thee?" (Psalm 85:6). But they do not ask, *how* will they be quickened? *How* will they be revived? Why must a Christian allow himself to get to that stage and those words, they are terrible words in those verses? As if God will merely *zap* them into revival, or *zap* them to holiness as they hoped. They were mistaken. If the Christian were careful, and resolved to remembrance, he would be quickened in grace *daily*. Drive a car as far as it might go, and at some point, it needs more gas; it will run out, stall, and be useless for nothing if that happens. It must be continually filled if it is to be used. My lawn mower works excellent, but it will not work at all if I do not tend it: gas, oil, spark plugs, fuel filters, *etc.*; I just want to cut the lawn when I need to, but without maintenance, the lawnmower will do nothing but break down.

Christians think that in their weakness and infirmities and afflictions, God will zap them by the Spirit to raise them up, that God will stir up their spirits and refresh them with spiritual life by nothing done by them. Many Christians live as though God does this apart from them. This is not what the psalmist believed.

The doctrine is set *soundly* on this phrase, which is an amazing phrase, "I will never forget thy precepts." Amazing! Is he *serious*? Assuredly. David stirs himself up with and by the word. It really deals with perpetuity; of a long duration, into the future, in fact, everlastingly, he uses that hard-sanctifying word, never ... never forget; and places on it, not the Spirit, as Reformed Christians would like, but places it in, "I will." He presses himself into a constant dependence on God and communion with him based on remembering. If the Christian did not need perpetual supplies of grace, would the Christian ever visit his prayer closet? If the Christian did not need "daily bread" and debts forgiven daily, and the need to be reminded of holiness, would they *ever* pray? God does not put his grace in the hands of Christians, as Thomas Manton rightly said, "God will keep his grace in his own hands, that ever we may have something to drive us to himself, some necessities upon us; for the throne of grace is for a time of need."[25] Is this not exactly what David said, and *is* saying? God desires his people to engage him.

---

[25] Thomas Manton, *The Complete Works of Thomas Manton*, Volume 6, (London: James Nisbet & Co., 1872), 329.

Chapter 6: Christian Resolve in Remembering the Word

So, he holds grace in his hands, and they must seek that grace out.

David resolves never to forget God's precepts. If he would never forget them, this does not necessarily mean he has a photographic memory. Luther had one of those, which is why he remembered most of the bible word for word. Calvin didn't; Jonathan Edwards didn't. Why were they so *smart* in the bible? What the psalmist is saying is that Christians are to frequently repeat and refresh the remembrance of those precepts by which God had particularly quickened him. What had happened to them, where they were once of the darkness, and then they were quickened? What had happened to them where they were once like dead Lazarus in the tomb and then Christ called them forth to life? It is the Christian's obligation to be thoroughly acquainted with those Scriptural places where he has met with God. To do so is to be preserved, but also to be rescued from falling into spiritual declension and laziness of life.

Such a resolve is not only with the mouth; people can vow all kinds of things before other church members. To make a resolution like this only with one's mouth is to start, right away, as acting hypocritically. To say one thing and not mean it, is what hypocrites do; remember, hypocrites, the very word, means to *pretend*. Hypocrites pretend to get into the Kingdom by being religious in front of others. But Christians are most religious when *only* God is watching. It must be of the quickened heart; which is of a different spirit than a hypocrite. "But my servant Caleb, because he had *another spirit* with him, and hath followed me fully," (Num. 14:24). It is a blessing for a man to follow God fully, with a right spirit, "...that they have their hearts come fully off in the ways of obedience, to fulfill the good will of the Lord; this is that perfect heart which God so often calls for in Scripture, and for which so many of God's servants are commended in the Word."[26] And listen to Acts 11:23 where Barnabas, "...exhorted them, that, with purpose of heart, they would cleave unto the Lord." Resolutions do not come to pass by men's mere speech. It should never be with a Christian, said of them, "For their heart was not right with him, neither were they steadfast in his covenant," (Psalm 78:37). They did not have a sanctified heart, and instead, they merely spoke the words, with some outward show, but what is that but hypocrisy? If I say I'm a Christian but I don't do things of a Christian, that makes me a hypocrite.

    Such a resolve to remember the word of God, and that which God has done for the soul in Christ, must not be in part, but in whole. What is a partial walking with Christ? What is partial reformation? What is it to love God with some of the heart, soul or mind? Spiritual duties that are half baked, are useless cakes not turned; can you recall Hosea 7:8? They are easily overcome by an immoderate love of the world.

---

[26] Jeremiah Burroughs, *The Excellency of a Gracious Spirit*, (London: Miles Flesher, 1639), 245–246.

Such a resolve is without delay. David says, "I made haste, and delayed not to keep thy commandments," (Psalm 119:60). This resolve is now, without haste, a resolution for the present time, not something he would put on a shelf for a later time; it is not like a diet, where someone says, I will begin tomorrow, next Monday. This is immediate and set in a perpetual remembrance, never forget, what God said and did in his sure mercies to him, the everlasting covenant of David.

Such a resolve is set on the character of the Word of God, which is sure, because God has given it, and given life through it; settled in heaven. The heart touched with the sweetness of divine truth, revels in it and improves it. Can a soul improve on what God gives in grace? Not in quality (grace is always grace), but most assuredly in *quantity*. It is there the soul meets with God and a quickened heart, striving for a blessed life, is resolved to continue the quickening and continue that meeting. When one draws near to God, they desire to draw closer and closer. That word from God does so much in this: mortifies sin, sanctifies the life, works joy in the soul, draws the soul nearer and closer to the Lord. "...strengthen thou me according unto thy word," (Psalm 119:28). And how? "I will never forget thy precepts: for with them thou hast quickened me," (Psalm 119:93). It brings them comfort. "This is my comfort in my affliction: for thy word hath quickened me," (Psalm 119:50). It soothes their soul in affliction. "I am afflicted very much: quicken me, O LORD, according unto thy word," (Psalm 119:107). David is very much about stirring up his heart to the quickening grace of God.

Such a resolve never forgets the word, and once it is gotten, that soul desires to keep it and improve it. Things that are valuable are kept with care. A rich man once said to me, "After one gains riches, he must do what he can to keep what he has gained." There is care in accomplishing that. What kind of watchfulness, then, accompanies such a resolve, to keep riches, which are sensitive to a worldly man's heart that when he loses them; he feels it. What kind of watchfulness must be employed to never forget thy precepts? What kind of diligence is there for a daily increase in grace? One soul outweighs all the riches of the world; gaining the world and losing the soul? Where is the watchfulness and diligence in that soul?

Where does this *daily increase* of grace come from but remembering the work and merit of Jesus Christ to the soul? The increase of grace, to obtain grace, in the life of the Christian is not fruit of their own merits, but the free grace of God in Jesus Christ. It's there for the plucking – the fruit is within hands reach.

David's resolution is by the sure mercies of God; by God's promises. "Incline your ear, and come unto me: hear, and your soul shall live; and I will make an everlasting covenant with you, even the sure mercies of David," (Isa. 55:3). This concerns the work of the Spiritual David in his people.

Such a godly resolve to never forget the word, and further such quickening influence, are according to Christ's covenant of grace. Eight times David entreats God's mercies in this psalm directly. What will he say next in this psalm? "I am thine, save me," (Psalm 119:94). Jesus me, *yasha*, deliver me, save me. He stirs himself to remember the word, and combines that with the desire to be furthered in grace, remembering what God had already done for him and what he would like him to continue to do; save me.

Christians ought to have a discernable sense of their insufficiency and dependence on Jesus Christ and his covenant of grace; David did. They are not confident, at all, of their own strength. "God is my strength and power: and he maketh my way perfect," (2 Sam. 22:33), said David. God's Christ is the place of strength and safety. "For when we were yet without strength, in due time Christ died for the ungodly," (Rom. 5:6); those who were dead and were quickened were made alive by God's Christ. "...the last Adam was made a quickening spirit," (1 Cor. 15:45). "Even when we were dead in sins, hath quickened us together with Christ, (by grace ye are saved;)" (Eph. 2:5).

What about faithful Christians in this? We often hear and talk about inadequate Christian professors, but what should be thought about in terms of Christians who, for all intents and purposes, are very faithful to Jesus, and who take up all kinds of holy duties and stir themselves to remembrance by the quickening word daily? How shall David's words relate to them in terms of their stunted growth at a time, or for a season? What do we do with immoderate Jacobs or immoderate Jonahs? Such Christians become resolved, and they do not want to forget his quickening presence in their life. Why do they not grow more, and that quickly, in this? It may be said that a lack of spiritual growth in Christ, for the Christian, is ascribed to a lack of knowledge and experience; they merely need direction and guidance in what will make them quickened. If they do not want guidance, if they do not want direction, it is at their loss.

And yet, in this, it may not be a lack of effort in trying to attain spiritual knowledge, or an exercise in spiritual things, but it really relates to their unacquaintedness with Christ, or their misuse of the means of grace, their unacquaintedness with his quickening means in the word. They often believe that the Spirit sanctifies them without rightly using the means; as if, they will just live, and the Spirit will bless them no matter what. But they are not further familiar with what they really have in Jesus, and so reach fundamentals of accepted Christian truths, and often do not go further experimentally, and sensibly, and practically. They do not tap into the virtue of Christ; they do not as they ought, suck virtue from him. They think, wrongly, as Nicholas Clagett said, They turn, "predestinating grace into impiety. It is a wrested conclusion from this glorious principle of election, that God has chosen me to life, therefore, I may live as I wish."[27] But that is not what the psalmist said; living as a professing Christian is not enough; he stirred himself up, and he was a very knowledgeable fellow according to God's precepts.

Do Christians often think about how much they do not know the Lord Jesus or stir themselves up to remembrance of what they have read in the word? How immeasurable he is as Savior. If drawing near to God is through Christ, what kind of spiritual impressions on the soul does the Christian consider in order to gain a greater understanding of the precepts of God's word? How might, as David did, Christians keep in line with a continual admiration and adoration of the majesty of Christ? Even those people, John Owen said, "of the most high and eminent attainment, of the nearest and most familiar communion with God, do yet in this life know but a very little of him and his glory."[28] Regardless of all that the Christian knows of God, or *thinks* he knows, they are as a child in comparison to God's unsearchable perfections. They must always be resolved to press further. Which is why Christ calls such people *violent*; *pressing* into the Kingdom. David, no doubt, loved God, honored God, believed in God, and obeyed God. Where did he find such wonderous thoughts of how he ought to do such? Had the Spirit given him everything he

---

[27] Nicholas Clagett, eBook, *The Abuse of God's Grace*, (Oxford: A. Lichfield, 1659) chapter 3.
[28] John Owen, *The Works of John Owen*, vol 6, (Edinburgh: Banner of Truth Trust, 1998) 66.

needed for life and godliness? Did he have the entirety of the spiritual blessing in Christ, for without which a man cannot be quickened, or go to heaven, (John 3:3). Most assuredly.

God consents and agrees to accept childish thoughts from David, and from all Christians. Christians see God's back parts; and know but little of him, much less the infinitude of the privileges that they have now in Jesus Christ.

Christians know so little of God, because it is God to be known. But should this cause them to distress in knowing him more? Where shall they find to know more of him, and his Son? Where shall they plumb more of the depth of quickening power of Christ and his Spirit? It is not merely by sense, but it is from the word to their sense. It is by the word, to their own practical experience empowered by the Spirit.

The understanding of the Christian is merely a slight apprehension of the back parts of Christ, and eternity and his infiniteness that they have a glimpse of; they merely see little sparks of his divine glory. Just sparks of Christ's divine glory they have in this life; but oh, such sparks are very full. Why is it that Christians are far more enamored with what Jesus does for them rather than who God is to them in Christ, but because they rather know him by what he does than by what he is. And they only know him by faith now, and not by sight, "We walk by faith, and not by sight," (2 Cor. 5:7). And yet, in "thy precepts," the Christian knows enough of Christ to love him, to delight in him and serve him, and believe him, and obey him and forget not all his benefits. David's plea was that in thy precepts, is quickening, and life, and all manner of delights. Christ is known, and truly known, even if in childish thoughts, and Christians may still glorify him as God; draw near to him, love him, serve him, believe and obey him, as David did. They can glory in him in this way.

    Do you desire a blessed life? Such is gained by lively thoughts about God's word worked by Spirit-power. Spiritual power is hidden in repetitive thoughts that are serious and lively; that is because the Bible is serious and lively; quickening; because Jesus is serious, lively and quickening. We often pray for spiritual power, and think that the Spirit zaps us so long as we have a few thoughts about God, not considering that such power comes in by way of our stirring to remembrance what Christ has done for us by his Spirit as so given in his word, who already dwells in us fully. This is why two personal factors (dealing with things *personal* here at this point in the psalm) are of utmost importance in this remembrance, in this Spirit-work to experience a blessed life by the word. *Personal devotions* and *family worship*; both of these are remembrance actions, things that stir us up. These two are critical areas for a blessed life, and for spiritual power. Reading, study, godly meditation on the word makes the fuel of the word of God burn in the heart and mind and the Spirit moves one to action by them.

Prayer harnesses that which is learned about God, and offers up arguments to God based on his word, for all daily necessities. ...as does singing if one is merry.

Family devotions, where all catechizing and learning in the home takes place, taking personal devotions and stretching it to family worship, is all based on the word of God, a stirring to remembrance.

You should be taken up daily with these things for two reasons: 1) if you are serious as the psalmist is about the word. 2) if you want a blessed life. Consider that as you look at your whole life. Thomas Manton said again, "...a weak impression is an argument of a slight apprehension because thoughts always follow affection. (what you love you do) I say, men thoroughly affected shall remember such a sermon for their whole lifetime. David said, "I will never forget thy precepts; for by them thou hast quickened me." Others let good things slip, because they never feel their power."[29] Power comes by *stirring*, couple with *resolve* and *resolution*, to take up the things of God by remembrance, and then, the Spirit will turn those truths to bless those efforts in a blessed life. Do you take the sermons and go over them in your family worship each week? Do you read the bible every year in whole without fail?

Do you meditate on the word each day in your daily studies? Is your prayer time heated with Spirit-power from this? As much stirring as you do in such

---

[29] Thomas Manton, *The Complete Works of Thomas Manton*, vol. 04 (London: James Nisbet & Co., 1871), 160.

Chapter 6: Christian Resolve in Remembering the Word

things is set in the point of God's considering what you consider to be important. If you pay no mind or little mind to him, what can you expect from him? Do you discern his power in your life? Quickening power? Do you hear the Christ speak to you in the power of the word and does he talk to you sweetly? Is his fruit sweet?

In daily reading of God's word we find our hearts warmed there. "I will never forget thy precepts: for with them thou hast quickened me," (Psalm 119:93); you have heated me up. What an impression was left on him to say such a thing? Strive to be affected with the word spiritually, every time you read it or hear it preached. Recall Jeremiah 23:29, "Is not my word like a fire?" Does it not heat you up? As much as it is a fire, it is also sweet. You can taste the sweetness of Christ in the word, "I have not departed from thy judgments: for thou hast taught me. How sweet are thy words unto my taste! yea, sweeter than honey to my mouth!" (Psalm 119:102-103). Who said this? David. In our psalm here, just a few verses from now. David's prayer was, "Open my eyes, that I may behold wondrous things out of your law," (Psalm 119:18); he said that 70 verses previous. Never be content with the bare reading of the Scriptures, but labor to find some spiritual improvement and profit from it, for those who profit by reading God's word are the best and most blessed Christians alive, and know the sweetness of his Spirit-persuasions to their soul.

Do not *forget* his word? Part of study is memorization, to work the word into the soul. "Thy word have I hid in mine heart," (Psalm 119:11). Hide it in your heart; it may not be easy, but what profitable things are always easy? It is what provides for your power, strength and comfort in Jesus Christ, as well as your shield against all the fiery darts of the devil. If you really knew the work of the devil, you would not let a day slip by to miss any stirring to remembrance. What made those in the Gospel to be foolish virgins, but that they did not make provision for eternal life? They were not really ready, and did not take heed as they should have. Consider, they were virgins too. Consider they were with the five wise. Consider they had some oil. Consider they had lamps. Consider they had means to light their lamps. Consider that they did not have oil after a time because they were not prepared. Consider that Christ called them, "foolish," (Matt. 25:2) for their lack of preparation. And what made the other five to be wise, but that their hearts and lives were adorned and beautified with grace and goodness to have full lamps of oil? Full of the Holy Spirit. It is interesting to me that Christ uses the word "wise", wisdom being the right application of what they knew to be true; so prepared, so diligent, so filled with remembrance. They could have done nothing if they did not stir themselves up to remember what they ought. Their knowledge made them prepared for the tarrying bridegroom to come in eager expectation of that union. What does your knowledge do, that you will not forget his precepts and things he has taught you by his word?

Chapter 6: Christian Resolve in Remembering the Word

Your affection to the word, its loveliness to you, its sweetness, is a friend to help you when you place it in your memory. Whatever you love most is what you will remember. Godly meditation is a help to that end, memorization is also, as is catechizing; which is why family worship is so vital. We must be often meditating on what we have placed in our minds concerning the Christ, and who but to help us with this than our family. Meditate on the questions of the confession and catechisms. *WSC*, Question 34. What is adoption? Answer: Adoption is an act of God's free grace, whereby we are received into the number, and have a right to all the privileges, of the sons of God. 1 John 3:1, "Behold, what manner of love the Father hath bestowed upon us, that we should be called the sons of God..." What fuel there is on such thoughts for weeks of remembrance at being brought into the number of the sons of God!

And consider, comparatively, the Bible you have by the revelation of Jesus Christ in the gospel is particularly glorious in comparison to the extent that David had; you wonder at David's zeal, yet, your bible is far bigger. It is more than what David had, though not of a different nature or substance.

It is glorious to you, though, in comparison to anything given in the Old Testament, not without it but in addition to it. David had shadows and you have clarity and sunlight. David had a night sky, and you have the Dayspring from on high who has come.

Has not Jesus Christ declared the Father to you if you are a believer? Shall you put those thoughts, and those precepts, and those commandments, into your memory that you may not forget them? What length and time and effort shall go into that remembrance? This is why Moses tells the church, it is your life? Devotions are your life, family worship is your life. Many professing Christians live as if it was not their life; by neglecting such they mimic the cursed families of the world. They have no time for it, or they exercise it but little, for life is far too busy for them to have time to remember such things; they are content with little, and sadly, will be little Christians in power and effect, if at all. Christ has revealed and declared the Father, and made known his mind by the Spirit to you as a believer. All the blessed effects of the Spirit reside in you. And in you he attests to the precepts of the word of God in clearer ways than he did with David, because this Light of the world has come, and the bible tells you all about him. What a privilege this is, even though we take time to see what David said in this psalm that pushes us and prods us to take up the same diligence he had about the word in our day. Jesus Christ by his word and Spirit reveals to the hearts of you who are believers, who are bought by him and endowed with his Spirit, quickened by him, that God is your Abba Father, Our Father, in covenant, to the saving of your soul, making dead things alive by his word; he makes you have a blessed life but not without the means to do so.

These are wonderful precepts, but as it regards things David had, they are better now; treat them as valuable; never forget how better they are. You have better promises of a better testament, (Heb. 8:6-7), to better, higher and more perfect covenantal blessings. A better explanation of God's Law and word, and better promises attached to it. Better knowledge of the Lord, and a better understanding of the remission of sins (Heb. 8:10-12). A better sacrifice by better blood of the Savior. A better tabernacle, and better intercession in heaven, by a better High Priest. You have a better and more sweet, perfect and comfortable fellowship among the saints, (Heb. 12:18-25). You have better and more clear and spiritual ordinances and sacraments. You have better, and more extensive and more powerful outpourings of Christ's Spirit, (John 7:38-39, with Acts 2). You have the hope of a better country, made by God. The conditions of the New Covenant church are better, for it is a better and more glorious testament, by the Son who has vigor and can put the testament to better and greater and fulfilled use, if you remember it. "I will never forget thy precepts: for with them thou hast quickened me." Do you see the force of it all, stated in that light? Christians are to be resolved never to forget God's word, for in it is found salvation and a blessed life, that of a better testament. Which is why the next thing David says, is, "I am thine, *save* me," (Psalm 119:94), which we will begin to consider in the next chapter.

Chapter 7: God's Election of His Own Special People

"I am thine, save me; for I have sought thy precepts." "I belong to you, save me (*or deliver me*); for I have sought out your precepts," (Psalm 119:94).

David believed himself to be of God's *special* people which have been saved out of the kingdom of darkness and brought into the kingdom of God. He is one of the special number of God's people, "I am thine," and he knew it. This is not an odd thing to say, to be saved. It would be odd for an unbeliever to say this, yes. No unbeliever, no hypocrite, no false professor, can say "I am yours," and know it, but the psalmist can say, "I am thine." Truly, "for whom are all things, and by whom are all things," (Heb. 2:10). The Psalmist knew, "For every beast of the forest is mine, and the cattle upon a thousand hills," (Psalm 50:10). All things in creation are God's. God has made all things, and he is Lord over all things, sovereign over all things, which he said in verses 89-91. Psalm 24:1, "The earth is the Lord's, and the fulness thereof." Even all things, regardless of their spiritual state, Ezek. 18:4, "All souls are mine." But not everyone can say what David is saying, because he was not making a generality. He is not saying that all things are God's by means of being created by him; that was his thought before, but not now.

All men cannot say "I am thine;" and here are the more particular words in light of the former, "save me." Certainly, God is sovereign over all things, rational and irrational creatures, but this is something more, in David's words, something peculiar and special. Also, consider, that those who are in covenant with God cannot say this, as it *generally* applies. All those that are part of the visible church, they might say, "We are yours Lord, we are your people, the sheep of your pasture," but they mean this in a *generality*. Those who have attached themselves to some local body, some church, and perform a number of religious and outward works, may say, "We are yours," *generally* speaking. This kind of thinking was given by the Jews, "They answered and said unto him, *Abraham is our father*," (John 8:39). Christ rebukes them, "If ye were Abraham's children, ye would do the *works* of Abraham," (John 8:39). There is something more in the justifying faith of those like Abraham that cause them to say, "I am thine, save me."

From out of the world, God has saved a special people for his own. These, and these alone can say with David, "I am thine, save me." Such a people are a peculiar people, a special people, saved from the city of destruction and brought into the Kingdom of light. They are those gathered up by God, "Gather my saints together unto me," (Psalm 50:5). "God is greatly to be feared in the assembly of the saints, and to be had in reverence of all them that are about him," (Psalm 89:7). "Precious in the sight of the LORD is the death of his saints," (Psalm 116:15). God says, "Yea, I will rejoice over them," (Jer. 32:41). "The LORD thy God in the midst of thee is mighty; he will save, he will rejoice over thee with joy; he will rest in his love, he will joy over thee with singing," (Zeph. 3:17). They are "the first-fruits" (James 1:18), the Lord's portion. God takes these people, from out of the world, to be his portion, and they are the apple of his eye. David says, "Keep me as the apple of the eye" (Psalm 17:8). "For thus saith the LORD of hosts ... he that toucheth you toucheth the apple of his eye," (Zech. 2:8). It is as if David were to say, "I am not my own, I am not sin's, I am not Satan's, I am not the world's, I am not the flesh's, but, I am yours; I am really, wholly, only, and always yours, and you are mine, and I know this." Thomas Brooks said, "I am thine to be sanctified, and I am thine to be saved; I am thine to be commanded, and I am thine to be ruled. Lord, I am thine own, and therefore do with thine own as you please, and dispose of your own as you please. I am at your feet, willing to be anything or nothing, as shall seem best in your own eyes."[30]

David uses "I", for his person. I "am" or "belong" as a possession to you. "Yours" or "thine" for God's ownership as a peculiar person, because he does not merely state the obvious, that all things are God's. He

---

[30] Thomas Brooks, *The Complete Works of Thomas Brooks*, Volume 2, (Carlisle, PA: Banner of Truth Trust, 1980) 99.

says, "save me" which brings in a very special ownership of a very special kind of person. "I am thine; *save me.*" David does not say, "Thou art mine, save me," but, "I am thine." That if David is God's, God is David's. And David knew God is his by giving up himself to be his and to seek his salvation.

God's choice and election of David is a secret until it is shown outwardly by David's choice of God, until David chooses God for his portion, and so he relies not only that he is God's, but that God will save him in temporary troubles and in eternal troubles.

Doctrine: God has elected a special people as his own from out of the world. Scripture teaches that there is a plan (or *purpose*) of God in relation to the salvation of men; God does not *wing it*. God has plans, and a plan supposes the following: 1) God's selection of some definite end or object to be accomplished. 2) God's choice of appropriate means to that end. 3) God's effectual application and control of those means to the accomplishment of his glorified end. God always gets what he wants. If the Bible teaches that a plan exists, then it is certainly important for human beings to know what that plan is and how it applies to them for God's glory. God's providence extends to all events great and small, so that nothing does or can occur contrary to his will, or which he does not either effect by his own power, or permit to be done by others. God is in control, and desires that his glory will be, and all his plans work, to that end. "For mine own sake, even for mine own sake, will I do it: for how should my name be polluted? and I will not give my glory unto another," (Isa. 48:11); that the glory of God, or the manifestation of his perfections, is the highest and ultimate end of all things; that *our God reigns*.

For that end, God purposed the creation of the universe, and the whole plan of providence and redemption; this is why David moves from his settled decree in heaven, to creation, now, to deliverance. Whoever is made to *differ* (1 Cor. 4:7) from the original condemnation of Adam by divine grace, there is no doubt, but God will do all that is necessary for them to receive the means of grace and be saved. Such a work and plan began before the foundations of the world. It is the work of God in Jesus Christ as free grace to elected saints, that grace is not earned or merited by their own works in any way. *The 1647 Westminster Confession of Faith* states, "Those of mankind that are predestinated unto life, God, before the foundation of the world was laid, according to his eternal and immutable purpose, and the secret counsel and good pleasure of his will, hath chosen, in Christ, unto everlasting glory, out of his mere free grace and love, without any foresight of faith, or good works, or perseverance in either of them, or any other thing in the creature, as conditions, or causes moving him thereunto; and all to the praise of his glorious grace (Ephesians 1:4, 9, 11; Romans 8:28–30; 2 Timothy 1:9; 1 Thess. 5:9; Romans 9:11, 13, 15–16; Ephesians 1:5–6, 9, 11–12; 2:8–9)." Any time the bible speaks of being "redeemed by Christ" "saved by Christ" "saved by God" "delivered by God" it is alluding to God's glorious covenant, and all God did in saving men in it. Man was in a most heinous position in being fallen in Adam. Adam was in paradise, and fell from life, into death. And he brought the whole human race with him. The old divines used the term, "woeful," for this, as a most "woeful condition."

Fallen man in Adam is not able to help himself, nor willing to be helped by God out of it. "And you hath he quickened, who were *dead* in trespasses and sins," (Eph. 2:1). In Adam, and the fall, men are not drowning, and they are not sick, but in fact, they are dead. Dead men desire and can do nothing; they are dead. They are so dead, and so wicked and so depraved, that they would, as a result of the fall and curse, rather lie still, insensible of its consequences, until they would perish at death into the second death, into hell, for all eternity; and they are happy to do so as it pertains to this life, for they suppress the truth of eternal realities in their fallen natures. But, would God leave all those perishing to perish? God, for the glory of his rich grace, has revealed in his word a way to save sinners; and this is by faith in Jesus Christ, the eternal Son of God, in covenant with him. This is according to the *Covenant of Redemption*, made and agreed upon, between God the Father and God the Son, in the counsel of the Trinity, before the world began; called, rightfully, the Covenant of *Redemption*, with all its benefits. "Even he shall build the temple of the LORD; and he shall bear the glory, and shall sit and rule upon his throne; and he shall be a priest upon his throne: and the *counsel of peace* shall be between them both," (Zech. 6:13). This is between the Christ, who is the Branch, the Mediator, and God. Is there peace between the members of the Godhead? Of course there is, for God is the ever-blessed God of the universe; they have eternal peace, Daniel 2:20, "Blessed be the name of God forever and ever." If this is true, then, where is this *peace* really needed? Peace is not needful between God the Father, Son and Holy Spirit. Rather, peace is needed between man and God. Zechariah is speaking about the Counsel of Peace, God's covenant, that will bring spiritual peace between men and God. To do this, an agreement was made between *the Branch* and the *Lord* called the *Counsel of Peace* that will bring that peace into time so that men can experience it.

Isaiah 4:2 again speaks of the Branch, "In that day the Branch of the LORD shall be beautiful and glorious; And the fruit of the earth shall be excellent and appealing for those of Israel who have escaped." The Branch (the Christ) will bring escape from the oppression of sin and the reign of Christ will reverse the fall, and those saved will see him as altogether lovely. People remain under sin's oppression until the Branch comes and delivers them. Such oppression is tolerated for a long time, "Then the Angel of the LORD answered and said, "O LORD of hosts, how long will You not have mercy on Jerusalem and on the cities of Judah, against which You were angry...?" (Zechariah 1:12). Christ is the

Chapter 7: God's Election of His Own Special People

Branch who is sent by God in the Counsel of Peace to relieve the burden of sin from off those he will save; he is the Prince of Peace. In this, God freely chose to life, a certain number of lost mankind, for the glory of his rich grace. So they will share in the sure mercies of David and say, "I am thine, save me." Are there any words more important for the believer than these? I tell you now, you do not realize the importance of this psalm and this verse; but by this chapter's end, I hope you will. Before the world began, before creation was created, God the Son, was appointed Redeemer, that, on condition he would humble himself so far as to assume the human nature of a soul and a body, to personal union with his divine nature, and submit himself to the Law of God, as Mediator for his own special people; he would satisfy God's justice for them, by giving obedience in their name, even suffering of the cursed death of the cross, he would redeem them. He was made sin, that knew no sin, that we might be made the righteousness of God in him (2 Cor. 5:21). It pleased Christ to put himself in this way under our guilt, and therefore it pleased the Father in this way to bruise him. How so?

The sure mercies of David are set in this wonderful covenant. This special counsel of peace is a *federal* transaction that was between God the Father, and God the Son from everlasting. It concerns redemption of men out of the mass of humanity going to hell because of the fall. In this covenant or counsel those bound to one another are the Father and the Son in the power of the Spirit. Later, in time, God will make this wonderful counsel, these *sure* mercies, applicable to men by a personal visit to the earth in his Son, where *he will be God with us*. He binds himself to believers through faith in his Christ; *I am Thine*. Such wonderful mercies are set in an agreement between God and Christ in the great work of man's redemption. It is called federal because it is between them on *certain terms*, with obligations they have to one another. Zech. 6:13, "The Counsel of peace shall be between them both;" the counsel of reconciliation. It shows how man, that is now an enemy to God, may be reconciled to God, and God to him. This counsel or consultation shall be between them both; that is, Father and Son, in the power of the Spirit. God the Father stands on being satisfied in himself for man's redemption; sinners shall be justified; but, first, God will be satisfied. Man is a criminal when he is born, and is an enemy of God, a God-hater. He must pay for the debt which he owes to God in Adam, but he has no power to do that being dead. Man is cursed, and by this fall he has sinned against God, and wronged God and God will have satisfaction to fix his honor, manifest his truth, and vindicate his justice and holiness. God's character has been offended by offending criminals. God's character must be satisfied, or man must go to prison, to hell, to pay the price, and stay there until they do, which for men, is impossible; that is why hell is forever, but the sentence is just; and the infinite God who is abused by sinful criminals must enact an infinite sentence against the sins against him; but he graciously decides to save some of them. For this end, the Father chooses Christ, and fore-ordains him, as it is in Romans 3:25, to make satisfaction, without which fallen man shall not be saved, and shall not be set in God's favor. These fallen men shall be redeemed and justified, but only in a way that God may declare his righteousness appeased, satisfied. This is the main argument of the entire book of Romans, God's righteousness must be defended. The Father demands satisfaction to his holiness, rightly so, for all men in Adam, as a rebel, have rebelled. God empowers his Christ that he would fit him for the work, strengthen him in the work, succeed and prosper him in the work by the Spirit, and then reward him for it with those the Father gives him. And all this the Father makes good to Christ. He fits him for this work by the graces and gifts of the Spirit on him, (John 3:34), and preparing a body for him, (Heb. 10:5). He strengthens him, and supports him in the work. Isa. 42:1, "Behold my servant whom I uphold." Isa. 50:7, "The Lord God will help me, therefore shall I not be confounded." Psalm 16:8, *etc.* "I have set the Lord always before me, because he is at my right hand, I shall not be moved," *etc.* The Father prospers Christ in the work. "When thou shalt make his soul an offering for sin, he shall see his seed, the pleasure of the Lord shall prosper in his hand," (Isa. 53:10). The Father gives believers to Christ and promises that believers in time should also give themselves to him as living sacrifices. And the Father will, and has, rewarded

Christ in his work to redeem man. "God hath exalted him" far above all principality and power, (Eph. 1:21-22), "hath put all things under his feet, made him to be head over all things to the church, given him a name which is above every name, that at the name of Jesus every knee should bow; (Phil. 2:9). These he has saved *gladly bow*.

Christ would, willingly ransom and redeem them all from sin and death, and purchase for them righteousness and eternal life, with all saving graces; so that there is now *no* condemnation for them in him. The Lord Jesus Christ engages in the work, accepts the terms and conditions set before him, and undertakes to satisfy his Father's demands. He brings in the satisfaction needed. Christ was willing to fulfill the whole Law, which was the rule, or measure, or standard for this satisfaction. Jesus accepted the task of this covenant, before the world began. 2 Tim. 1:9, "Who hath saved us, and called us with an holy calling; not according to our works, but according to his own purpose and grace, which was given us in Christ Jesus before the world began." Here is the purpose of God, here is grace given in Jesus Christ; but how? In the covenant between the Father and him; when was this given? Before the world began, *i.e.* from all eternity. Titus 1:2, "In hope of eternal life, which God that cannot lie, promised before the world began." How was this life promised before the world began, but in this everlasting counsel of peace, in which the Father promised to Christ eternal life for all his seed? God had been dishonored by the violation of his Law, which made an infinite breach between the sinner and God. God would only be satisfied and reconciled if that Law were fulfilled, and Jesus fulfills it all. By his own appointment, at a specific point in time, for every believer, this eternal life is effectively applied to every one of them. The Father demanded the fulfilling of the Law, and Christ undertakes to do it; and he willingly puts himself under this Law. "When the fulness of time was come, God sent forth his Son, made of a woman, made under the Law, to Redeem them that were under the Law, that we might receive the adoption of sons," (Gal. 4:4-5). And he willing submits not only to the duty of the Law, but also to the penalty of the Law; not only to do what the Law enjoins, but also to suffer what the Law threatens for all believers. Every sin was in the cup he had to drink on behalf of his people.

And in this covenant, made before the world began, Christ is in all ages, since the fall of Adam, still working to apply the actual purchased benefits to his own special people as he redeems them in time. He does this now by entering into a special relationship with them. This special relationship, this covenant in time is called the covenant of free grace. "...the LORD thy God hath chosen thee to be a special people unto himself, above all people that are upon the face of the earth," (Deut. 7:6). Christ being "...the Lamb slain from the foundation of the world," (Rev. 13:8). "Forasmuch as ye know that ye were not redeemed with corruptible things, ... but with the precious blood of Christ, ... who verily was foreordained before the foundation of the world," (1 Peter 1:18-20). And, "he hath chosen us in him before the foundation of the world, that we should be holy and without blame before him in love," (Eph. 1:4). In this gracious relationship in time he reconciles them, by faith, in himself. And when they are found to be in him, every believer has a right and interest to Christ, and to all his blessings, that they may say, according to the sure mercies of David, "I am thine." Christ comes to do the Father's will and his own special people gain the benefit from his work, as he fulfills the covenant he made with his Father.

If Christ was given for the redemption of his people, then their redemption is rendered certain, and the operations of the Spirit are successful. If that is the design of Christ and the nature of the Spirit's influence, then those who are the objects of the one, and the subjects of the other, must persevere in holiness to the end; they will be saved. If the fall brought mankind into a state of sin and misery, then it follows that salvation must be of grace. God graciously saves his own special people out of the world for himself, and his glory, and it is certain that, "I am thine." It is not the work of men, lest any should boast. The work of God through Christ is effectual and renders certain the salvation of his people so that they cannot fall away from God's power and grace, if they are his. If the death of Christ renders certain the salvation of his people, if election is not of works, then the whole plan of God must be admitted as true. In God's plan of salvation (or any other part of his government of the created order) nothing can be unexpected, and nothing happens contrary to his purposes for his glory.

God intended in eternity what he actually does in time. Why? The psalmist said in the beginning, "For ever, O LORD, thy word is settled in heaven." (Psalm 119:89). Ephesians 1:3-6 is exceedingly clear, "Blessed be the God and Father of our Lord Jesus Christ, who hath blessed us with all spiritual blessings in heavenly places in Christ: according as he hath chosen us in Him, before the foundation of the world, that we should be holy and without blame before him in love: having predestinated us unto the adoption of children by Jesus Christ to himself, according to the good pleasure of his will, to the praise of the glory of his grace, wherein he hath made us accepted in the Beloved." The Apostle Peter says believers are elect, "unto obedience and sprinkling of the blood of Jesus Christ," (1 Peter 1:2). "God hath from the beginning chosen you to salvation through sanctification of the Spirit and belief of the truth," (2 Thess. 2:13). And, "We give thanks to God always for you all, making mention of you in our prayers; remembering without ceasing your work of faith, and labour of love, and patience of hope in our Lord Jesus Christ, in the sight of God and our Father; knowing, brethren beloved, your election of God," (1 Thess. 1:2-4). And, "If by grace, then is it no more of works: otherwise grace is no more grace. But if it be of works, then is it no more grace: otherwise work is no more work," (Rom. 11:6). In Romans 11 it is said that election is "not of works, but of him that calleth." "So then, it is not of him that willeth, nor of him that runneth, but of God that showeth mercy." Romans 8:30 demonstrates this unbreakable chain, "Whom he did predestinate, them he also called, those he called, these He also justified, those He justified these He also glorified..." (cf. Gal. 1:15-16; Eph. 1:12; 2 Tim. 1:9; James 1:18; 1 Pet. 2:8; Jude 1:4; Rom. 9:22).

Christ equally emphasizes God's work, choice and purpose in salvation in everything he taught. Christ speaks of those whom the Father had, "given him," (John 17:2). He gives them eternal life, (John 17:2 and 24). He prays for them, (John 17:19). He loses none of them because of the Father's preservance of them, (John 6:39). They hear his voice as sheep hear a Shepherd. "My sheep hear my voice, and I know them, and they follow me: and I give unto them eternal life; they shall never perish, neither shall any man pluck them out of my hand. My Father, which gave them me, is greater than all; and no man is able to pluck them out of my Father's hand," (John 10:27-29).

As sheep, God chooses them, gives them to Christ and *they* hear his voice. *Goats* do not hear his voice. Only sheep hear the Shepherd's voice. There are sheep, and there are goats. "All that the Father giveth me shall come to me; and him that cometh to me I will in no wise cast out," (John 6:37). Christ says, "No man can come to me, except the Father which hath sent me draw him: and I will raise him up at the last day," (John 6:44, cf. verse 65). God is the one with whom rests saving knowledge of the truth, for those saved, they must listen to Christ's words, "It is given unto you to know the mysteries of the kingdom of heaven, but to them it is not given," (Matt. 13:11, *cf.* Matt. 11:25), for our God reigns over the fall in his eternal covenant plan to save a special people as his very own and he gives such knowledge to people. Such is the Gospel preached to men as seen in Acts 13:48, so, "As many as were ordained to eternal life believed."

If God has his own special people in Jesus Christ, they are cared for by God. "I am thine, save me." "I am thine, therefore, save me." Was this not David's desire in a time of danger and affliction? The Lord Jesus, as the good Shepherd will hazard all to gain his sheep, and rejoice in doing so. "What man of you, having an hundred sheep, if he lose one of them, doth not leave the ninety and nine in the wilderness, and go after that which is lost, until he find it? And when he hath found it, he layeth it on his shoulders, rejoicing," (Luke 15:4-5). Sheep do not come wandering back. "I have gone astray like a lost sheep; seek thy servant," (Psalm 119:176), David says. John 17:6, "Thine they were, and thou gavest them me; therefore keep them through thine own name." There is great confidence with David in God's election of his own special people. He will preserve them, and care for them and help them and hazard much in his incarnation for them to be with them. How does this really help David? Why does it give him assurance?

God knows his people, he has a great interest in them as the apple of his eye, to care for them. 2 Tim. 2:19, "The Lord knows those that are his." He has a particular and intimate knowledge of all the elect, and all who shall be saved. They are said to be inscribed in his flesh, "Behold, I have graven thee upon the palms of my hands," (Isa. 49:16). John 10:3, "He calleth his own sheep by name." Christ knew their names while he hung on the cross for them. Christ knew their names, and all their sins, and all he would need to do to rescue them, before the world began. His special people are consecrated, set apart to him, for himself, Psalm 4:3, "The Lord hath set apart him that is godly for himself." People often like the "set apart" speech, but do not often like the latter which informs the former, him that is godly, for himself. God holds them as the apple of his eye. "...for he that toucheth you toucheth the apple of his eye," (Zech. 2:8). The Scriptures describe his own special people as the apple of his eye. The eye is very tender. Will he allow the apple of his eye to be touched? He has a very special eye to his own because God is known, glorified and owned in and through them. None, then, can look for life and salvation, but they that are of God's household, who alone can truly say with the Psalmist, "I am thine, save me," (Psalm 119:94). They remind themselves of this work of God again and again, hold it, and look on themselves as the Lord's, never to forget it, (verse 93). So the church says, "I am thine, save me." Song 2:16, "My beloved is mine, and

I am his." The spouse says that Jesus Christ is mine. They can with the greatest confidence and boldness affirm it, without wavering. He is my head, husband, Lord, Redeemer, Justifier, Savior, *yeshua, yesha, save me*. And they are equally confident because they are his. Thomas Brooks said, "I am as sure that I am his, as I am sure that I live. I am his by purchase, and I am his by conquest; I am his by donation, and I am his by election; I am his by covenant, and I am his by marriage. I am wholly his; I am peculiarly his; I am universally his; I am eternally his. This I well know, and the knowledge of this is my joy in life, and my strength and crown in death."[31] David could say, "The Lord is my portion for ever," Psalm (73:26), why? Because "I am thine, save me." The condescension of Christ in covenant is an amazing thing, that God would want his own special people out of the mass of fallen humanity, and claim an interest in them. "O, behold what manner of love the Father hath bestowed upon us, that we should be called sons of God!" (1 John 3:1). I own a lawnmower. It is mine. I own a house. It is mine. I own a truck. It is mine. People take joy in what they own. Do they take joy in salvation in the same way? If God has his own special people, taken from out of the world to himself, these too have God as their own.

"I am thine, save me." The Mediator reconciles men to God that they may have an interest in God, continually. When people lay hold of the Christ by faith, the Lord has never yet refused, at any period of the

---

[31] Brooks, vol. 2, 321.

human race, nor to the time of the last judgment, *will* he ever refuse, his healing and salvation to those he has elected out of the world to be his own, that come to him for rest. And this the saints know that they have their names inscribed by an immutable pen of iron in God's book of salvation if Christ has saved them. "Rejoice that your names are written in God's book of life," Christ tells his disciples. God has chosen his saints for salvation, elected them to glory, even before the foundations of the world in Jesus Christ; it is settled, in heaven, forever. God has promised them eternal happiness in the Son; joy, *forever*. It is a promise of eternal life, ever sure, the sure mercies of David; and this they know. They know the truth of the word, and the Spirit of God testifies to their spirits that they are sons and daughters of the most high. But I bring a question up to this point to light for you, why are we studying Psalm 119:89-96? It is because of this verse.

I want to explain something important about these verses by way of application. This whole series on Psalm 119, in these particular verses from 89-96, were originally set down as a result of my consideration, or meditation on these particular words, "I am thine, save me," which was attached to some thoughts I had about Martin Luther. Why so? I need to tell you about Luther. You can appreciate this comforting verse by what the word of God says, I think, but I also think you will appreciate what is being said here by David, with a *real life*, a *practical picture*, of what the power of this verse is, and what it has entailed even on history. The impact of Johannes von Staupitz (c. 1468–1524) on Martin Luther is extremely important for the magisterial reformation. This fellow is so important, in fact, that you may very well be sitting in a Popish church if it were not for God's Fatherly providence on this point, and from these words in the text of this Psalm. "I am thine; save me." Staupitz was elected the cleric general of the reformed Augustinian Order in 1503. Between 1504 and 1506 he had the *order's* constitutions printed for the first time, which was about the time when Luther became an Augustinian monk. Luther followed Staupitz, and as such Staupitz sent him from Wittenberg to Rome as the travel companion of the chief negotiator for his spiritual benefit. He saw many abuses in Rome that angered and confused him. Upon Luther's return, he became Staupitz's successor as professor of biblical theology in Wittenberg; their relationship was critical.

In his preaching, Staupitz was celebrated as the "tongue of the Apostle Paul" and the "herald of the gospel," one who stood up for evangelical truth. He was a Roman Catholic without the rites, and an evangelical without becoming Protestant. He wrote much. Luther sent his mother a copy of the first edition of Staupitz's work, "On the Love of God" published in 1518, giving his endorsement; a year after the Reformation begun. Luther gave his endorsement to subsequent editions of that book, which is essentially a book about "grace alone" and "Christ alone" for salvation. In this book

Christ's suffering is "for us," and God is made sweet and pleasant to us by grace, which Luther loved. Staupitz was Christ centered in this, following 1 Corinthians 1:23, "We preach nothing else than Christ crucified," as all good preachers are in heralding the "how" of the Gospel.

Toward the end of his life Luther, in a letter to Elector John Frederick of March 27, 1545, summed up his indebtedness: "Doctor Staupitz is first of all my father in this doctrine and gave birth to me in Christ." Luther said, "If it had not been for Dr. Staupitz, I should have sunk into hell." What counsel would Staupitz have given Luther in this to make him so admired and thankful for him? Prove out your *election* in Christ? Prove out that you are one of the *chosen*? No. Luther was terrified of God in the beginning of his walk, and wrestled vehemently with God being an angry Judge; so much so there were fits that Luther had, almost to the point of breaking him mentally. He often attended the confessional for hours in the monastery, confessing his sins in agony. How was he helped by this man?

Here were Staupitz's words to him, paraphrased as such, "when the Law threatens you, when you begin to think that God is angry with you, or, when you take your eyes off Jesus, learn to say, "Lord, I am thine. Save me." (Psalm 119:94). Luther, later, understood this verse to mean, "Thou hast given me life."[32] "For, unworthy as I

---

[32] Martin Luther, Luther's Works, Vol. 11: First Lectures on the Psalms II: Psalms 76-126, ed. Jaroslav Jan Pelikan, Hilton C. Oswald,

am, you will save me in your great mercy, and I will praise you continually all the days of my life."[33] For "if Christ is the bread of life, then I am convinced that my work will not save me and give me eternal life; for they are not Christ. My life is something else than my works; therefore they will not give me life."[34] What a verse to memorize; simple yet profound, on which the entire reformation swung for Luther. "I am thine, save me."

Staupitz was telling him, give yourselves up to Christ, to be saved by him, then give yourself to Christ in service for his glory. Our very taking of Christ in covenant requires this giving ourselves to him, and this taking him as our Lord and Savior. "No one can say save me except one who understands and acknowledges himself to be condemned."[35] When did you give yourself over to God? We could say it this way if you don't like that language, "When did God's electing plan manifest itself in your life?" When did you give up the key of your hearts to God, and lie at God's feet, and say, "Speak, LORD; for thy servant heareth," (1 Sam. 3:9). Those that

---

and Helmut T. Lehmann, vol. 11 (Saint Louis: Concordia Publishing House, 1955), 478.

[33] Martin Luther, Luther's Works, Vol. 39: Church and Ministry I, ed. Jaroslav Jan Pelikan, Hilton C. Oswald, and Helmut T. Lehmann, vol. 39 (Philadelphia: Fortress Press, 1999), 47.

[34] Martin Luther, Luther's Works, Vol. 23: Sermons on the Gospel of St. John: Chapters 6-8, ed. Jaroslav Jan Pelikan, Hilton C. Oswald, and Helmut T. Lehmann, vol. 23 (Saint Louis: Concordia Publishing House, 1999), 113.

[35] Martin Luther, Luther's Works, Vol. 10: First Lectures on the Psalms I: Psalms 1-75, ed. Jaroslav Jan Pelikan, Hilton C. Oswald, and Helmut T. Lehmann, electronic ed., vol. 10 (Saint Louis: Concordia Publishing House, 1999), 395.

are God's own special people come in this way, and hear the voice of the Shepherd beckoning them, and directing them and saving them, because they know they belong to him. God has a peculiar people for himself. What do you have in this but special mercies and special grace, for God's own special people have very special mercies and very special grace? "Let thy mercies come also unto me, O LORD, even thy salvation, according to thy word," (Psalm 119:41). "Let thy tender mercies come unto me, that I may live: for thy law is my delight." (Psalm 119:77). "Great are thy tender mercies, O LORD: quicken me according to thy judgments," (Psalm 119:156). Are you looking and longing for the tender mercies of God's covenant promises in Christ? Luther said, "I must have his grace, his Christ, his Spirit." Don't be deceived, people in the world may have common mercies and go to hell, and not be among God's own special people. There cannot be a profession in your mouth, without a walk that convinces both yourself and others that you *are* indeed of God's own special people. This is why Scripture never tells you to prove out your *election*, but prove out your *profession*, and then never doubt your election.

God has opened the floodgates of everlasting life in Christ to you. The blessings which are conveyed to you as one of his own special people are privileged. Matt. 22:14, "Many are called, but few are chosen." By the power of his Spirit, he applies to you all saving graces that he purchased in the covenant of redemption. He makes a change in you, converts you by spiritual life, in opening your understandings, renewing your wills, affections, and mind, for giving the gift of spiritual obedience to his commands. He gives you saving faith, by showing you the plight of sin and death, deserved condemnation, that you would then give your consent to the covenant, and to embrace Jesus Christ with sincerity. He gives you repentance, by making you, with godly sorrow, in the hatred of sin, and love of righteousness, turn from all iniquity to his service in worship. He sanctifies you, by causing you to persevere in faith, and spiritual obedience to his Law. He makes you fruitful, in all duties, and doing good works, as he allows, by his Spirit, which he graciously has sent to you, and fills you, and dwells in you. He brings you, by faith, into a special relationship, where you know you belong to him and he to you. He justifies you by his work, reconciles you, and makes you his friends, who were once his enemies. He adopts you, that you would not be bound by Satan in the Kingdom of darkness any longer, but you are now his children, given all spiritual privileges as sons and daughters. And in the end, you will be joyfully joined together in the resurrection with Christ and made to see him face to face, and will be students of holiness with him forever, in the state of glorification.

    What a high admiration of the great and infinite love of God, of God the Father, of God the Son; what manner of love has the God of grace revealed in this counsel of peace! Admire the love of the Father as a wonderful, superlative love! "God so loved the world, that he gave his only begotten Son," etc. (John 3:16). That the thoughts of the Father should be on lost man, to save him, through killing his Son, is incomprehensible; and yet glorious. Admire the love of the Son; he is willing to engage in this covenant, he knew its terms, what the redemption of man would cost him, even his innocent life and innocent precious blood. Yet, he willingly and freely binds himself to redeem sinners, whatever it would cost him, to drink of the Father's wrath in the cup to the very last drop. You should think, "Blessed Jesus, that you should ever agree to lay down your life for me, to wash away my sins in your own blood, (1 John 3:16; Rev. 1:5), to give your soul as an offering for sin, that you might save such a poor worm as I, to bring me near to the Father. What shall I, what can I say to all this? but fall down, and wonder at that love which can never be fathomed!"

Admire the love of the Spirit who shines Christ into your heart. All his heart work, his covenant heart work, to motion you to stir yourselves up to service; it is by the Spirit of truth, in the truth and by the truth. Understand this work of Christ, in this redemptive covenant, encourages your faith. You sometimes question the blessings of Christ, and wonder what he is doing in your life, especially during times of affliction. But know, the blessings of his work to you are sure. They are called, "the sure mercies of David," (Isaiah 55:3), for a reason. God has ratified it by his oath, (Gen. 22:16; Heb. 6:13-18). Thomas Case said, "His promise is enough, but surely his oath must put all out of question; there's no room for unbelief, now that God has sworn to it,"[36]

If you would gain comfort and strengthening from this, you must find out if you are the elect of God, chosen of him to be vessels of his mercy before the world began; but to do that you cannot think about it backwards. Christ undertook to give his life only for those whom the Father had first given to him; only these he prayed for in John 17, and only these he died for.

You might think this is hard thing to know, Peter says, "To make their election sure," (2 Peter 1:10); are you sure? You should, then, have an interest in this covenant; to know Christ's work better. To demonstrate the work of the Christian so you can have assurance, to make your calling and election sure; to know you are his. Because from knowing this comes assurance; the Spirit works that into the soul through the word; and who doesn't want that? Then, to know where there is safety, is where we turn to consider how the believer may safely stand before a satisfied God on the day of judgment. This we will consider in the next chapter. That even they would know, right now, God's election of his own special people in them, as David did, "I am thine, save *me*."

---

[36] *Essentials of the Christian Religion*, (Crossville, TN: Puritan Publications, 2022), 165.

Chapter 8:
Election in Christ, the Ground of the Sinner's Safety

"I am thine, save me; for I have sought thy precepts," (Psalm 119:94).

It's personal, "I belong to you, save me," It's ownership, "thine." It's a current reality, "am". It's concerning God's means of salvation, "save me." "I am thine; save me." David is God's, for God has bought him with a price, and he relies on God for his salvation; and desires to be saved; there is safety in God and his means of salvation which is through the Spiritual David, the Messiah.

Doctrine: Saving faith trusts in the safety of the righteousness of Jesus Christ alone at the day of judgment.

In a work given by preachers to set forth the truth of the Gospel, in the middle of the 17th century, there were a number of points written down. 16 to be exact, which the 16th was this: 16thly. *That the dead shall rise; and that there is a day of judgment, wherein all shall appear, some to go into everlasting life, and some into everlasting condemnation.* 1 Tim. 1:19-20, compared with 2 Tim. 2:17-18; Acts 17:30-31; John 5:28-29. 1 Cor. 15:19.[37] In

---

[37] Neal, Daniel, *The History of the Puritans*, Volume 2, (London: B. Griffin and Co., 1837) 622.

preserving one's soul, one must watch and take heed; consider the future judgment to come; how will they be safe at judgment? Scripture teaches that there is a God who has set a day in which there is a day of judgment in which all men must answer to all that they have done in thought, word and deed. "The Lord knoweth how to deliver the godly out of temptations, and to reserve the unjust unto the day of judgment to be punished," (2 Peter 2:9). There is a judgment coming, and one would be wise to consider how they may escape the day with blessing rather than cursing. "...we may have boldness in the day of judgment," (1 John 4:17).

God has a peculiar people that he owns, which he rescued out of the fallen world, as the apple of his eye, a most tender expression of his love for them; and this was considered in light of that everlasting counsel of peace, set down by the Triune God. The question that comes from this, is how this Counsel of Peace made between the Father and the Son in the Spirit, is now applied to men? How are they made partakers of this peace?

When considering what God did before the world began in that blessed plan to save his people, next is to see how that salvation is *applied* in time to *particular people*. The covenant exists, and now, sinners want to know how they can be part of it. It is one of the most important questions and studies they can ever have. It is why we call this kind of a study having a true interest in Jesus Christ; to have faith in his righteousness. An interest in both who he is and what he has done. And how this is applied is what is called the Covenant of Grace, the covenant between God and believers. It is the same question to ask, how can a person say, "I am thine, save me," and know it and mean it? Christ, as Mediator of the elect, was subject to earn eternal life and pay their debt of sin to the Father. The Father needed to be satisfied for the transgression and omission of his holy Law by criminals who sinned against him. Christ came to fulfil the Law, both in upholding it against transgression, and fulfilling it in righteousness against any lack of conformity to it. And as a result of doing all that the Father desires of his elect Servant, Christ, then went to the cross as a willing sacrifice, to fulfill the debt that must be paid to God as a result of sin; someone had to die for it. His work in fulfilling all that God requires according to his Law is called, his active obedience. His work in fulfilling all that God requires as a sacrifice for sin on the cross, is called his passive obedience. In the first, his active obedience, he fulfills the Law perfectly during his entire earthly life, in every point, in every way. He fulfilled the Law in every respect. With all the heart, soul and mind, and that to an infinite degree as the God-man. In the second, his passive obedience, he suffered from the time of Gethsemane, to the time he died on the cross and was willingly under the power of death for three days. Without both aspects of his obedience working on behalf of the believer, the believer can never be saved and they can never be justified. Nothing can ever be applied to them if the Law is not perfectly upheld, and God is not perfectly appeased. Someone must come and fulfill all righteousness on behalf of the crimes of the elect, or, the elect must fulfill all righteousness on their own, which they can never do because they are criminals and rebels. The active and passive obedience of Christ accompany each other at every point in the Savior's life. Romans 10:4 declares, "For Christ is the end of the law for righteousness to everyone who believes."

Christ is the "termination" or *telos* of the law for all who believe (by faith) that his obedience justifies them eternally as they believe in him by faith. This obedience of Christ fulfills the covenant breaking of the Law that the first Adam failed to uphold. The second Adam succeeded in perfectly fulfilling the demands of the covenant by his obedience. This does not liberate Christians from keeping the Law – in terms of sanctification and holiness – but does release them from having to keep the Law perfectly to satisfy divine justice and secure their own salvation which they cannot do; they cannot save themselves. The only means by which the sinner can say "I am thine, save me," is being justified by faith alone in Christ alone to the glory of God alone. It rests solely on what Christ did.

The obedience of Christ was performed by him in the stead of the elect in order that they might receive eternal life. Romans 5:16–19, "And the gift is not like that which came through the one who sinned. For the judgment which came from one offense resulted in condemnation, but the free gift which came from many offenses resulted in justification. For if by the one man's offense death reigned through the one, much more those who receive abundance of grace and of the gift of righteousness will reign in life through the One, Jesus Christ. Therefore, as through one man's offense judgment came to all men, resulting in condemnation, even so through one Man's righteous act the free gift came to all men, resulting in justification of life. For as by one man's disobedience many were made sinners, so also by one Man's obedience many will be made righteous."

The merit of Christ (i.e. that which was gained by obedience) is perfect righteousness, so God rewarded him for his work and labor, and it is that merit that is imputed to the elect in this covenant of free grace. Romans 4:6, "just as David also describes the blessedness of the man to whom God does not impute iniquity." Romans 4:8, "Blessed is the man to whom the LORD shall not impute sin." Romans 4:24, "It shall be imputed to us who believe in him who raised up Jesus our Lord from the dead." Imputation means that God accounts Christ's work as the elect's work, just as impute means God counted Adam's sin as humanity's sin. The sins of all kinds of believers, are "covered" by Christ's work; he is their covering; he is their Mercy Seat.

Christ's righteousness is "imputed" to the elect; credited to them when they believe in him by faith. *The 1647 Westminster Confession of Faith* says in 8:5, "The Lord Jesus, by his perfect obedience and sacrifice of himself, which he through the eternal Spirit once offered up unto God, hath fully satisfied the justice of his Father, and purchased not only reconciliation, but an everlasting inheritance in the kingdom of heaven, for all those whom the Father hath given unto him." God accepts the elect if they believe this. What are they to believe? They are to believe that the obedience of Christ was sufficient for their salvation, in all its parts; they bring nothing to the bar of justice on judgment day other than the righteousness of Jesus Christ; only there is safety. His obedience is of inestimable value to the elect, and to God. The elect's infinite sin, against an infinite God, needs an infinite sacrifice; I cannot tell you how many Christians do not understand *that*. Any sin committed against God's infinite majesty is considered an *infinite* transgression; a *limitless* sin against him. Only Christ can deal with such sins because he is both God and man. He is *man* to offer his flesh, and *God* to make it of infinite value for good. Christ's deity enabled him to offer such a sacrifice of inestimable worth for the elect; infinite in point of fact. His humanity enabled him to obey in the place of the elect, but his deity gave it its infinite power. The blood of bulls and goats cannot save, rather, it must be a human sacrifice for sin that atones for the sins of humans (Hebrews 10:4). And yet, even though Christ's sacrifice was infinite, and infinitely atoned for sin, and infinitely satisfied the wrath of God, the obedience of Christ does not take away the elect's responsibility to obey him in and after their conversion. Many times, people use the "righteousness of Christ" as a means to sin. *Look at all he did for me, I need to do nothing more than just believe that he did this for me and leave it at that and I will go to heaven.* But what does the psalmist say? "I am thine, ... save me." What contradiction this Scripture is to such notions that nothing more after justification is to be done!

The Psalmist was confident in the worth of the Messiah's work, God's work, so he could be confident in being God's, and continuing along this path of salvation, that would "save him." What was this worth? The worth of Christ's satisfaction in this salvation is considered in two ways in this: 1) Christ obtained for himself, as Mediator, a right to all of his elect. For example, "Ask of me, and I shall give thee the heathen for thine inheritance, and the uttermost parts of the earth for thy possession," (Psalm 2:8). "In whom also we have obtained an inheritance, being predestinated according to the purpose of him who worketh all things after the counsel of his own will: That we should be to the praise of his glory, who first trusted in Christ," (Eph. 1:11-12). Such people are special to him, "For the LORD hath chosen Jacob unto himself, and Israel for his peculiar treasure," (Psalm 135:4). "I am thine," the psalmist knew. 2) Christ obtained for the elect a protection (a safety) from all misery and a right to eternal life to be applied to them. "For this is my blood of the new testament, which is shed for many for the remission of sins," (Matt. 26:28). "Who gave himself for our sins, that he might deliver us from this present evil world, according to the will of God and our Father," (Gal. 1:4). "Who gave himself for us, that he might redeem us from all iniquity, and purify unto himself a peculiar people," (Titus 2:14).

In today's Christian culture, it is unfortunate that many believe Christ only accomplished a "way of salvation" instead of "actually saving" anyone to call his own. The Bible teaches that Christ did not achieve a bare possibility of salvation but actually obtained salvation for his people; that is why his very name means Savior. Otherwise, the psalmist could have been confident in nothing. The idea of redemption, ransom and the price of redemption demonstrates the reality, and not the possibility, of salvation. This salvation of God is never uncertain. When Christ gives himself as a ransom for sin then sin is effectually removed. Otherwise, if he was a ransom for sin, and that did not actually take away sin based on his work alone, then the work of the Mediator is counterfeit. The Psalmist would never be able to say, "I am thine," he might say, "I hope I am thine..." "I might be thine..." "maybe I am thine." Christ would then be a dying Mediator who does not actually mediate anything, and who actually saved no one in and of himself. But Scripture declares that the effect of redemption is actual salvation; because it is there and only there that the sinner can be safe on the day of judgment. "Being justified freely by his grace through the redemption that is in Christ Jesus," (Rom. 3:24). "In whom we have redemption through his blood, the forgiveness of sins, according to the riches of his grace," (Eph. 1:7). The elect were purchased, "For ye are bought with a price," (1 Cor. 6:20). "...that we may have boldness in the day of judgment," (1 John 4:17). On judgment day there is safety in Christ alone. In other words, there is no possibility of Christ losing anyone that he died for. Part of the Holy Spirit's work is to reward Christ by applying the saving work of Christ to his people for all time; he will never fail in this.

Scripture never speaks of Christ's death as a possibility for the remission of sins; what safety is there in a possibility of something? "I am thine..." with no question about it, and he even gives proof for it in the latter part of the verse, which is that word "for". To many modern-day Christians Christ being the Savior is an absurd idea. They want some part in salvation. They want some natural man's way into heaven; I did this, I believed this Gospel and my friend didn't and that is the difference between me and them, that I believed and they did not. Christ is not the difference to them; they are the difference. Scripture refutes them thoroughly at every turn, "For other foundation can no man lay than that is laid, which is Jesus Christ," (1 Cor. 3:11).

It is absurd to believe that Christ died for someone who would eventually be sent to hell and that

Chapter 8: Election in Christ the Ground of the Sinner's Safety

God did not have a specific elect group in mind for Christ's death to give him as a reward for his merits. That makes his work and his power ineffectual. It makes him a non-Savior – a Savior of no one. It makes the lost sheep in the wilderness now caught in the mouth of the lion, under the paw of the bear, in a situation where they escape in order to go to him by something they do. They are not rescued out; can the sheep outwit the bear, or the lion; it is an absurd picture. The Shepherd waits for the sheep to set themselves free from the lion and the bear? Some people like to put salvation into the hands of men. Why? Fallen men love to, "do things for themselves." Salvation for them isn't about "I am thine," it is not about safety in Christ's righteousness alone, but rather, it is about, "I did something myself and feel good about it." Because *they* did it, in a temporary and shallow way, it comforts their flesh; it's tangible to them because the true way of holiness is *foreign* to them. And if they do not have a point of reference to experience something, then it is not real for them and they do not like it. This is often because they are devoid of true faith. Man *cannot* save. God *must* save. God alone saves, because there is safety with him. This is why the Psalmist, in ages past, said, "I am thine, save me." It is the only place one can be safe, in God's hands. "My Father, which gave them me, is greater than all; and no man is able to pluck them out of my Father's hand." Oh, ...and let me tell you one more thing on this, "I and my Father are one." (John 10:29-30). God is bound to his promise, and faith and repentance are part of the blessings (Ephesians 1:3; Phil. 1:29) bestowed upon the elect on the merit of Christ's satisfaction alone. It is a failure to understand what God was doing with the sacrificial system in the Old Testament that often brings people to wrongly interpret passages in the New Testament about "whosoever" believing in Christ (John 3:16). Faith and repentance are not required conditions before some effects of Christ's death are communicated to a person; that comes after. People are born again, first, by the Spirit, (changed) based on the sovereign work of the Spirit – not based on a condition of whether they have faith or not. Being born again is a sovereign act of the Spirit based on Christ' work for the sinner. Jesus told Nicodemus that unless men are first born again, they do not have the ability to have faith at all, as a matter of fact, they do not have the ability to understand anything about the kingdom without being born again first (John 3:3, 5), "Unless a man is born again, he cannot..."

In the Old Testament when sacrifices were given for the people, they did not save those outside the camp; there was no atonement for people outside the camp. Its effectualness resided in God's application of that sacrifice as a shadow to the work of Jesus Christ. Joe Israelite was not the maker of his own destiny; God was.

Objection: if salvation is really accomplished by Christ in the past, and the sins of those for whom he died are actually forgiven in him, how is it that people are still sinners when they are born? Answer: The benefits of salvation are not bestowed on the elect before calling, faith, repentance and actual union with Christ in time occurs. It's true, God *eternally* loves the elect in Christ, and yet, they will have the means of the Gospel given to them at a *certain time* in their life. While they are yet under sin and its power, they are called, "children of wrath" (Ephesians 2:3) as they reside under the sin of Adam. But, they will one day be saved at a specific point in time in their life. They were once this way, and then they will be now that way. They were once in the kingdom of darkness, and now they are brought by the Spirit into the Kingdom of Christ. Keep in mind, why the elect, are able to come before the throne of grace boldly. God's elect can boldly ask for blessings because of what Christ has done. No one can ask for those blessings unless he has first been converted; unless the Spirit has applied those things to them. Pagans and heathens cannot ask for blessings from God. God counts such requests as abominations. "The sacrifice of the wicked is an abomination to the LORD," (Prov. 15:8). Yes, they might pray for some change in their life, or some bad circumstance to turn into a good one. God sees asking him for things without faith in Christ as abominable. What, then, makes one person to differ from another? As the Apostle Paul stated, "God." First God changes the heart, then the changed heart asks accordingly by the power of the Spirit of God, to be saved. God never requires faith and obedience as the means to earn the right to ask for eternal life because the right to gain eternal life is based upon the person and work of Christ alone. It is based on the application of that work by the Holy Spirit first. Faith takes place immediately after the Spirit's work on the heart.

"What is faith?" What makes the psalmist say with great faith, "I am thine, save me"? He believes he is God's. He's confident of it; it is a very confident statement. Faith is to believe Christ, that all he accomplished in salvation is based solely on his righteousness. Faith is among the graces of God, given as a gift. Faith injects men into Christ. Hab. 2:4, "The just shall live by his faith." Faith quickens graces. Faith excites repentance. Faith looks to hope. Faith is the oil which feeds the virgin's lamps. ...faith in the righteousness and work of Christ. Even the believer's obedience is the result of faith. For all believers live by faith in the Son of God. Faith is believing the good news of the reigning King, which looks to the promises of God found in Christ alone, and includes a real trust and reliance on him for salvation. That the elect believes what Christ says, and believes that what he says is both true and good. "For by grace are ye saved through faith; and that not of yourselves: it is the gift of God: Not of works, lest any man should boast," (Eph. 2:8-9). Grace comes first (through Christ and the Spirit's application of his work) and faith afterwards (after the man's heart is now born again). There is an evil heart, the Spirit changes that evil heart to be a born-again heart, and then that heart believes what Christ says; it cannot help to do so – it must! Salvation is given to the elect in respect to

Chapter 8: Election in Christ the Ground of the Sinner's Safety

their right of ownership before they believe anything; the Spirit changes them first. Why? Because in Jesus Christ they are saved from even eternity past; there is safety at the judgment seat only in him. Faith and salvation become theirs actually by possession (in time) they know it, when they believe. It is like a prisoner in a jail cell that had his bail paid (he is a free man) though he does not know it yet because he's still in the cell. The jailer has not walked down the hall and released him yet. But his "state of being" is one that is freed, not one that is jailed; he's a free man by the view of the authorities. It is simply a matter of time before the jailor walks down the hall to release him. But rest assured, he will be released; and he will know it when it happens.

At a certain point in time past, Christ has saved all his elect by his work. In time, men have those benefits applied and declared true about them, and they realize their freedom. Is not his life, death resurrection, ascension and present intercession of not the most important topic for sinners? "I am thine..." with confidence, and boldness, in holy safety; but wait, why does he say right after "save me?" Does this not seem odd for him to say if he is saved by God and is God's? He says, "I am thine;" but then he says save me. Does he not understand what he is saying? Consider this phrase, "Save Me." Time is always moving forward, it is the place where people live and exist and experience life moment by moment; salvation takes on certain characteristics, in which saints experience the affects of being saved by faith alone in Christ at a certain moment in time. The benefits of such a salvation applied to them by faith, are extensive. "Blessed be the God and Father of our Lord Jesus Christ, who hath blessed us with all spiritual blessings in heavenly places in Christ: According as he hath chosen us in him before the foundation of the world, that we should be holy and without blame before him in love," (Eph. 1:3-4). Many spiritual blessings could be given. The psalmist is blessed in God's work in him, with every spiritual blessing being given by God, and saved by God. So why this, "Save me?" He's God's, but still needs to be saved? Are these real benefits that he's gained or only imaginary if he says he's God's and yet, still needs to be saved? Doesn't the first part of this little verse answer the second part? As if to say to him, "David, you are asking God to save you, but you already confessed you are his. Why the apparent contradiction?"

There are three aspects to salvation throughout the bible: (1) true believers *have been saved* by Christ, (2) *are being saved* by Christ and (3) *will be saved* by Christ; one may summarize this more theologically by saying, they are justified, sanctified and glorified. Certainly, one chief role given to ministers of the gospel is to be used of the Lord through the preaching of the word every Lord's Day to bring Christ's flock all the way to heaven. People ask me, what is purpose of your church? I give them a twofold answer, "To worship the Trinity in spirit and truth without compromise", and, "to get everyone in the congregation to heaven." It is true, believers are God's, "I am thine." They are Christ's and they are his sheep, his people, his church, his reward, given to him by the Father, which he can lose none of them that are truly given. And yet, it is also certain that true believers are being saved, and will be saved enduring to the end. That language is just as fitting; justified, sanctified and glorified. It is *certain* that the Lord uses the means of the word of Christ, the sacrament of his body and blood, his intercession in the means of grace, to bring his own people home, all the way to heaven. Here a distinction is to be drawn in terms of position: David is saved, "I am thine," and he is being made more holy (being saved) (John 3:36; Ephesians 1:3; 2:3–6; Romans 4:25; 8:9–14; 1 Corinthians 1:2) and awaits the ultimate glorification of the body (will be saved) (Romans 8:29–39; 1 Corinthians 15:50–58; Philippians 1:6; 3:20–21), based on what *Christ* has done. In terms of their current daily experience believers (saved) are to be sanctified (being saved) (Ephesians 3:14–19; 5:3–8, 33; 6:4, 18; Philippians 2:12–13; 4:6–7; 2 Peter 2:16), with a hope to the end that he who has begun this work in them will complete it (will be saved.)

It can be said that believers are saved, are being saved, and will be saved, and are safe in this Jesus who does all these things in and for and with them. "I am thine, *save* me." As if he were to say, *it's all of you Lord, and not of me; work in me that I may see your salvation, and that I may please you in all things you give me to do.* All this is by faith alone in Christ alone, the only place of the sinner's safety.

What are redeemed sinners in this safe from at the Day of Judgment? There is safety to appear in the righteousness of Christ on the day of judgment from God's wrath. The only means of escape from the wrath of God in hell is Jesus Christ; Jesus saves people from God. 1 Thessalonians 1:10 says, "even Jesus, who delivers us from the wrath to come." Jesus has the ability to save men from hell, and he is doing that very thing right now in every believer. Christ suffered in the garden and on the cross for the sins of his people. He drank the cup of God's indignation for those he died for, and suffered the pains of hell's torment on the cross for them. He alone, in his work, is able to save men from the hell of God's wrath. He alone holds in the palm of his hand the way of salvation. He alone takes away sin and wraps men in the robe of his righteousness. He alone covers men with his blood, and, through his work, men are accepted before God. Yes, there is great safety in standing in the righteousness of Christ on the Day of Judgment. In fact, there is no other way to be saved. Oftentimes people make the mistake of trying, on their own, to "escape the wrath to come," without having a sincere interest in Jesus Christ. Without a true interest in Christ, "escaping hell" is impossible. People escape hell as they love the Lord Jesus Christ in sincerity and have a true interest in his person, not just the gifts he gives them in salvation, because he saves them. These people are owned by God, they are his, and they are saved by him and for him; and they know it. Those washed in the blood of Christ, and those not washed in the blood, will have a day of judgment. For those not washed in the blood, it is a day when Adam's sin in them will be brought to a frightful light at Christ's judgment seat. Exposed in light. It is appointed to these people once to die then to judgment they go.

There the books of their life will be opened, and the Son of Man will reveal the depth their sin. *I want to be rich*, you should have wanted me more. *I want to be famous*; you should have wanted me more. *I wanted status and power*; you should have wanted me more. *I wanted to carve out my own destiny*; you should have wanted me more. He will show them original sin, and then turn the pages of the books page by page and tell them all things they thought, did, said, and acted, which will in turn aggravate the sentencing they will have to their eternal misery. Going to judgment outside of Christ's blood will be a terrible day, the first of many terrible days without end. And they will have no excuses, and nothing to say, because everything they will experience will be in the light, by the truth, and they will know it; but they will know they are without a covering; and they are exposed; there will be no debate. But judgment day will be very different for those washed in the blood of Christ, who are God's. God will require the believer's life too at judgment, but if they are trusting in the righteous blood of Jesus alone, the outcome is very different. It may be today, tomorrow, in six months, in twenty years, it may be before this day is done. But to judgment believers too will go and there is no better place to stand before the Christ but in his righteousness.

The saints are covered by the everlasting blood of the covenant of Jesus Christ. And there is great safety in appearing at the day of judgment in the covering provided by the Christ; he is their mercy seat; God has accepted them because he has accepted the work of Christ for them. Christ has so purchased salvation, he has made saints, "his", for, "I am thine, save me," that the elect cannot fail in what Christ has done for them. The first Adam made men heirs of death and hell. Christ (the second Adam) made believers heirs of life as it is impossible that they should fail in being saved. Christ's purchase gives them such a title to having been saved, being saved, and that they will be saved, that there can be no failure in it. "Now our Lord Jesus Christ himself, and God, even our Father, which hath loved us, and hath given us everlasting consolation and good hope through grace, comfort your hearts, and stablish you in every good word and work," (2 Thess. 2:16-17). God has given believers everlasting consolation and eternal hope through grace. Men shall be blessed in Christ, according to his promises, and all the families of the earth should be blessed in his seed, and the promise made to believers realizes that very promise to them.

Christ saved the psalmist, was saving him, and would in fact in the end save him, because he was God's.

It was so certain a salvation that God considers what the Messiah did for David was as if David had performed that righteousness himself. He gains all the benefits of life, for God demonstrates all through the Bible, no less than in Psalm 119, that his Christ should bring his people to salvation by his righteousness, and it is safe to appear before the holiness of God, in his work and merit. All others who appear in some other way, or think in some other way, will meet a horrible end at judgment.

Are you God's and have you asked him to save you? This is the same question as asking if you have faith in Christ. Faith in the righteousness of Christ alone. David prayed this after his conversion. It was a means to stir him up to assurance. Faith is a subject that could be written about for millions of pages. Actually, it has, over the span of two thousand years on various continents by thousands of great theologians and preachers throughout church history. Are you assured of *your* safety, do you feel safe? Why would you need to feel safe? Why would you need to stand in safety? Because left up to yourself you are in a precarious position, a terrible one that will not end well, because being an enemy of God is a terrible state to be in. It's not a theological state, it is a practical one. God counts those who are not washed in the blood of Christ as enemies. And if God does that, he does that to its fullest and perfect extent, and will show you that to the greatest degree at the day of judgment. Without someone to come and intercede on your behalf, that has all power and all holiness, two things you do not have, you will not stand safely before God's Christ on judgment day. Faith acts on the knowledge of something to be believed. When you know this, you throw yourselves wholly on Christ. Faith involves something you are to know, and faith causes you to act. The Psalmist knew he was God's, and that for various reasons. Most atheists love to toss around the stupidity of "blind faith;" Oh these Christians believe with a blind faith. No, they don't. How ludicrous. Yes, blind faith is stupid and it's even more stupid for atheists who don't know what they are talking about to apply blind faith to the Christian faith. The Christian faith is rational, it's not blind. Why? God is sound and sensible and reasonable by things he has told them; and the entire Christian faith is based on God's promises and word; on inspired God-breathed evidence written down for them. The Christian faith, therefore, does not contain an ounce of blind faith. Any Christian that tells you otherwise, or says otherwise, that they believe in Christ blindly, doesn't know what they are saying, or is completely ignorant of the Gospel.

Scripture testifies that your faith involves knowledge. Jesus said in John 17:3, "And this is eternal life..." What is eternal life? "This." What is "This?" He continues and says, "...that they know you the only true God, and Jesus Christ whom you have sent." Peter confessed in John 6:68-69, "You have the words of eternal life, and we have believed, and have come to know, that you are the Holy One of God." The very nature of faith dictates knowing what you believe. If we are to believe something, faith then rests on something to be believed. We have to assent to something we know or understand. If we assent to something, then, that presupposes knowledge. Where does knowledge come from? In this case, concerning salvation, it comes from the word of God; from God's precepts. Where have we heard that? "I am thine, save me; for I have sought thy precepts," (Psalm 119:94). The psalmist will use this to prove out his faith, which in turn, gives him assurance of his election. Faith is stirred up externally from the preaching of the word and internally by the teaching of the Holy Spirit all based on God's word. There are specific things that one must believe in order to be saved. It is absurd to think that you can feel safe in the righteousness of Christ without believing something. The very nature of what faith is dictates otherwise. We have to believe the Scriptures – that they come from God. If we don't believe that the Scriptures are divine then there is nothing to believe in. The Sum of Saving Knowledge states in 2:1, "Albeit man, having brought himself into this woeful condition, be neither able to help himself, nor willing to be helped by God out of it, but rather inclined to lie still, insensible of it, till he perish; yet God, for the glory of his rich grace, hath revealed in his word a way to save sinners, to wit, by faith in Jesus Christ, the eternal Son of God, by virtue of, and according to the tenor of the covenant of redemption, made and agreed upon, between God the

Father and God the Son, in the counsel of the Trinity, before the world began." John 21:24 states, "This is the disciple who is bearing witness about these things, and who has written these things, and we know that his testimony is true." We believe what is true (*i.e.* the Scriptures) about the Christ and his salvation; his testimony is true. But after that hurdle, there are certain truths with respect to salvation in Christ that must be believed. We must believe we are sinners, and that sin is abominable to God. We must believe that the Jesus of the Bible is the only Savior (and know what that means). We must believe that salvation is obtained through faith which is a gift of God. We must believe that faith is accompanied by the substance of the truth of God. It is not a hollow faith, or an empty faith, or a blind faith; it is a true faith which believes the truth, empowered by the Spirit in a person. In believing the Gospel and having faith we have an assent to and have a conviction of the truths of the Gospel. Hebrews 11:1 says, "Now faith is the assurance of things hoped for, the conviction of things not seen." Not that faith does not have substance – but that faith is not yet seen; that's not blind faith, that is hope-filled faith based on the word of God and his promises, and his oath. When Christians go to heaven and see Christ, their faith is made sight; the substance doesn't change, just the mode of reality changes. Right now, though, that faith is a belief on something that the Holy Spirit convicts the soul is true out of the word of

God based on evidence; it's not a blind faith. It is a conviction which is based upon the truth.

We must love the truth. Some people do not love truth and they are *not* Christians, "...because they received not the love of the truth, that they might be saved," (2 Thess. 2:10). We must have a hunger and thirst after Christ's truth, "I am the way the truth and the life." This is where we love Christ as God and Lord of our salvation, (was saved, being saved, and will be saved) by his work and merit. "But as many as received him, to them gave he power to become the sons of God, even to them that believe on his name," (John 1:12). And Paul says "As ye have therefore received Christ Jesus the Lord, so walk ye in him," (Col. 2:6). In this kind of believing, you are applying the promises of the Gospel to yourself; making the promises personal to you, and walking in them. Where have we heard that, the psalmist does this very thing, "I am thine, save me." That's eminently personal, and the opposite of any other kind of worldly faith or nominal faith that does not save.

Consider non-saving faith. As much as someone may have true faith, there is also a non-saving faith that will not bring someone to heaven, and is not safe to appear at the judgment seat in, though it may be laden with facts about Christ and God. We might call this "historical faith" or "theological faith". You can be theological and never get into heaven, just like the devil is theologically correct in his understanding of Christ but will not go to heaven. With fickle human beings, this kind of faith is really temporary faith, because it has no depth, and engages the heart only for a little while and then dies. It cannot save anyone, oftentimes it deceives them and corrupts their mind. They believe they are saved, but in fact, they have been fooled; they are nominal Christians, meaning, they have a little bit of religiosity about them, but they have no depth; and they do not grow.

There are, then, some important distinctions between non-saving and saving faith. Non-saving faith does not properly see the beauty of Christ. Non-saving faith does not see or love the truth of Christ. Non-saving faith does not engage in self-examination as to whether one is holy or not; they want nothing to do with holiness. Non-saving faith does not produce the love of God. Non-saving faith does not produce the Spirit's fruit. True saving faith is the opposite of all of these. If you have true faith, "I am thine, save me," you have peace with God. That is an easy test, do I both believe and feel I have peace with God?

The consequence of spiritual peace is friendship with God. That is an easy test, is God my friend and do I know it, experience it? Is it just the words that are spoken or is there a reality for you in it? "In whom we have boldness and access with confidence by the faith of him," (Eph. 3:12). Where might we look in Scripture to see this boldness in God and his salvation? "I am thine, save me." A statement, a prayer, a confidence, a boldness, a plea, a desire, a testimony, a witness; true saving faith.

This gives you as an elect believer peace of conscience. A saint's election in Jesus Christ and in his righteousness is the ground of the sinner's safety at the day of judgment, and you can be confident in it. Safety from God's wrath. Safety from the world, the flesh and the devil. Safety in salvation, safety in sanctification, safety on the day of judgment, safety in the hope they have to one day be glorified. This is because the ground of the sinner's safety is God in Christ alone, and his power to execute his saving benefits to their fullest extent. Because the sinner's safety is set in Christ alone, in his righteousness alone, and there is great safety in that, for it is the only thing that God accepts.

Seek this safety in Christ alone, for peace. You are saved, no doubt, in what Christ has done. But you are being saved and sanctified and made more like him daily by exercising that faith. You are his, but you need and require his power and his Spirit and his work to continually be applied to you for your daily good. What will you do on the day of judgment? What, will plead with God? Will you plead a good work you did, how much you went to church? Will you plead being children of covenant homes? Will you plead that you did so well at memorizing the catechisms? Will you plead something you prayed so well for one time? Will you plead anything but the blood of the Savior? Only the red hand and his blood alone can cover you under the mercy seat of his grace at the day of judgment. In doing this we confess our sins before God, believe in Christ alone for reconciliation with the Father, and continue to humbly submit ourselves to God in all things. We are to preserve this spiritual peace, because it can waiver, and it can be lessened. "I now write unto you ... which I stir up your pure minds by way of remembrance," (2 Peter 3:1). As with Luther, when you feel not so stirred up, a very excellent verse to memorize and speak out loud to the devil when he comes against you to make you doubt of that true safety in Christ alone, "I am thine...save me." The devil is very busy to hinder you from entertaining that truth. He is very industrious in this, because when you consider this truth of Christ, and the safety of Christ in salvation, that you are God's and he is the Savior, contemplating this truth will always deliver you from the shadows of the devil's dominion. He is always about casting in objections, and fortifying your heart against the spiritual persuasions of the word of Christ, because the word produces assurance. I ask you now, are you going to heaven? You must consider both why and what is your safety? From answering this successfully there is an assurance of faith possible for you, a confidence. Paul was sure of his faith, "For the which cause I also suffer these things: nevertheless I am not ashamed: for I know whom I have believed, and am persuaded that he is able to keep that which I have committed unto him against that day," (2 Tim. 1:12). There was also someone else who was very sure of their faith, "I am thine, save me." The Psalmist's argument for assurance begins with the truth that he is God's, asking God to keep him, save him, because his faithfulness and devotion to God is seen by his outward works of righteousness that God began in him, "for I have sought thy precepts."

There are many occasions where you doubt your faith. Faith stands upon what you know, what you are convinced of in your heart, and what you see in your life. If what you know is wrong, or weak, faith will waiver. This is why error is such a hindrance to your walk. A wrong notion of saving faith will cause you to doubt; not having the Spirit, the blood and the water, will cause you to doubt. If you have an inability to properly understand the appropriate acts of your own heart, that will cause you to doubt these words, "I am thine..." If you compare your faith with the level of faith that you aspire to, your faith may waiver. If you compare it to other's faith, it might waiver. You must always strive to gain a full assurance of faith. Safety in Christ produces assurance. Faith in Christ, produces assurance. And then assurance produces gratefulness to God for his electing plan and power to save you.

It is consoling to our hearts and a consolation for our mind. And how shall we increase in such an assurance as the Psalmist had, such a confidence and boldness of faith, continued to the very end so that we may be safe in Christ's righteousness on the day of judgment? We will look at assurance in this verse in the next chapter, for the psalmist sets assurance on proving out true faith, by works, "for I have sought thy precepts."

Chapter 9: Assurance of Election in Christ Considered by Spiritual Fruit

"I am thine, save me; for I have sought thy precepts," (Psalm 119:94).

"I belong to you, save me (or deliver me);" why should God pay *him* any mind at all? Is he obliged? If David is God's, yes, God is obligated to do it; he is God's and God is his. But what is David's reasoning here, his personal proof? "...for I have sought thy precepts." David believed himself to be of God's special people which have been saved out of the kingdom of darkness and brought into the kingdom of God. "I am thine; save me." Why? "...for I have sought thy precepts," (Psalm 119:94). The Hebrew word "for" is more helpfully translated as "because;" *that, because, for, in that light*. "Know therefore, that the LORD thy God, he is God, the faithful God, which keepeth covenant and mercy with them that love him and keep his commandments to a thousand generations," (Deut. 7:9). "And I will walk at liberty: for I seek thy precept," (Psalm 119:45). "The earth also is defiled under the inhabitants thereof; because they have transgressed the laws, changed the ordinance, broken the everlasting covenant," (Isa. 24:5). Henry Hammond, Westminster Divine, translates this verse and combines it with a comment on it in this way conveying the idea,

Chapter 9: Assurance of Election in Christ Considered

"These advantages assuredly belong to all your faithful people, that sincerely attend and perform obedience to you. I can confidently place myself in that number: that you would be pleased to reach out your promised deliverance to me."[38] David places the latter part, for I have sought thy precepts, after the statement, to prove out that he is God's and God is his. There was assurance in that proof.

Doctrine: Assurance of salvation in Christ can be considered by the saint's spiritual fruit. There is a difficulty among Christians in certain circles to think about sovereign election as the *proof* of salvation; this is reversed. They would rather reverse it, because the reverse is easier to consider. They would much rather simply say, "You are mine," changing the psalmist's words to fit their emotional need. But then, they want to prove out their election in Christ. They talk about election, they think about the theory of election, and then they say, "How do I know whether I might be counted among the elect?" This is not a bad question to ask, but they try to prove out election in their life which causes them some trouble. They hear verses like these: "...but rather rejoice, because your names are written in heaven," (Luke 10:20). But how do I know? "...brethren, give diligence to make your calling and election sure," (2 Peter 1:10). How shall I do this? "...knowing, brethren

---

[38] Hammond, Henry, *The Works of the Reverend and Learned Henry Hammond, D.D.*, Volume 4, (London: T. Newcomb and M. Flesher, for Richard Royston ... and Richard Davis, 1684), 345.

beloved, your election of God," (1 Thess. 1:4). *How might I gain an understanding that I am of that number?* "For many are called, but few are chosen," (Matt. 22:14). *Am I chosen?* "...that the purpose of God according to election might stand, not of works, but of him that calleth," (Rom. 9:11). *Am I called of God?* They hear Scriptures like that, and then they wonder, *am I elect?* They think, "I need to prove out whether I am elect or not." "I have to figure out whether I am elect, or whether I am reprobate." But they have missed the fundamental article of understanding election in that they take the theory of election and place it practically before saving faith. And the reason this happens is because they mix in their mind thinking about the order of God's decrees to save someone, with the practical work of how that salvation actually works out in time. They think in this order, "I consider myself elect, therefore, I have saving faith," but they cannot *prove* that out. Where does the bible tell them to do that? They've reversed it, and it turns to trouble.

Where Christians often deeply feel their infirmities and the weakness of their faith, they in turn think about election, and might in fact doubt whether they are partakers of that happiness, instead of thinking about good works. "I'm a sinner, am I one of the elect, am I really saved? I'm a terrible person because I have done such and such things today. I wonder if I'm elect, because elect people don't do the things I do. I wonder if I am saved." They have the order confused. They may be very well assured even if their faith is no larger than a grain of mustard seed, being true faith, it joins them to Christ and makes them partakers in his redemption, having their sins washed away in his blood of righteousness; if they think rightly about salvation. They have a union and communion with Christ in salvation regardless of how large the fire of salvation is kindling in them. It might be a spark, it might be a raging inferno; grace is still grace. Their faith believes in the covering of the obedience of Christ and makes them heirs of the kingdom of glory. True faith provides a sure and stable foundation on which they can stand, even the righteousness of God and of the Savior Jesus Christ; even safe on the day of judgment. But how do they know this? How can they take those saving ideas, and not merely mouth the words, but have it personally applied to them in way that they know, and can say, "I am thine..." and know it to be true? How can they know they have been saved, they are being saved and will be saved?

In Psalm 119:94 David tells God, "I am thine," Yes, but how does he *prove* it? God owns him, *I am thine*, and yet how does he prove out the reality that he knows God owns him? Through his *actions*, "for I have sought thy precepts." Keep in mind that he does not only say, "I have kept your precepts, I have done them," but, "I have sought them." There is some *action* stemming from his heart and mind and soul that assures him he is God's, that proves salvation out. To seek God's precepts is much more than merely looking into them, for it resides in hearing and doing; it is a statement of outward obedience. He seeks the precepts of God, which is in complete contrast to the wicked who seek to sin. He seeks God's word, where sinners seek to sin. When his mind is at rest, and is in repose, and desires to relax, what does his natural mind, since he is God's, default to in his thoughts? What joy does he have? Where does he find all satisfaction? In God's precepts. Such an action holds in it an earnest desire to know them; and not merely for head knowledge. He does not say I am thine because I know your word, or that I read it once. He seeks it out, as a disposition in him; a common occurrence. This is great evidence of an upright heart and a sincere love to God, to be inquisitive into the will of God and the word of God. It suggests a holy affection to God. No one will ever seek what he does not love. He is God's, he seeks God's precepts, this is because he loves what God loves. The psalmist does not rest confident in past action. I went to church, I've read the bible, I've witnessed a few times before, I used to serve the church, I went to youth group, I went to Sunday school, I used to be in ministry. He rests confident in actions which stem from the past that continue for the present. It involves a constant endeavor to practice them; for the end or goal of seeking is keeping. Psalm 119:2 says, "Blessed are they that keep his testimonies, and that seek him with the whole heart." He's already said that in verse 2 of this psalm. It involves earnest desires after a higher measure of grace for strengthening obedience. That is seeking: earnest desires after a higher measure of grace for strengthening obedience to serve Christ the King. Such a seeking is a sure evidence of choosing God for themselves, since God has chosen them. Saints know God to be theirs by their giving up of themselves to be his. The psalmist places equal footing in this, having a respect to all the commandments of God. I have sought thy precepts, and continue to do so, and keep them, and strive to uphold them, and it is apparent to me; I seek them out all the time, I am possessed of them, obsessed over them. "Blessed are the undefiled in the way, who walk in the law of the LORD," (Psalm 119:1). "Make me to go in the path of thy commandments; for therein do I delight," (Psalm 119:35). "I will delight myself in thy statutes: I will not forget thy word," (Psalm 119:16). "Open thou mine eyes, that I may behold wondrous things out of thy law," (Psalm 119:18). He desires to know the whole will of God in all things that concern him to know who God is, what God has done in saving him, and what God requires of him. He desires to know God in one thing as well as in another, so long as it is stated in his word. In all things that concern him to know as God has set down his will in his word for him to know. If a professing believer does not seek out God's precepts, it is a sign of insincerity, contrary to what the psalmist is saying about his own actions. The Psalmist is not interested in things that will not profit him; conjecture and such. Things that are not edifying, and are in no way useful in faith and obedience to God, they are excluded in this "seeking." Such desire is to walk in a way to please God. This was the knowledge that David desired, Psalm 119:66, "Teach me good judgement, and knowledge." The Psalmist does not want to offend God in anything, but obey his will in all things, he desires to know the whole will of God, so far as it concerns him and may be profitable for him to know it. "I opened my mouth, and panted, for I longed for thy commandments," (verse 131); as if he had said, "I seek them out continually, to know them, to know their depth, so I don't break them." A wise and prudent Christian will say, "I am thine, save me for I have sought thy precepts," meaning those very same things.

How might a Christian be afraid to offend God in anything, or desires to do the will of God in all things, that is not careful to enquire and know what the will of God is in all things? As if a person would say, "I don't want to sin, I don't want to displease God, but I don't want to study the bible or memorize or learn my catechism, or do those things that are necessary *for* seeking." That is to live in a very unhappy contradiction. David charged his people, those he summoned not long before his death, and said this, "Now therefore in the sight of all Israel the congregation of the LORD, and in the audience of our God, keep and seek for all the commandments of the LORD your God: that ye may possess this good land, and leave it for an inheritance for your children after you for ever," (1 Chron. 28:8). The order is first, to know, and then do his commandments. Then by doing his commandments he knows his salvation in God. "I am thine, save my," why? "For I have sought your precepts." I show my sincerity in following you and can be sure I am yours because of the fruit that I see in my life as it surrounds the will of God based on his word. I live out the word of God; I do what God says. My life is a sermon before my very eyes, and others. And it is not so with the wicked, for they will go to church but be devoid of fruit and have no growth in Christ. The question is never, am I elect? To run that errand and try to solve that riddle is a great difficulty.

The question is always "Am I assured of my salvation?" *Assurance* is drawn out primarily on sanctification. Assurance of election, assurance of one's justification, perseverance, and glorification (*hope*), cannot be without *assurance of sanctification*, this being the outward sight and inward personal experience of their assurance. They cannot have the one without first having the other. Is God tightfisted in his salvation? Or does he act very liberally to his people in helping them to know true salvation? Then, why do they not know assurance more; why is that question so hard for most people to answer? It is because they are thinking about it in the wrong way. There people rest in theory, and think, "I am elect," and yet they find *no closure* in that because it is theory to them; or people rest in works, and salvation depends on what *they* do, and they find they are *never satisfied* on their works, so on both ends of the spectrum they *doubt*.

Christians ought not to ask, "Am I elect, and how might I prove *my election*," but, for purposes of assurance, "Am I being sanctified?" and then they never doubt their election having its proof in their life that they see and experience. In particular, the Christian must labor (for I have sought thy precepts) to draw forth out of the sure word of Christ, the infallible characters and clear descriptions and evidences of the new creature that they see in themselves, and of the sincerity of true grace in their life. They then meditate and ponder these sure evidences and right Scripture-filled descriptions given of the new creature and sincerity of grace, so that they can come to as clear and distinct an understanding of what is held forth in salvation as they can. What the bible says about true believers they see in their own life. They know their minds have been changed from what they were; they think about the heinous aspects of sin and wickedness in all their conduct and communion with God. They hate sin and love holiness. They hate everything contrary to God, and seek out his precepts to know his will for them in their lives; they love what he loves and hates what he hates. Where shall they find such things but in God's word? They have a universal liking, and an allowance of all good, of all known truths, and all known duties; truths as revealed by God, and to be believed by them; and duties commanded by God, and to be performed by them.

If they are skilled in knowing what those things are, and they seek to further their understanding in

Chapter 9: Assurance of Election in Christ Considered

them, they do it to work them out, and so discern their presence in their life. What do they see in their life? They see the fullness, beauty and excellency of Jesus Christ working in them by the Spirit and find Christ precious. "Unto you therefore which believe he is precious," (1 Peter 2:7). They see Christ working his might to save them in all respects; they have been saved, they see him working in them to save them, whether by temporary affliction or in eternal realities, and they know they will one day be saved. The excellency of grace, holiness, faith and love in them contributes to their happiness; because that spiritual fruit causes them to see the Spirit working in them. They see a new principle working in them for holiness. Nominal Christians have a *very* hard time with this. "The natural man knows not the things of God, nor can he, because they are spiritually discerned," (1 Cor. 2:14). So nominal Christians panic and they end up entertaining *a natural religion* based on what they do in works to be saved, without ever knowing the first part of what the psalmist said, "I am thine," They say, "I am thine because I have sought your precepts so I consider myself saved," which is not what the Spirit is teaching here. David often mentions his will, his choice, his purpose, his firm and rooted resolution. "I will keep your statutes. I have chosen the way of truth. I have sworn, and I will perform it, that I will keep your righteous judgments," (Psalm 119:8, 30, 106). "...for I have sought your precepts."

A sinful, unconverted heart is described by choosing things that are sinful and provoking. A holy heart chooses things that are holy. The change of the will to desire holiness by the word is a very high evidence of sincerity, a choosing of God to be their God, a choosing of Christ, his offered grace, above all, "him" as their righteousness and justification, their wisdom, their sanctification. Coming to him, trusting him, is an act of the will, in choosing him, a choosing the holy ways of God universally out of a principle of love. David says in verse 6, of this psalm, that he gives "respect to all thy commandments," (Psalm 119:6). Not merely knowing, but as a purpose of heart for keeping all of them to the glory of God. What else do they see in this, but a new creature in a new will, and a new will in a new aim. They are no longer that old, sinful, carnal self. They are not out to satisfy only or chiefly themselves, and being satisfied in worldly and carnal things. Self-love is taken down and crucified with Christ. God's precepts are now their chief aim. *I am thine...for I have sought thy precepts.* In this there is a new master-aim, a new mark to which it designs, and principally drives at, God and his glory, serving and pleasing him. This evidently appears in the saints in Scripture. They exalt God, called such to seek God, serve God, live to God, to Christ, and deny themselves. "Alive to God," (Rom. 6:11). They do not live to themselves, but to him that died for them, (2 Cor. 5:15).

An objection is given, "Wherefore the rather, brethren, give diligence to make your calling and election sure," 2 Peter 1:10 says, "and does it not tell me to make my *calling and election* sure? It says to make it *sure*. It says to give *diligence* to doing so. If one is to be diligent in doing so, it must be something important." These people fail to first quote the whole verse, and then they misapply it. "Wherefore the rather, brethren, give diligence to make your calling and election sure: for if ye do these things, ye shall never fall," (2 Peter 1:10). What things? Are the things the inquiry into election, to make one's calling and election sure? Are *they* the things? No, theoretical theology is not the answer. Consider the apostle's order, calling first, then election after. It does not belong to the Christian to make their election sure unless their *calling* is sure. You see how easy it is, right there, to just slow down a little, and ask a question or two about the text and its order. They are not to seek assurance of election until they seek their calling. How will they know their calling is sure? They will seek assurance of election in vain and will never find it if they do not first seek their calling. Where do they find the evidences of their calling? What does the Lord do in this? He calls them to believe. He calls them to the highway of holiness. He calls them to obedience. He calls them to repentance. He calls them to diligence to follow the way that God prescribes for them through Christ. To follow their own way, will never prosper them. Anything in theory will never prosper them. If they give all diligence to pursue the former things that the apostle lays down, they will know their calling, and the incomparable benefits will be a true assurance of salvation. Assurance is an essential element of salvation, for without it there is no right faith, no willing obedience, and no soundness of joy. They will never be able to say or know or have confidence in "I am thine." 2 Peter 1:5-7, "Therefore give even all diligence to join virtue with your faith: and with virtue knowledge: and with knowledge, temperance: and with temperance, patience: and with patience, godliness: and with godliness, brotherly kindness: and with brotherly kindness, love." That is what one looks at first, which is what they are called to, so they can say, "I am thine." Assurance is based on seeing the work of joining virtue with faith, and knowledge with temperance, and patience with godliness and brotherly kindness with love, etc. Assurance is never first joined to election. Assurance of election is the *fruit* of a godly sanctification; *assurance is the fruit of holiness*. Assurance of election in Christ is considered by the saint's spiritual fruit of the Spirit. And it is very easily seen why people don't think this way about salvation and election, because if they cannot discern such real spiritual fruit, if it is not *tangible* to them, if it is absent to them upon inspection, they need something to cling onto. That leads them right down the path of salvation by works, because they can touch that and feel that, though they are devoid of virtue, faith, knowledge, temperance, patience, godliness, brotherly kindness, and love. They can cling to their one-minute prayer. They can cling to their church attendance. They can cling to participating in the potluck suppers. Social religion is easy to cling to because it is visible to them, because it is self manufactured.

But, if David is not seeking out God's precepts, if he is not deep into the word, he will never say he's God's; why would he? He will never ask for God to save him if he is not a changed man. Wicked men will barter with God all the time, but they have no desire after *holiness*. Bless me in this thing, and I will be a good person, for a time. They have no desire after seeking out God's precepts, constantly and universally. They want their own form of religion that makes them feel good.

Now listen here, God increases all gifts and graces by the Spirit in those who diligently seek him. He promises to do so, and there is no possibility of it not occurring. Why? This proves out their salvation, it then gives them assurance, and God is for them in this, and desires it for them. "For this is the will of God, even your sanctification," (1 Thess. 4:3). George Gifford said, "Faith must be in place first, and then all other characteristics of godliness are added to it because without faith we cannot in any way or by any means please God. Faith alone is what justifies us before God. But once true faith is born in a man, it does not remain there dead and fruitless. Virtue is added to a lively faith, that one may attend to all the duties of a godly life."[39]

---

[39] Gifford, *Faith*, 44.

That's why the apostle James makes the distinction of a faith that is alive and faith that is dead (James 2). Dead faith doesn't save, for it doesn't prove out anything; how can it, it's *dead*. It's just religious talk, and holds in it, not one ounce of assurance. It makes people professing Christians *and that alone*, without being *true* believers. Walking in the way God has prescribed, the psalmist comes to the assurance that he is called and among the chosen people of the Lord. Because the assurance of salvation in Christ is considered by the saint from his spiritual fruit which is discernable to himself and others.

Are you assured of your salvation? Election itself rests on the unchangeable purpose and counsel of God; yes, true enough. But, we are not to gain assurance of it in ourselves from some personal revelation. How can you do that? Maybe your emotional feeling of election in theory comes from an underdone potato or a blot of bad mustard, as Scrooge thought his vision of Marley was. He couldn't trust himself. Neither are we to attempt to ascend into heaven to search the counsel of God, to determine whether our names are in the book of life. There is no celestial elevator to ride up and to peek at the book to see if your name is written in it. But we are to gain assurance from the fruit of the Spirit, that Spirit who dwells in us; those are discernable and evident. We must look within ourselves and outside of ourselves in action in order to judge whether those things are in us, and whether they are exercised. They are given to all those whom God saves. You see here the importance?

You gain assurance because of the seal of God by which he has sealed us, which is the Spirit of sanctification, the Spirit of holiness. Many people do not like biblical ideas like this because *they* are devoid of those things in their personal life, so they feel panicked, because there is no spiritual power in them. George Gifford again said, "For we cannot come to the assurance of our faith without a great attention to godliness, abundance of virtue, and plenty of all good works."[40]

Ask yourself, does your resolve appear in living and acting for God like the psalmist? Not according to your own taste, but the way the word of God lays it out? Is holiness written in visible characters on all you do? "In that day shall there be upon the bells of the horses, HOLINESS UNTO THE LORD; and the pots in the LORD'S house shall be like the bowls before the altar," (Zech. 14:19). On everything down to the bells of the horses, holiness is found for the people of God. "The impress of God is upon his People, it is upon the Horse Bells, upon all the Pots of Jerusalem; it is upon all they have, all they enjoy, Holiness to the Lord; they spend their time, as being dedicated to God; they spend their estates, as being dedicated to God. Do you use your selves as those that are Christs, improving your Time, Relations, Talents, Interests for his glory?"[41] The impression of God is on his people, so much so that it is

---

[40] Gifford, *Faith*, 70.
[41] Thomas Manton, *One Hundred and Ninety Sermons on the Hundred and Nineteenth Psalm* (London: 1681), 607.

on the bells of the horse that bring them from one place to another; it is even on the menial tasks of cooking pots. Is that impression on all you have and do? Is it on all you have, all you enjoy? If you are Christ's, do you improve your time, talents, and interests for his glory in this? You must be persuaded to dedicate yourself to Christ, and to live as those that are God's people. I think professing Christians do not know what that means. To live as God's people. I made reference in another work, to this verse, "...take hold of the skirt of him that is a Jew, saying, We will go with you: for we have heard that God is with you," (Zech. 8:23). The woman afflicted with the disorder of the blood who was looking to touch the hem of Christ's garments, and why would she touch him? Take hold of them and go with him.[42] Take hold of the commands and precepts and statues of God, dedicating yourselves to him, with all of God's people. "And God spake all these words, saying, I am the LORD thy God, which have brought thee out of the land of Egypt, out of the house of bondage. Thou shalt..." (Exod. 20:1); he saved them then commanded them to live a certain way You owe yourselves to God, and should give up yourselves to him. He rescues you first and then commands you to obedience second, and if you obey you show yourselves as those who belong to him. And so you can have assurance that you do if you know what he commands and if you do what you know he commands.

---

[42] See my work *I am For You: God's Power in Supporting His People*.

God ordains your whole life for good as a believer, *for good*, and you owe all that you have to him. You have nothing but what he gave you first. Christians often become myopic, too focused on little things in this, to miss the big picture. For example, you ought not to dismiss the work of Christ in your life for a single sin that you haven't repented of. Christians often do that; "oh I sinned today, same sin, ... am I saved?" Rather, they ought to look at their whole life every time, and see and remember and discern God's work throughout their whole life. Not merely at one instance and one point. That will never give you a good idea of your spiritual change. God gives you salvation, and his Son, he offers himself to you; and will save you and deliver you out of all your troubles, as David prayed. Is it not reasonable for you as a Christians, then, to give up yourself to God? In the Covenant of free Grace there is a reciprocal engagement between God and you to be each other's. The Father, Son, and Holy Spirit are our everlasting portion; you then live as one who had dedicated themselves back to him in a regular and consistent practice. You live as though you are God's. You are not your own. "What? know ye not that your body is the temple of the Holy Ghost which is in you, which ye have of God, and ye are not your own?" (1 Cor. 6:19). You don't live according to your own will, your own end, your own interests. You are the Lord's and your whole business should be to please God and honor God; because now, God's interests are your interests. It is easy to say, "I am thine..." but do you make it your practice, "for I have sought his precepts." His glory is to be the compass of our entire life. Phil. 1:21, "To me to live is Christ." You don't seek your own things, but the things of Christ Jesus. Do you give up yourselves to be governed and ordered by his Spirit, his word, his will, his precepts, acting and living for his glory? We love to say "Lord, I am thine!" But then we do not act like it; we often act like we are of the world, the flesh and devil. "Lord, I am thine, for... I have sought they precepts." Thomas Manton said, "It is not words, but affections and actions that must prove us to be the Lord's; then we are his when we seek to please him in all things. Judas was Christ's in profession, but the devil's in affection. David saith, 'I am thine,' but presently adds, 'I seek thy precepts,' I endeavor to do thy will. Oh! then, live not as your own, as of Satan and the flesh, but as the Lord's."[43] That is the place where your soul will then say, I am thine, and I know it to be true, save me, and you have, you are, you will, because I know I am of your flock, how do I know, but that I seek your precepts, your Spirit testifies to my spirit that your word which I know is true, and it is true for me and about me, and I am of your sheep because I can see the fruit of your work in my life. I can certainly prove out "I am thine" it is because of the fruit I see of your Spirit in me working for my good and your glory. I see it in my daily life all the time. Even when I sin I see

---

[43] Thomas Manton, *The Complete Works of Thomas Manton*, vol. 7 (London: James Nisbet & Co., 1872), 444–447.

Chapter 9: Assurance of Election in Christ Considered

it; because I'm ashamed, and saddened and resolved to seek you out, and that very quickly. Even when a good work is done, I see it, for I see your Spirit motioning me to more and more works of holiness. I prove out my election by my faith, which is exercised constantly, and seen always. My faith, my life, my acts line up with your word and I'm confident in my calling so my election is sure, for "I am thine, save me, for I have sought thy precepts. And I know, then, I am saved."

What follows the fruits and effects of true faith? Various comforts like, peace of conscience, joy in tribulation, an increase of hope, a hearty love to God's house and people, *assurance will follow*; a joyful life waiting for a crown of glory; and many other joys which are true tokens of true faith, and signs to examine it by, both for our own good, and the glory of the Redeemer. ...which you can possess right now.

You can be assured that you have true faith by the testimony of God's Spirit in your heart, soul, and mind, and the signs that accompany them. What are such assuring signs? Seeking God's precepts, which tells you about ... putting off the old man and putting on the new man. The works of the Spirit, death to sin, and living to righteousness. Not walking in the flesh, but in the Spirit, and the renewing of the mind. They are holy and righteous acts according to the commandment, acting like a new creature, and all good works before God. They are for the glory of God and his Gospel because they show your change and your conformity to

Jesus. They testify you have true faith. They confirm you're Christ's. They adorn the Gospel with the beauty of grace. They show forth your salvation. God will crown these works with eternal glory. If a person has assurance, they have holiness. "The assurance of election is a significant means whereby sanctification is promoted."[44] Because it is not merely conjecture, assumptions, guesswork, speculation. It is an unfailing assurance, founded on the divine truth of the promises of salvation in Christ alone. It is true, you can be saved and not have assurance, many Christians are. But the reason is because they fail to see how to consider the spiritual process of assurance; the tools which God uses to prove it out in their life. They are trying to peer into God's book where they should be peering into their own heart. Yet, one will ask, "Can you be saved without these good works in your life?" Just think, no works, no assurance. No assurance, then, *doubting* of one's election. "Am I thine?" *who knows?* No one can be saved without good works as a fruit of Christ's work in them. It is impossible; the entire second chapter of James explains that. You are not saved by good works, but you cannot be saved *without* good works. They testify we are in Christ made safe, and have God's Spirit with us, working holiness, and so we cannot be idle, but fruitful in him. Assurance of election in Christ is considered by the saint's spiritual fruit. Which is why most people

---

[44] Wilhelmus à Brakel, *The Christian's Reasonable Service*, vol. 1 (Morgan, PA: Soli Deo Gloria Publications, 1993), 250.

today don't even want to think about this because it is evidence based. They would much rather set their assessment of themselves on theory and say, "I believe I am saved, because that makes me feel good." Election is certain and unchangeable, personal and you know it. You can certainly know that you are saved. By descending into your own hearts, examining the book of conscience there, and finding out in yourself the fruits of salvation and the Spirit. If you can know you have faith, you can be sure of your election, because faith is the effect of election. You can know you possess faith, by looking at your life and seeing if it lines up with the psalmist, or any of the other Biblical writers. Paul says you can know whether you are the children of God, for "the Spirit itself beareth witness with our spirits, that we are the children of God," (Rom. 8:16.) All the children of God are said to be "sealed by the Holy Spirit unto the day of redemption," (Eph. 4:30,) which could not take place without being sensible of it. The Apostle John says, "hereby know we that we dwell in him, and he in us, because he hath given us of his Spirit," (1 John 4:13.) The Spirit is given to the elect, and you can know it if you have him. Yet, sometimes, you may not always be certain of it. Sometimes your belief is stronger than at other times. That is because afflictions can weaken it; and that is because you waiver in where your focus is. Temptations and assaults by the world and the flesh and devil weaken it. You might even feel as though God has forsaken you for a time, or not paid you any mind.

But go back to the psalmist, go back to these words, go back to Staupitz's direction to Luther, turn the words of the psalmist to prayer. "I am thine, save me," and he will; that in and of itself is seeking his precepts.

Out of any dark condition the believing soul comes forth, when God restores to it the joy of his salvation, to a shining light. If your soul sometimes groans, struggles, doubts, and fears, yet afterwards it sings, trusts, rejoices, and triumphs, as over a conquered enemy; which is seen in this very psalm, in these very words of the text. But such an assurance cannot operate without following after holiness. If you persist in sin, and yet persuade yourself that "you possess eternal life, and will be certainly saved no matter what you do," well, you cultivate a false and deceitful hope which will never give you any assurance.

Prove out your faith, assurance will come after. Are you sure of your faith, and consequently of your salvation? "I know whom I have believed," (2 Tim. 1:12). And "he that believeth on the Son of God hath the witness in himself," (1 John 5:10.) Whoever is sure that he has the Spirit of God dwelling in him, can be sure of his faith, since where the Holy Spirit is, there is faith. The faithful say, and are reminded of and continue to stir themselves up with the words, "for I have sought your precepts" and they may certainly know that they have that privilege. The same arguments which prove that the faithful man can be sure of his faith, prove also that he

Chapter 9: Assurance of Election in Christ Considered

can be sure of his salvation. Why? Because assurance is connected with the pursuit of holiness. To have one means you have the other. This turns into, interest in the word of God as a gracious means of divine encouragement to the soul concerning salvation, which we will consider in the next chapter.

Chapter 10: Interest in the Word a Means of Divine Encouragement to the Soul

"I am thine, save me; for I have sought thy precepts," (Psalm 119:94).

All men cannot say "I am thine;" and here are the more particular words in light of the former, "save me," which are very important in this light, especially as these relate to assurance and divine encouragement. "Save me" brings in a very special ownership of a very special kind of person; a person whom God owns. "I am thine; save me." David is God's, for God has bought him with a price, and he relies on God for his salvation. Why is this? There is a reason. "...for I have sought thy precepts," (Psalm 119:94). *That, because, for,* in that light *of this*, I know the truth of it. The psalmist continually sets this same idea down time and time again as it relates to the word of God. Psalm 119:38, "Stablish thy word unto thy servant, who is devoted to thy fear." David is concerned about God's "precepts." Rules, commissions, charges; they are committed to men by God, with a charge carefully to keep them. "Thou hast commanded us to keep thy precepts diligently," (Psalm 119:4). Good precepts of God's appointment and sending are life to

Chapter 10: Interest in the Word / Encouragement

the godly. Evil precepts of the world, the flesh and devil, are a hindrance to the godly.

These precepts the psalmist speaks of are something given as a charge: or the knowledge of the Law, and these can certainly be applied to be the doctrines of Christ, (Romans 7:8-9; John 12:50), or the whole of the word of God. There is no part but either directly or indirectly requires something, which is not in man's choice to do, or not to do, but to do as God so instructs. They have a choice to obey or not, but God does not give them a choice to follow him or not. God never says, you can obey, or not obey, it's up to you. He commands them to obey, and to seek his word and to follow it and to uphold it to its highest degree; to love him with all the heart, soul and mind, to take him as their God. All God's laws are kept in mind in the psalmist's word for "precepts" in this verse. What is he getting at when he says, "I am thine, save me; for I have sought thy precepts?" I have sought your precepts, so, this shows me I am yours. Save me; for...he had a grand interest in the word of God as a means not only for proof, but encouragement and stirring up of his life as he lived before God's face.

Doctrine: Interest in the Word of God is a means of divine encouragement to the believing soul. What does it mean to have an interest in something? A feeling that accompanies or causes special attention to something or someone; a matter for deep consideration; to persuade to participate or engage in something. To be absorbed, gripped, immersed, involved, and even occupied in something; and for the Christian, supernaturally so. Everyone on the planet, everyone that has ever lived, whether for good or evil, has had an interest in something. Some have an interest in the basic needs of life; food, shelter, clothing. Some have an interest in video games. Some have an interest in relationships. Some have an interest in their phones. Some have an interest in cats. Some have an interest in fashion. Some have an interest in horticulture. Some have an interest in their course of life, what they will be when they grow up. And whatever the interest is, there is a great amount of consideration and persuasion to make what they are interested in successful. Interest is not had for the sake of interest, but for some end or goal; and they spend a great deal of time considering their interests. In this example, the psalmist is directing the stirring of his mind on ideas surrounding, God's decrees, salvation, affliction, and assurance; he does this by acting on that which he can sensibly discern, which is aided by the supernatural power of God's Spirit within him. What does it mean for something to be sensibly discerned? It means to be noticeable to the senses or to the mind; it has with it a form of appreciation, to be sensitive to something. What does it mean to discern? To observe and decide about something. What does it mean to be supernatural? Ascribing help to a power that goes beyond natural forces; in this case, the Spirit of God.

To be *sensibly discerning* in a supernatural way means that the psalmist is able, by his seeking of God's precepts, by sense, by touch, by feel, by sight, by labor, by work, to discern that he is God's, aided by the Spirit's work in his heart; it is a mixture of both the natural, and the supernatural working to a common goal. In this case, he is sensibly discerning that an interest in God's word is a great encouragement to his confidence that he is God's. That seems to be oversimplistic, but that is what he is thinking. "I have a great interest in God's preached word, I seek it out, I continue to do so, I desire it to be fulfilled by me in all things, and I am persuaded that such a seeking shows I am God's, for ungodly men do not do this." Ungodly men and women do not have a sensible discernment of the Spirit of God working in and through them. Ungodly men and women do not have an interest in God's word, God's precepts, God's will or holiness in searching out God's precepts, and will never be committed and attentive to God's word preached, as David was.

The Christian must consent, first, that the word of God in this way ought to be highly esteemed; for it is God speaking to them. "So they read distinctly from the book, in the Law of God; and they gave the sense, and helped them to understand the reading," (Neh. 8:8). They read – they recited the word of God. They explained it. They caused them to discern its meaning, literally, in its reading. Here we have the true scriptural idea of the preacher's function: to cause the people to understand what is in God's word by reading it, explaining and applying it. This is highly esteemed by all Christians.

Christians ought to diligently esteem the ministry of the word for there they find God's precepts. Question 157 of the *Westminster Larger Catechism* asks, "How is the word of God to be read?" The answer, "The holy scriptures are to be read with an high and reverent esteem of them; with a firm persuasion that they are the very word of God, and that he only can enable us to understand them; with desire to know, believe, and obey the will of God revealed in them; with diligence, and attention to the matter and scope of them; with meditation, application, self-denial, and prayer." There is certainly much in that answer. The word of God reveals God's will in what are called, propositions. What is a proposition, but a thought or idea, a statement? An expression in language, that can be believed. God had his will written down so that men could understand what he requires of them in faith and practice. God, "at sundry times and in diverse manner spoke in time past unto the fathers," (Heb. 1:1). Now, he has spoken with a clear voice through the ministry of his Son, the Living Word, that comes down from heaven to declare the Father (John 1:18). He does not want people to guess at his will, so he had it written down; and then he commissioned preachers to preach it. It was necessary for a written word to be given to the church that a Bible containing a compilation of true doctrine might be constant and unmoved for the believer for all time about the Christ. It may be in one part of Scripture God reveals his nature. It may be that in another part it reveals an action of his providence; some form of blessing, some warning, or some prophecy. From Scripture, these statements or assertions come from God. In Nehemiah 8, Ezra, the preacher, read his Bible, that is where he went to find God's words. This was the Law of God. He had more than just the Law of Moses, Joshua, Judges, Ruth, Esther, 1 and 2 Samuel, possibly Job, some Psalms, various Proverbs, the Song of Solomon. But he read the Law, it took 6 hours to read the Law and generally explain it. The word is simply a reflection of the character of God. They took time to discern it, and consider it.

God is seen clearly when the Law is heard and understood. Why are we even talking about *this*? Does this have anything to do with the psalmist? Much! Where is the word of God to be sought? Where are the precepts sought? Where would the psalmist have sought the word? Did he go to his local Walmart and buy a bible and read it? Did he wake up in the morning, and pull a lamb skin scroll off the shelf and open it up and read through it as he drank his morning coffee, sitting on his couch? Where did he find God's precepts? He didn't have a personal bible, he had teachers. "For the priest's lips should keep knowledge, and they should seek the law at his mouth: for he is the messenger of the LORD of hosts," (Mal. 2:7). "And that ye may teach the children of

Israel all the statutes which the LORD hath spoken unto them by the hand of Moses," (Lev. 10:11). David was confident that he was God's, by paying attention in church to God's word, which he sought, in the tabernacle, in the synagogue, in God's house, from the lips of those who taught the word of God; as well as being a prophet himself. When he heard the word read, and explained by the priests, and he was caused to understand its meaning, he sought those precepts, to do them. This implies that which David sought in his obedience, was the fulfilling of God's will. He heard it, remembered it, meditated on it, desired to do it; wanted more of it. He desired to profit from diligently esteeming God's preached word. It would be an exercise in futility for him to go and hear the word read, preached and given its meaning, without some spiritual benefit or profit for him to gather from it. What a waste of time, so many Christians go to church and do not profit by the word because of their negligence to diligently esteem it as God's voice, and sensibly discern its meaning, to retain it in their memory because they are far more interested on what they are Googling on their phone or texting other people than listening to the word. Preachers do not preach to fill up time in a service of worship just so people can say they attended the service. If preachers are charged by God to preach well, people are charged by God to hear well, and hearing is seeking and seeking's aim is *doing*, and that cannot happen without knowing, and remembering. Every time the word is preached, there should be some spiritual profit gained; every time. If there is not, there is no way the psalmist would ever be confident to say, "I am thine, save me for I have sought thy precepts." He would have to say, "I heard something sometime, and I guess it was important, but I can't remember what it was. It could have been on the temple street corner, or maybe by one of the merchants selling doves as I passed by." This is the importance of the congregation's diligence in attending the word rightly; they should be desiring the word rightly read, preached and explained. So, they get a good night's sleep, they are prepared in their hearts, put down their phones, and are ready to listen attentively without distraction. Distractions *alienate* them from God. That is why Daniel Burgess said, "Irreverence at a sermon is a public call to God for damnation. It is a call bidding God to damn you,"[45] That's heavy; but it's true; *I don't need you God, nor care what you have to say.* If there is no profit in hearing and understanding, one of two things has happened; either the minister did not do his job in reading and preaching well, or the Christian is not doing their job in diligently esteeming the word in hearing it and listening to it, and further, to do it. Listening, seeking, searching, means, to the psalmist, exercising obedience to be *prepared* to hear his word. And if there is no interest to hear it, then there is no interest to fulfill it, consequently, there is no interest in what God really says. Pew sitting is not what

---

[45] Daniel Burgess, eBook, *Directions for Daily Holy Living*, (Crossville, TN: Puritan Publications, 2017) chapter 3.

the psalmist is saying. Taking up space in church or falling asleep like Eutychus did during Paul's preaching, or talking in the pew with a neighbor during the service is not what the psalmist is driving at. One must profit under the preached word, for spiritual benefit can mean a number of things as they are attached to the work of the Spirit. The preached word is the means of conversion. If one is brought from the kingdom of darkness into the kingdom of the beloved Son of God through conversion, that is of great profit. The preached word is the means of illumination. If the Christian understands a passage more clearly, more plainly than before, and is illuminated to the truth of the word, that is of profit because they know Christ more. The preached word is the means of sanctification. If the Christian is changed by the word, to be more conformed into the image of the beloved Son, that is of great profit.

The preached word mines out and exposes heart sins that tread deep into the heart of a Christian. True Christians desire to be further sanctified in putting to death the deeds of the body by knowing what to do in those situations, and that is of great profit for them. Distractions from that, disrespect the majesty of King Jesus as he speaks through his word to the people. The word, then, must be understood and practically applied for spiritual profit; for the Spirit of God cannot use what is not in the heart of a person. Why? Because as the psalmist thought, being God's is shown by having an interest in things of God, and in this case, the words that come from his own mouth.

The Scriptures are the foundation of religious life and practice. If the psalmist wants to know that he is God's, he seeks out and desires to fulfill the precepts God has given him. Assurance of salvation is not something the Spirit merely zaps a Christian to be; I am suddenly assured. No one has ever testified that the Spirit *zapped* him into such a sensibility; *I was not assured one minute ago but now I am assured and did nothing towards that end, the Spirit zapped me.* The Spirit never does that. He *uses* the preached word. If the psalmist seeks the word at the mouth of the priest, and yet, does not have the sense and meaning of a passage, it will not profit him. He does not say in this psalm "I have heard your word," "I have heard the preacher in my ears," ... that will not do; he does not say I have done my duty and attended church. He says, "I have sought your precepts." The communication of that word from the Creator to the saint, is of utmost importance. It instructs the saint how to live well before God's holy face, and so they hear it and do it. They do it gladly, and are encouraged by others in the same way. "They that fear thee will be glad when they see me; because I have hoped in thy word," (Psalm 119:74); which he said in this psalm.

The Scripture's foundation, is Jesus Christ, the Living Word. The highlight of the psalmist is knowing he has an interest in God by having an interest in the preached word, and knows that God will save him because he is God's. The revelation of the word of God to man is absolutely necessary for salvation, for it lays out the coming of the Christ; who he is and what he does. And if God thought it was good to place this word of Christ in the mouth of the minister, or to write it down, as the church has it in our day, he thought it would be good for Christians to hear it read, and to have it explained, and for them to understand it; for them to seek it out that they may know it, and be assured by it, through the Spirit. It is the seed by which sinners are born again. 1 Peter 1:23 says, "since you have been born again, not of perishable seed but of imperishable, through the living and abiding word of God." It is the light by which God's covenant people are directed. Psalm 119:105, "Your word is a lamp to my feet and a light to my path." It is the food upon which the covenant community feeds. Hebrews 5:14, "solid food..." It is the foundation upon which God's covenant people stand. Jude 1:3, "the faith once delivered to the saints..." *The 1647 Westminster Confession* states, "The Supreme Judge, by which all controversies of religion are to be determined, and all decrees of councils, opinions of ancient writers, doctrines of men, and private spirits, are to be examined, and in whose sentence we are to rest, can be no other but the Holy Spirit speaking in the Scripture." If this is true, and it is, it is necessary to seek out the preached word so that Christians may know God's mind on life and godliness.

Chapter 10: Interest in the Word / Encouragement

It is necessary, then, to have an interest in the preached word. If a person wants to know if they are saved, if they are converted, if God owns them, they seek out, hear, understand and apply the word daily to their hearts; that is a *natural process* for all Christians; to prepare them for God's voice in the preaching of the word. They look to fulfill it because they are interested in what God is interested in. If people confess that they are saved out of the world, and are now in the Kingdom of God's Son, that they are delivered from the Kingdom of darkness, they are no longer part of the world, they love the things of God. One cannot be delivered from the world and still be part of the world. The apostle says, "Love not the world, neither the things that are in the world. If any man love the world, the love of the Father is not in him," (1 John 2:15).

This is where such high esteem of the preached word will lead Christians to gain spiritual profit from it, and they know they have been changed, because the reprobate do not seek out the preached word or will of God. And when Christians highly esteem the preached word of God, when they seek it out, they highly esteem the Lord Jesus Christ, the Eternal Word – who is the Logos of God; and that is part of worship. The Father is seeking worshippers, "But the hour cometh, and now is, when the true worshippers shall worship the Father in spirit and in truth: for the Father seeketh such to worship him," (John 4:23). "One thing have I desired of the LORD, that will I seek after; that I may dwell in the house of the LORD all the days of my life, to behold the beauty of the LORD, and to enquire in his temple," (Psalm 27:4); only one thing is needful. How would David see the beauty of God, but in the beauty of God's worship, which surrounds at every turn, the word from God's mouth. It is then, impossible to learn about God, or the Savior Jesus Christ, or the instrument of righteousness, the Spirit of Truth, without understanding his word. Sinclair Ferguson said, "Christians today are all about sermonettes, and sermonettes beget Christianettes."[46] Fast and quick and summed up; that is not a diligent searching and seeking. The Psalmist would take God at his word no matter where it took him; the more the better, in fact, he sought it out. Whatever God says he desired to receive the engrafted word with meekness, to esteem it highly. It is rather amazing that professing Christians will have words come out of their mouth like, "I just don't want to believe that. I just don't like that teaching. I've never heard that before and so I reject that. That's not the way I've always understood things. I will never believe that." What an outrage and offense to Christ and his word to think that way, or to speak that way. The psalmist loved God's word so much that he sought it to fulfill it, to have an interest in it, to sensibly discern that interest and then to be assured of what that word said in his life, no matter where it took him. And in doing so, he said, "I am thine, save me." And then he said he was divinely

---

[46] 2012 *Ligonier Conference*.

encouraged by the preached word because, "I have sought they precepts."

What does it mean to be divinely encouraged? Without the searching there is no divine encouragement. Divine encouragement and instruction are combined with human faithfulness to accomplish total victory in their life by the Spirit, *abundant life*. Jesus comes to give life and that more abundantly. There is a great need for the psalmist to be sure he is God's. Nominal Christians are not sure. Pew warmers are not sure. Christmas and Easter Christians are not sure. The psalmist was very sure. He was so sure that it was a means of divine encouragement to him, because he knew he was God's. The process of knowing, and seeking, and seeking and knowing and seeking and doing were part of his new interest in the things of God.

As a side note, Jesus warns casual seekers about the word being abused in this way. "When any one heareth the word of the kingdom, and understandeth it not, then cometh the wicked one, and catcheth away that which was sown in his heart. This is he which received seed by the way side. But he that received the seed into stony places, the same is he that heareth the word, and anon with joy receiveth it; yet hath he not root in himself, but dureth for a while: for when tribulation or persecution ariseth because of the word, by and by he is offended. He also that received seed among the thorns is he that heareth the word; and the care of this world, and the deceitfulness of riches, choke the word, and he becometh unfruitful. But he that received seed into the good ground is he that heareth the word, and understandeth it; which also beareth fruit, and bringeth forth, some an hundredfold, some sixty, some thirty," (Matt. 13:19-23). People may have a false interest and it will not last; it is not durable because it is not supernaturally fueled by the Spirit. There is a great need of divine encouragement from God to his people while they live in the world; because temporary things impact eternal realities in the Christian mind, and make life very difficult. "Save me" is not merely, save me eternally, but it also has connotations of David speaking this in the midst of adversity and his enemies, being in trouble. It is difficult to be a faithful Christian in the midst of calamity and difficulty, which is why, often, such times are "considered joy when you face trials of many kinds." Calamities give way to discouragements which requires one to be divinely encouraged. *Where* shall one turn for this divine encouragement? Most Christians pray in hopes of gaining a feeling. Prayer is good but divorced from the constituted means God gives is a kind of negligence; it is neglect because praying is easy, but may be unfruitful without the preached word diligently sought. One must use the right means in the right way for the right purpose to gain the right affect. Let me tell you a story – there was a Samurai warrior, and a Buddhist monk who were in a class with a Master martial artist, as the story goes. It was raining profusely, and the three of them were standing under the porch

Chapter 10: Interest in the Word / Encouragement

watching the rain. The Samurai said, I could jump out into the rain, swing my sword over my head and not get wet. So he did, and swung his sword fiercely and then jumped back in. The Buddhist monk looked at him and said, *you have a drop of water, right there on your shoulder*. *You do better*, the Samurai said, so the monk jumped into the rain, sat down, closed his eyes and hummed a bit, got up and walked under the eve with them again, but wet. The Samurai laughed at him, *you are soaking wet. But in my mind*, the monk said, *I am completely dry*. The Master pushed them both aside, took out his umbrella and walked two feet out in the pouring rain, turned around and said to them both, *this is how you deal with the rain*. The Christian is often in a quandary and will pray, Lord, rescue me from this rain and help me not to get wet. God says, *grab your umbrella*. One might say, that's not very supernatural and Spirit filled and led. Quite the opposite, of course it is Spirit filled and Spirit led if God has *told* the Christian by his preached word to grab his umbrella. If that is God's way that is the right way, then the Christian must use God's ordained means to accomplish whatever God has given them to know, seek or do.

    Where might this divine encouragement and instruction be found? Divine encouragement is found in God alone, in his word alone. Until the psalmist knows that God is mine, and I am his, he would dread God's presence. The wicked dread God; they hate the thoughts of God because he is all wrath and judgment to them. But when David knew God, and the more he knew God, the more he would gain peace and comfort from him, he would seek out his precepts to be greatly encouraged. Such a peace and comfort come from the love of God to his dear children, those who are the apple of his eye. Do Christians believe they are the apple of God's eye? Are they filled with the encouragement of the Christ? Would they testify as such, could they testify of it? The assurance of God's love is his greatest encouragement to the soul seeking his precepts. If the psalmist knows God loves him and he is his, he will be divinely encouraged by that notion, even when calamity and trouble strike, because he can look to his word, hear his preached word, hear his sweet voice, words from that love letter sent from God to him to know God's mind in all matters. The encouragement this gives is not only in some kind of idea, but it is sensibly discerned as a fact and reality no matter what is occurring in their life. The weak Christian is encouraged by finding himself becoming strong in the strength of God (Isa. 40:29; 2 Cor. 12:10). And the one who thinks he is strong, is deceived, by turning away from God and exercising his own strength. "Cursed be the man that trusteth in man, and maketh flesh his arm, and whose heart departeth from the LORD," (Jer. 17:5). How shall the psalmist obtain such a divine encouragement to his soul? How will he be confident in God? By the word of God, as he receives it in humility. "...but to this man will I look, even to him that is poor and of a contrite spirit, and trembleth at my word," (Isa. 66:2).

The psalmist could be filled with God's divine encouragement if he is emptied of his own self-confidence. He even turns the encouragement into a prayer, "Save me." He does that by a confident faith, "I am thine." He is roused to believe it, why? "for I have sought your precepts." A prayer set in the truth of the preached word, exercised for divine encouragement.

For the Christian, divine encouragement is to take the word of God for their rule, the Spirit as their guide to that rule, and the promises of the Christ for their encouragement. 2 Cor. 7:1, "Having, therefore, these promises, dearly beloved, let us cleanse ourselves from all filthiness of the flesh and spirit, perfecting holiness in the fear of God." 2 Peter 1:4, "Whereby are given unto us exceeding great and precious promises; that by these you may be partakers of the divine nature, having escaped the corruption that is in the world through lust." The opposite to this is Romans 8:5, "For they that are after the flesh do mind the things of the flesh..." Christians should gain all the divine encouragement they can from the word preached and read, and as they do, it is a sign to them that they are in God's way ; and when they seek out God's encouragements they will be divinely encouraged.

What does Question 5 of the *Shorter Catechism* say? "What do the scriptures principally teach? A5: The scriptures principally teach, what man is to believe concerning God, and what duty God requires of man." In other words, "Hold fast the form of sound words, which thou hast heard of me, in faith and love which is in Christ Jesus," (2 Tim. 1:13). Hold fast, seek them out, "for I have sought thy precepts." The Scriptures come from God by divine inspiration, they are necessarily true, the psalmist and the Christian ought to know and believe what it says, rest on it, and be divinely encouraged by it for it is God's inerrant, infallible and inspired will for his people.

If the Christian's heart is like the psalmist's, where it ordinarily, consistently, lies under the word, then God's words will bring a great means of divine encouragement to the soul everyday no matter how they may be serving Christ; holiness will adorn the horse's bells and the Christian's cooking pots. If the word carries the soul, aids the soul, lifts up the soul, encourages the soul, it is sensibly discerned by them.

How is it discernable, and how is it encouraging? I find the example of Cain and Abel to be very telling in this. Abel, tending flocks, and Cain tended the ground. In the span of time, at the appropriate time, the time of worship, on the Lord's Day, they bring sacrifices. Abel listens to God and brings an appropriate sacrifice, Cain does not, and brings what he wants to bring. The church at large should take note of that. Cain covers up his wickedness both by listening to the instruction of his parents as if he took an interest in the word and by bringing an offering just as his godly brother does; but *not quite*. Cain is rejected because he had no interest in what God has said and did not bring a proper sacrifice.

Chapter 10: Interest in the Word / Encouragement

He wanted to do what he wanted to do. But Abel is listed in the hall of faith, as faithful. "By faith Abel offered unto God a more excellent sacrifice than Cain, by which he obtained witness that he was righteous," (Heb. 11:4). What a *rockingly glorious word* that is of Abel. Luther said of these two, "This is an example of the twofold church, the true church and the hypocritical one."[47] Cain neither discerned the word, nor was made sensible to it though he acted like he did, he was in church, he offered something, but had no real interest. Abel both discerned what God said, and did it, to fulfill it; for he had a divinely encouraging faith.

The instrument which the Holy Spirit uses in the administration of the means of grace, to divinely encourage the soul is the word of God; God's instructions. For the word is the word of life. The declaration of the Father, by the begotten Word of the Son, in the person of the Spirit encourages the hearts of all God's saints.

The Holy Spirit works grace in the heart by the word and the preached word then causes Christians to love it and so highly esteem it. In fact, like the psalmist, it should cause them to prize it above all things. It holds in it the inspirations of God. "O how I love thy law! it is my meditation all the day," (Psalm 119:97). He loved it

---

[47] Martin Luther, *Luther's Works*, Vol. 1: Lectures on Genesis: Chapters 1-5, ed. Jaroslav Jan Pelikan, Hilton C. Oswald, and Helmut T. Lehmann, vol. 1 (Saint Louis: Concordia Publishing House, 1999), 247.

exceedingly. He will say later it is a light to the feet; the rule of the life; it tends to perfection; it cures all calamities (Psalm 119:105, 151.); it's the ground of his confidence; it keeps him from perishing in affliction, (verse 92), it quickens him, (verse 93), it causes his heart to rejoice because it divinely encourages him (verse 111). To love the preached word, as with the psalmist one must highly esteem it, see it as lovely, meditate on it, practice it, to know it and know its Giver better.

Since the word is the very inspirations of God, it should cause God's people to embrace the Scriptures, and as the psalmist, as Jesus said, John 5:39, "...search the Scriptures..." The word holds forth the Living Savior Jesus Christ; on every page, in every pattern, in every precept. This is the main reason that divine encouragement to the soul can be found in it. Jesus Christ is the living word of God; it breathes him. It is in the Scriptures that God's Christ is found. He is the one who encourages the soul. "...that they might be encouraged in the law of the LORD," (2 Chron. 31:4). It is how saints are strengthened and encouraged, by the ministry of the word to their soul. "But charge Joshua, and encourage him, and strengthen him," (Deut. 3:28), God told Moses to encourage Joshua by the word he would tell him. The Scriptures show that Christ is God, the word is Christ, and that Christ lifts up the soul to God. They show Christ has life in himself (John 5:26). That angels worship him (Heb. 1:6). That he created the world, and all things (Col. 1:6). That he upholds all things by the word of his power, (Heb. 1:3). That he is the first, and the last, (Rev. 1:8). That he was before the world, (John 17:5). That he is a mystery, (Col. 4:3). That he is expressly God: Christ is the mighty God, (Isa. 6:9). Very God, (John 5:20). The very Word was God, (John 1:1, 14). God over all, (Rom. 9:5). "Unto the Son he saith, Thy throne, O God, is for ever and ever," (Heb. 1:8). That he is in all believers by his Spirit, (Col. 2:27). He is the one that is the divine encouragement of the soul. "For the Lord himself shall descend from heaven with a shout, with the voice of the archangel, and with the trump of God: and the dead in Christ shall rise first: Then we which are alive and remain shall be caught up together with them in the clouds, to meet the Lord in the air: and so shall we ever be with the Lord. Wherefore comfort one another with these words," (1 Thess. 4:16-18). I am thine, save me, for I have sought thy precepts. This is what divine encouragement is all about. And as a side note, ministers are happy when the congregation seeks the preached word, hears the preached word, embraces the preached word, follows the preached word, and are divinely encouraged by the preached word. "I have no greater joy than to hear that my children walk in truth," (3 John 1:4).

The Bible is a *manual* of divine encouragement. God gives himself over to us by that deed of gift, Christ, and gives himself to us. He says to the believer, "I am yours, and you are mine, and all that I have is yours! I have written it down for you, and commissioned preachers to preach it; look to the preached word, and be of great encouragement in your soul as you learn what I have for you, for my Spirit is with your minister who preaches glad tidings, warnings, threatenings, promises, encouragements, to you." This is a mountain of divine encouragement! All that is in God is ours! All that is Christ's is ours. His wisdom is ours to teach us; his love is ours to pity us; his Spirit is ours to comfort us; his mercy is ours to save us. His preached word is ours to divinely encourage us, if we have an interest in it.

The preached word of God deserves your love and interest. It's yours, as a saint, it has been delivered to you by the blood of his Son. Rare gifts are often handled delicately, and this is the rarest of gifts. The good things contained in it, the more you believe and have an interest in it, the more you love it and him. Who said, "Great peace have they which love thy law: and nothing shall offend them," David did in Psalm 119:165.

No affliction is beyond the reach of divine encouragement to the soul; you see, this is very practical to you. God never deserts us in any trouble. It does not matter how heavy the affliction is, the smallest amount of divine encouragement alleviates the hardest affliction in this way; but he uses the preached word and warms the heart by it. It points you to look heavenward instead of on the earth. The mind is set on Christ instead of things swirling about them here in times of trouble. We are even commanded, "Set your mind on the things above...where Christ is seated at the right hand of God..."

Chapter 10: Interest in the Word / Encouragement

in Col. 3. The only discernable difference is that the greater the affliction, the greater the divine encouragement is to the soul that is interested in his precepts.

Christ will never leave his people without divine encouragement for them, if they have an interest in it. Divine encouragement to the soul is the opposite of trouble; it is why it is encouraging instead of depressing. You might think to yourself, "I don't have this divine encouragement." Examine your question, and merely ask, "why so?" "I don't seem to taste and discern the word as I ought." You must have an interest in it, first. You say, "Oh, but I do now! I want to be divinely encouraged, and persuaded of my salvation, with God's help, with an abundance of assurance in Jesus. Won't the Spirit just impress me into feeling that way at some point if I come to church enough or pray to him for it enough?" No. He won't. You think he will, but he won't. And this is the reason why most Christian churches and Christians today are a mile wide and a half an inch deep. The Spirit saves you with you; yes, certainly, he saves you in spite of you, if you are a believer ... but never without you. Thomas Brooks said this, "Divine encouragement is a delicate thing, and is not given to him that admits of any other."[48] To find encouragement to the soul, in any other way that the psalmist has laid out, and fulfilled in Christ, through the preached word, they will not find encouragement. It will be something

---

[48] Thomas Brooks, *The Complete Works of Thomas Brooks*, vol. 2, 372.

else; it will be counterfeit. Whatever they find or think they have will not last. It will not be spiritually helpful. It will in fact be the opposite to what the psalmist has said, because divine encouragement is delicately handled through the preached word. How does a curator deal with an ancient vase? Delicately. How do new parents deal with a newborn child? Delicately. Such things require careful treatment.

Interest in the preached word of God is a means of Divine Encouragement to your believing soul because it shows you where your love lies, and that is a very delicate thing; and you must handle it delicately and carefully. God grants his saints the joy of spiritual success, the guarantee of his defending care and providence, the assurance of his salvation in Christ, through the preached word. But wait, one objects, they say, "But God is not physically here, it is not God's mouth, it is your mouth." Ministers are only valuable insofar as they preach God's word, and cry out God's voice to you; otherwise they are useless, good for nothing (Jesus told his disciples that when he compared them to useless salt to be thrown and trampled). Ministers are called: Ambassadors for Christ, (2 Cor. 5:20) Angels of the Church, (Rev. 1:20; 2:1), Defenders of the Faith, (Phil. 1:7), Elders, (1 Tim. 5:17; 1 Pet. 5:1), Laborers, (Matt. 9:38, with Philem. 1), Lights, (John 5:35), Ministers of God, Isa. 61:6; 2 Cor. 6:4), Ministers of the Lord, (Joel 2:17) Ministers of Christ, (Rom. 15:16; 1 Cor. 4:1), Ministers of the word, (Luke 1:2), Ministers of

Chapter 10: Interest in the Word / Encouragement

Righteousness, (2 Cor. 11:15), Overseers of the souls of God's people, (Acts 20:28), Pastors, (Jer. 3:15; John 21:16–18; Eph. 4:11), Preachers, (Rom. 10:14; 1 Tim. 2:7) and a variety of other important designations. When they speak, God is speaking, "The LORD'S voice crieth unto the city," (Micah 6:9). God cried through Micah. It was Micah's voice, no, it was the Lord's voice. How rude you would think it if you were speaking to someone, giving some important life-giving direction – most important words you may ever speak - to a child, a wife, a husband, a friend, brother , sister, and you were pouring out to them something exceedingly important, and they looked down to their phone to start texting a friend, or they turned around and walked away to busy themselves with something else, or they turned and sat down and put on the TV and started watching a show, while you were speaking to them; how terribly rude you would think that is. When the preacher preaches God's word, he is God's voice; what does Christ think of that when you do that to him speaking to you? God says, I have a word for you, listen, hear, listen intently, with diligence, seek these precepts, listen carefully to what I am about to tell you, I am the sovereign God of the universe who has... And the person in the pew gets up and leaves. One would never do that at the movies because they *paid* for it; it is of *interest* to them. One would never do that to a famous person if they visited them at their home; they are of interest to them. Why affront God in that way? Is it so hard to be adequately prepared to seek out his precepts for a time?

The word dictates the material for the message of the preacher; seeking precepts is the same whether it's preached to 10 or to 100 or to 1000, or 10,000. "For this reason we also thank God without ceasing, because when you received the word of God which you heard from us, you welcomed it not as the word of men, but as it is in truth, the word of God, which also effectively works in you who believe," (1 Thess. 2:13). Christ's church will never ever grow, there will be no improvement to holiness, no revival, until Christians are *serious* about God's word; ... *where is revival today?* We do not have revival; we have coronavirus. Where is revival in you today? Consider it, you have been part of many churches, I would suppose, have you ever been part of revival? Why is that? For the psalmist, salvation and assurance both caused him to have a divine encouragement by God's preached word, to seek those words, understand them, to fulfill them. Christians, today, often think the Spirit is a kind of magic that electrifies them into feeling a certain way, without them, and just on them, so that they suddenly feel different by no work of their own. The psalmist has no part in that fantasy. He will seek out God's precepts at the mouth of the preacher, because to forfeit that, to reject that, is to reject God's counsel to them; and to reject God's counsel, well, where will that leave you? The psalmist will be encouraged by the preached word. There the

Spirit will work the word into his soul. There he will know, confidently, "I am thine," without which he would have known nothing.

What measure of divine encouragement will you gain from the preached word? Do you have an interest in divine encouragement for your soul in this way? Earnest Christian effort in seeking a blessing at God's precepts never fails, did you know that, for Christ says through the apostle, "In due season we shall reap, if we do not lose heart." It never fails; then one wonders why they do not have it? Many Christians begin well but grow tired, lose heart, end poorly. They lose heart because they have taken a wrong turn, and have lost interest; they may spend years in Doubting Castle because they have forgotten the key of promise is in their pocket; or that they were never told it was even there; they don't know where to look; they were never instructed well.

God promises to give you divine encouragement, if you have an interest in it. He will respond to your prayers, and grant you sensible and discernable signs of his presence and favor as you look to him in the preaching of the word, and that even, daily, in its reading and study. God promises, to his seeking children, to bless them; and to negligent children they go backward and not forward in holiness, "But this is what I commanded them, saying, "Obey My voice, and I will be your God, and you shall be My people. And walk in all the ways that I have commanded you, that it may be well with you." Yet they did not obey or incline their ear, but followed the counsels and the dictates of their evil hearts, and went backward and not forward,'" (Jer. 7:23-24). Listen closely, he does not promise blessing to those that *go backward*; he will not give divine encouragement to Christians that *neglect* him, or do not have an interest in him, those that might even merely hear the word, who do not *diligently* seek it out, as David said, "sought thy precepts," to hear them, keep them and do them. Those that think in this other way, forfeit his blessing because they are more content with some other worldly things; or they are content *not* to be taught; they believe they have arrived, and have enough; how much of Christ is enough? God's promises that are in Christ are directly attached to the preached word that has come from his mouth; they teach his sweetness. And like the psalmist he will, with all those who seek out his precepts, then say and be confident to say, because they know it to be true, for certain, "I am thine, save me, for I have sought thy precepts." He will give them the assurance of his presence, he will give them power to act as his witnesses, success in all their labors, rest and joy of heart in him and in his service, and he will do so liberally, and abundantly, by the word, in the power of the Spirit, as he spiritual persuades you to know the Christ you have come to seek out and understand in his preached word; and your interest he will turn to divine encouragement. And, then, regardless of what is happening to you in the world, all worldly affliction is arrested and brought into subjection by the comfort you gain in the Word of God, and this we will consider in verse 95 in the next chapter.

Chapter 11: Worldly Affliction Arrested by the Comfort of the Word of God

"The wicked have waited for me to destroy me: but I will consider thy testimonies," (Psalm 119:95).

The wicked have waited and expected, and hoped, to destroy me, or for me to be destroyed; but I discern, or consider, or am prudent, regarding your testimonies. David turned to the word of God when afflictions arose. He considered God's testimonies. *Consideration* includes interest, seriousness of thought, application; it is a parallel word to *godly meditation*. This was a very serious work, with earnestness, and motioning his power of consideration. Whatever his thoughts about this were, so his consideration would be. Light thoughts yield light expectations. Serious thoughts yield sober truths that lift up the spirit. Meditating in Scripture is sometimes expressed by the term "considering." "I will consider your testimonies," Psalm 119:95; that is, give them a serious and thoughtful pondering.

There are many parts to the word of God to the psalmist here as he considers it, ponders it, meditates on it. God's word cleanses (119:9–16). God's word is saving (119:41–48). God's word gives hope (119:49–56). God's word is faithful (119:81–88). God's word is sure (119:89–96). God's word is sweet (119:97–104). God's word is a light (119:105–112). God's word is wonderful (119:129–136). God's word is righteous (119:137–144). God's word is true (119:145–152). The psalmist had a great love for God's word (119:153–160). And he rejoiced in it (119:161–168). Because it is God's means of deliverance (119:169–176). If David had afflictions, trouble in the world, and he was a carnal man, what would he have thought about? A lost person in times of trouble considers his property, his wife and his children, his life; his stuff. When danger or uncertainty occurs, the carnal heart runs after the world, tries to fix it by the world's means. When David, a godly man, has worldly troubles, when wicked men advance against him to kill him (possibly the greatest of worldly problems), he considered the testimonies of God. And in such a consideration, he will say not but two verses later, "O how I love thy law!" (verse 97).

Doctrine: Worldly affliction is arrested by the comfort of the Word of God. Whatever the world, the flesh or the devil can cast at a person, the word of God is of grand comfort. And it will never fail. The godly will have worldly affliction while they are in the world. "These things I have spoken unto you, that in me ye might have peace. In the world ye shall have tribulation: but be of good cheer; I have overcome the world," (John 16:33). Christ centers the gaining of peace on his word, and on him. "These things I have spoken unto you." He gives a promise that is often left out of all those contemporary books of promises, which is that Christians will have tribulation in the world. But the comfort of his word shows he has overcome the world, for God rules the world, for God reigns over the world. And if God is for them, what could possibly be against them? What shall a Christian rest in while they are in tribulation, while they are in promised tribulations? For, the people of God are promised worldly afflictions while they live in this world. There are, in many ways, hard afflictions for many of God's children (think of the Christians who were in Afghanistan, or the Ukraine, at the hands of the wicked). David, throughout this psalm, mentions afflictions *many* times. People are given a false conception that when a person becomes a Christian that somehow the trials and tribulations stop, and life becomes *a bed of roses*. Many preachers preach that way, come to Jesus and all will be well. Yes, it will be well with your soul, but who knows what God will do in sanctifying the Christian, and placing them in Christ's school of affliction? Christians can have very fiery trials. 1 Peter 4:12, "Think it not strange concerning the fiery trial which is to try you, as though some strange thing happened unto you." That somehow being a Christian frees them from sickness, danger, hardship, poverty; such a message is a devilish lie, and will turn many people into *Orpahs*, those with good intentions at the start, but when afflictions arise, go back to the heathen and to devil (see Ruth 1). Christians will have affliction, and they will be sorrowful in the world, as their Master, Jesus, was a Man of Sorrows and acquainted with grief. Shall the student be less than the Master? Christ drank deeply of the cup of affliction, Matt. 27:46, "My God, my God, why hast thou forsaken me?" So do Christians who follow their Master. Jeremiah had "...bitter weeping" (Jer. 31:15). "Even to day is my complaint bitter: my stroke is heavier than my groaning," (Job 23:2). "And she said unto them, Call me not Naomi, call me Mara: for the Almighty hath dealt very bitterly with me," (Ruth 1:20).

But comfort may be had and comfort is also an outreach of God's providence to receive consolation through a particular means God has specially set up in his church: it is found in considering the word of God and seeking after it. It is comforting to God's people to read and meditate on the word. They are to be picked up by Christ through his means; his ordained way of comforting them.

God is a God of pity, and has written down things for pitiable creatures to know and embrace and consider. He is the, "Father of pity," or, "The Father of compassion," The Father of all mercy," and is the one who brings comfort. "...even the Father of our Lord Jesus Christ, the Father of mercies, and the God of all comfort," (2 Cor. 1:3). The description shows the pitiableness of the object. It is not simply that Paul wishes the reader to understand that God is to be blessed, but he moves from God, through Christ, the only Mediator between God and man, to descriptions that capture the heart. *Pitiable* creatures know they *need* pity. Pity, in a supernatural and spiritually beneficial sense, is only accessible through Christ, and Paul praises God as the Father of compassion in this way who has given Christ. *Pity* is looking upon a creature who is miserable, and in light of 2 Cor. 1, gaining comfort from God's looking to them. But how and when will God look to them? Christ is the visible manifestation of God in the flesh as Redeemer and Savior. The spring of pity overflows from God's view of the redeemed sinner by way of covenant. *Pity* is to look on the object as miserable and have compassion for it. "No eye pitied you, to do any of these things for you, to have compassion on you; but you were thrown out into the open field, when you yourself were loathed on the day you were born. And when I passed by you and saw you struggling in your own blood, I said to you in your blood, 'Live!' Yes, I said to you in your blood, 'Live!'" (Ezek. 16:5-6). How does God take pity on ugly things infected by the fall and downtrodden by affliction? God is described by Paul as the, "God of all comfort" in this pity. "All" comfort? – how much is that? It includes every aspect of biblical comfort; nothing is left out. It may include inward comfort by the Spirit, and outward comfort in various circumstances through people whom the Spirit uses to minister to others. All comfort; whatever kind of comfort is brought, God has a monopoly on it; he has it all.

Chapter 11: Worldly Affliction and Comfort

And his word is filled with comfort for people in times of trouble for souls that need comfort. "Comfort," God brings comfort; where the root word is the idea of nearness. It literally creates a picture of a compassionate Father who is concerned about working through the One and only Mediator to bring comfort to miserable creatures wallowing in their own blood in a field abandoned by all others, and this God draws near to them. God comforts his people, "in all our tribulation," (2 Cor. 1:4). Why do the righteous suffer? Why does Job sit on the ash heap, why is David overwhelmed with tumults and downcast, why does Paul have great tribulations from within and without? That's practically easy to answer, so God can minister comfort to them through Jesus Christ and his Spirit for his glory and their good. So they can experience more comfort from the Father of mercies. So they can be further sanctified; and the word is God's ordained means to do that.

Life is filled with *promised misery*. *The Westminster Shorter Catechism* asks in question 23, "Into what estate did the fall bring mankind?" Answer, "The fall brought mankind into an estate of sin and misery." What is misery? Unhappiness, distress, suffering, anguish, anxiety, torment, pain, grief, heartache, despair, despondency, depression, gloom, woe, sadness, sorrow. Pick the term that fits best. "He has filled me with bitterness, he has made me drink wormwood. He has also broken my teeth with gravel, and covered me with ashes," (Lam. 3:15-16). The lamentation of a godly soul in bitter affliction. What Christian does not need comfort? What? Do disciples think once they are converted they no longer feel the effects of sin? That the affects of the fall somehow go away? Have they been so delivered by Christ that they experience no turmoil, no difficulties, and that the Christian life is a walk in the park? Is it a bed of roses? To be a Christian disciple is to suffer and have tribulation because they still live in a fallen world; it may even be said, tribulation is a mark of the godly. But, the smallest amount of joy in God's comfort is greater than the heaviest affliction or suffering. A drop of Christ's comfort alleviates a mountain of affliction. Mountains in Scripture refer to the massive magnitude of sin. "...and though I have all faith, so that I could remove mountains," (1 Cor. 13:2); that is in relation to moving sin; sin is the mountain that faith moves. Faith in Christ overcomes sin. Sin brings misery. God brings comfort in misery if one is faithful. It does not matter how heavy the affliction is, the smallest amount of divine comfort alleviates the hardest affliction in this way. It points the Christian heavenward instead of on the earth. But where will comfort in affliction come from? It will come by considering the word of God. "...but I will consider thy testimonies," (Psalm 119:95).

Affliction and comfort have varying degrees. Some are heavy, and some are light; so some comfort is given to deal with those things that are light. But affliction is still difficult at any level. But the psalmist said, "For ever, O LORD, thy word is settled in heaven,"

Chapter 11: Worldly Affliction and Comfort

(Psalm 119:89). As the torrents and waves break upon the head of the drowning Christian, so a hopeful hand that raises him up above the water is a blessing. His word is settled, and the Christian can hope in it; because as his word is so is God. There is nothing out of his control. God is infinitely loving, tender, and compassionate towards his people in all their afflictions; big or small; of even in what they think is big or small. He governs and orders their afflictions. Oftentimes, Christians are fine saying that God *comforts* in afflictions; but they will have nothing of God's supremacy over tribulation where providences seemingly turn frowning or bad in a Christian's life by God's ordination. Abraham, go sacrifice your son for me, your only son. *Job, sit in the ash heap for a while, I've given the devil leave to afflict you.* And, *Paul, you will do well to be in prison, and then beheaded.* David had affliction, in fact, men waiting to kill him, waiting to destroy him, waited to see his demise. But God is in control of such things, even things that seem very evil, "But as for you, you meant evil against me; but God meant it for good, in order to bring it about as it is this day, to save many people alive," (Gen. 50:20). Was God with Joseph? Was he with him only as chief steward over all Egypt, or was he with him *even* when he was thrown into the pit, or sold as a slave, or thrown into prison? Was God with him in all those circumstances too? God is sovereign over all suffering and affliction of every kind. He will send leprosy into the house of Israelites as in Lev. 14:34, strike Miriam with it as in Num. 12:10, or with Job on the ash heap as God instructed Satan as to what he could physically do to Job in 1:12? "For whom the LORD loves He chastens, and scourges every son whom He receives." If you endure chastening, God deals with you as with sons;" (Heb. 12:6-7). God governs and oversees all of it. Nothing befalls his children except by his command or permission. For David, the trouble which he sustained by persecutors, drives him to search more deeply into the word of God, and to harden himself against all that the persecutors can do: and every comfort given to him from the Word, should do the same.

A carnal heart would have considered his house and land, wife, and children, or at least his life, which seems to now be in danger; but David's heart was on a better subject, he considered the testimonies of God, and so much sweetness pours in on his soul in that meditation, that while he is pondering them in his mind, that he cannot but help and say, "It is exceedingly broad (it covers everything, verse 96) and, "O how I love thy law!" (verse 97). And God even travails with them in their distress. "And it shall come to pass, that as I have watched over them to pluck up, to break down, to throw down, to destroy, and to afflict, so I will watch over them to build and to plant, says the LORD," (Jer. 31:28). "'They shall be carried to Babylon, and there they shall be until the day that I visit them,' says the LORD. 'Then I will bring them up and restore them to this place,'" (Jer. 27:22). He sees them, cares for them, afflicts them, and

Chapter 11: Worldly Affliction and Comfort

rescues them. He knows how to comfort them because affliction is part of a refiner's fire. "He [God] is like a refiner's fire," (Mal. 3:2). Fire is hot and it hurts to touch, much less to be drowned in molting metal, and to come up refined, new. But what shall happen to all those he refines? "Then shall the virgin rejoice in the dance, both young men and old together; For I will turn their mourning to joy, and will comfort them, and make them rejoice from their sorrow," (Jer. 31:13). But how will he do this? "Let my teaching drop as the rain, My speech distill as the dew, As raindrops on the tender herb, And as showers on the grass. For I proclaim the name of the LORD: Ascribe greatness to our God. He is the Rock, his work is perfect; For all his ways are justice, A God of truth and without injustice; Righteous and upright is he," (Deut. 32:2-4). Raindrops of biblical teaching, the word of God is consolation in tribulation, and there, God makes the heaviest afflictions bearable, and he often makes them light; or at least considered light in comparison to eternity and glory. So, the smallest amount of comfort bestowed is able to alleviate such difficult providences through considering the word of God, and its message of the God of all comfort.

Tribulation and comfort are glorious messengers from Jesus Christ to his people. People agree with the latter, comfort, but they do not really like the former, tribulation. It is not enough to simply say that God ordains trials and afflictions for the good of believers. Tribulations and troubles are messengers of Christ to try the Christian. He sends them this to see how they will respond to his governing of their life. Will they say, "curse God and die?" as Job's wife did? Or will they say, "All the paths of the LORD are mercy," (Psalm 25:10). "I will consider thy testimonies." (Psalm 119:95). Think on it, is there any suffering and trial greater than the cross of Christ? His suffering was so great, that before the actual time of his curse and death, the very thought of such a curse and death caused the Christ to sweat great drops of blood in intense agony in the garden. He sweat blood. It is unfathomable to the finite mind to understand how the Christ endured such suffering and torment; willingly; for the joy set before him. Incomprehensible was the prospect of undergoing infinite wrath, not for his own deeds (which were perfect and without blemish) but for the deeds of others – for Adam's curse and the Christian's personal sins. Earthly minded people put up with little to nothing for others.

Why did Christ suffer? "For the joy that was set before Him endured the cross, despising the shame," and what was the comfort? "and has sat down at the right hand of the throne of God," (Heb. 12:2). Christ was exalted in due time, with an exaltation also as remarkable as the cross was horrific. And if one reads through the passion narratives, there is much prayer, there is much consideration, there is much of the word of God, much quoting of scripture done by the Christ in his tribulation, even from the cross.

Chapter 11: Worldly Affliction and Comfort

But such things as affliction, tribulation, they are messengers of Christ to his people for their good. *Comfort.* No doubt, through the word of God, comfort is a sweet messenger from Christ. It is always available. One never has to wait for it, in the sense of there is no line to stand in. They do not need to climb a mountain to get it. They do not need to make a pilgrimage to find it. They simply need to be stirred up to consider it. Was there any earthly man more afflicted than Job? I think not. Crushed, yet comforted. And he said, ""shall we receive good at the hand of God, and shall we not receive evil?" (Job 2:10). "Though he slay me, yet will I trust in him," (Job 13:15).

This comfort is delivered by means of the word of God both inwardly and outwardly. Inwardly, the word is used by the Holy Spirit in the Christian to supernaturally deliver comfort. This is gained by the Christian when they believe the word by faith when it is heard or read. And when they read it, the Spirit presses them to know, this is true of you. They are refreshed and comforted with particular favors God has assured them of in his word. He will not deal with us after our sins, "nor reward us after our iniquities," (Psalm 103). It is great comfort. He will, "spare us, as a man spareth his son that serveth him." It is great comfort. No father can show compassion like God is bound to show to his children, (Malachi 3:17). It is great comfort.

At all times they find they have, "access to the throne of grace," to go boldly to ask, "in the name of

Christ, and it shall be given," (Hebrews 4:16). It is great comfort. "In all their affliction He was afflicted, And the Angel of His Presence saved them; in His love and in His pity He redeemed them; And He bore them and carried them All the days of old," (Isa. 63:9). What great comfort is this? "He giveth power to the faint, and to them that have no might, he increases strength. They that wait on the Lord shall renew their strength," (Isaiah 40:29, 31). It is great comfort from great promises.

By way of notation, the world, the flesh and the devil lie in wait to *steal* that comfort away; the wicked look to destroy this comfort. "...sin lieth at the door," (Gen. 4:7). Psalm 119:61, "The bands of the wicked have robbed me." Psalm 119:69, "The proud have forged a lie against me." Psalm 119:85, "The proud have digged pits for me." The Christian's troubled soul in all situations must be to turn to the word of God, his testimonies will comfort them. Where shall the afflicted soul find comfort in trouble? In highly esteeming the word of God above all things in the world. What Christians honor, that they love, what they love, that they labor for, what they labor for that is where their interest lies. Whatever people love they labor for. This is where such high esteem of the word will lead Christians to gain spiritual profit from it. It is to have a heart inflamed with a sincere love to the truth of the word of God, to come to know God more, and the providence of his ways.

To know *about* God is *conjecture* until it has some practical way of working itself out in one's life. To know about God can be done by *here say*, but to know God, truly, is by *personal experience*. What should the word of God do in times of affliction that would make the Christians as confident in tribulation about God's comfort as David was? Often they go to God in the prayer of illumination before looking to the teaching as "take us into the protection of your word." Such a protection in the word moves the mind of the Christian from off himself, from off the world, from off the wickedness of sin and temptation, to the word. It is a mortifying work because it is not easy. Such a protection brings the Christian to God and to Christ. It is a vivifying work; it makes life stirred up in them. "And be not conformed to this world: but be ye transformed by the renewing of your mind, that ye may prove what is that good, and acceptable, and perfect, will of God," (Rom. 12:2). The Christian's love to the word shows his desire to kill sin, and be drawn closer to Christ, to be like him; the mind transformed, so that one may see and understand and do, God's will in the word while tribulation swirls about. They gain a greater sense of God's work in their lives, and what God is doing in his providence with them, and they know it when they look to the word, for that shows his character, and his will as it pertains to them. They are safe there; he is a Strong Tower. The word teaches them how to think and act and walk and talk and carry themselves. They can measure their responses in their life to what it says, and they find comfort when their lives coincide with the word. They know God's word is the place they find Christ speaking to them, "...for thou, LORD, only makest me dwell in safety," (Psalm 4:8). This is why Luther said, "Understanding safeguards."[49] *Understanding* makes people *safe* if they understand the word, because God comforts them by it in the power of the Spirit.

Consider the Word as David did in afflictions. You must take time to view your afflictions from the perspective of providence. Afflictions of all kinds will come; it is a promise of Scripture that tribulations will be a regular part of your Christian walk. You will have many Potiphar's wives to contend with, many Hamans, many Pharaoahs, you will have many *devils*. There are always two walking with you wherever you go, Christ and devils.

Afflictions might come in all kinds of shapes and sizes. They may be of the body. They may be of the mind. They may be of the spirit. They may be outward. They may be inward. How will you respond to them all? With David, you must turn to the word and be mesmerized by it. You must be very strong and readied in the faith to do this. When temptations come, and trouble come, and afflictions come, if you are not ready, if you are not prepared, you will find afflictions to be sharp and hard.

---

[49] Martin Luther, *Luther's Works*, Vol. 11: First Lectures on the Psalms II: Psalms 76-126, ed. Jaroslav Jan Pelikan, Hilton C. Oswald, and Helmut T. Lehmann, vol. 11 (Saint Louis: Concordia Publishing House, 1955), 479.

Tribulations should find the point of your spiritual sword of God's word sharp. First, prepare to hear and read the word. "For Ezra had prepared his heart to seek the Law of the LORD, and to do it, and to teach statutes and ordinances in Israel," (Ezra 7:10). The minister takes time to prepare to preach it, you should take time to prepare to listen to it. That may mean taking time the previous night or early in the morning to prepare your heart. Pray, read, meditate, get in a frame in which you are thinking, today I expect to be spiritually revived by the word of God, because today, by the word, I will be armed with what I need for the week. Today I expect God to show up when I hear the word. Today I expect to be transformed further by it; so prepare.

Second, hear the word of God attentively and without distraction. Each person in the church should be of the mind that when worship begins, everything else falls by the wayside. God is going to speak to us this morning. Remember, for, "one Achan, the church suffers." The entire church should be of the mind that nothing will rob you of the kernel of truth to be handed out during that time of considering the word of God. Revelation 2:7 says, "He that has an ear, let him hear…" If he is hindered from hearing, how can he hear? If he is distracted from hearing how can hear? Take the kernel, the fundamental truth that the entire service should be built on, hide it in your Christian bag of jewels to pull it out when you need it once you have it. But to use it is to first know it and understand it. It is to consider it; it is to hear it without distraction, with focus, for profit.

Thirdly, cultivate the word of God read and explained. Talk about it. Talk about it after church. Talk about it when you go home. Go over the sermons. Take notes, compare notes, consider it. Use it in family devotions; test your family members on it. Consider it in your personal devotions. Is it not an odd thing that Christians often don't talk about the word preached, the message, meaning or intent of the entire worship service, during the week in family worship, when they are all together. At that time, it is fresh in your mind, use it wisely. Christ has ministered some sweetness to you. Take the Lord's Day and make it work the good of your soul. Encourage one another while it is still called today.

One cannot be so distraught about tribulations and afflictions that they do not use God's constituted means to better their walk, and better the walk of those around them, especially in their homes. Here is a practical way of doing it: treat the word of God, as worldly people treat a movie. Service on the Lord's Day is, what, an hour and a half? That's shorter than 90% of most Hollywood movies. Think about the movies for a moment; and then what happens after. A person goes to the movie, sets themselves up for it: they paid good hard-earned money for it. Some plan way ahead, a month ahead, and Google the possible characters in the movie ahead of time, finding out what they can about how good the movie might be, watch a trailer, read a few reviews to be sure they are spending money wisely. They

Chapter 11: Worldly Affliction and Comfort

plan out a day in which they will go to the movie, to get there on time; there is a time table, and they will be on time. They get their popcorn, candy, buy their drink. They use the restroom ahead of time, because they're not getting up once it starts; they've *paid* for it; they don't want to miss a moment. They are engaged in considering so many things. They have planned so well that they are there in a good seat, in full view, in the middle, so they can see best, and they arrive early to even watch the coming soon trailers. Then the movie starts and they hang on every word and every sequence, the whole story; they are wide eyed about it. And then after the movie has ended, what do they do with others? They talk about it, they further consider it. "Did you see when so and so did such and such." They talk about it when they go out, when they come in, when they lie down, when they get up. They love to consider it ...until the next one comes to town.

Scripture exhorts you to consider God's word more than a worldly person would consider anything. It is why God says, of godly households, concerning the word, "speaking of them when thou sittest in thine house, and when thou walkest by the way, when thou liest down, and when thou risest up," (Deut. 11:19). It is because the word of God alone is what is used by the Spirit to encourage you, to cause you to grow, to protect you, to help you, where all worldly affliction is arrested by the word, and brings you into subjection to God's will; for the world is filled with tribulation. If there is affliction, there must be a time of consideration for you. If there is a time of affliction and trouble, Thomas Manton said, "let us provide for a time of exercise."[50] In other words, to think about it, and see how God might give comfort by the word; to search it out. And if there is a particular situation that you deal with, ask the pastor about what you ought to read, and what you ought to seeks out, seek the law at the mouth of the priest. David, a saint, is afflicted, so he considers God's testimonies. What has God done, what is his witness with others, through the history of his people, so I can see how I might be comforted in my trouble. That is where he finds comfort and help and aid and spiritual strength; and then he has the ability to help others in affliction by using the word in his own testimony to them. A person might object, "But I don't have affliction, really of any kind," Well, hear how that works out in these verses: "If ye endure chastening, God dealeth with you as with sons," (Heb. 12:7). "For whom the LORD loveth he correcteth; even as a father the son in whom he delighteth," (Prov. 3:12). Afflictions and tribulations are part of being sons and daughters. To be without afflictions and tribulations is not the property of a son or daughter of God. This is not the same with everyone. Godly children may not have the tribulations of a parent at the same moment in the same way, but later they may.

Every Christian has afflictions. Where will you go for comfort and what will you do to find it? Everyone

---

[50] Thomas Manton, *The Complete Works of Thomas Manton*, vol. 8, 96.

Chapter 11: Worldly Affliction and Comfort

wants comfort, but does everyone want to consider, as God instructs them, to consider? "...but I will consider thy testimonies," (Psalm 119:95). This is an interesting word, "testimonies." It means the witness of God for himself. The witness he has left behind for people to consider based on who he is and what he does. Do you see how all that fits together? Not merely facts, but a full witness as to how God acts personally. How Jesus acts personally with a saint. They are considered by the godly to gain comfort in the midst of all and any tribulations.

But when we deal with the subject of considering God's word, this concerns how Christians can be happy, even when afflictions come; it argues contentment. The practical dimension engulfs the Christian here in application. When we study, the end of study is to have practical knowledge of some kind on a particular passage so that it may profit our spiritual growth. When we consider the word of God, the end of that is sanctification or to be more holy; that it works something into our soul so we act and think a certain way while the world terrorizes us. The Apostle James read Psalm 119, and was familiar with it, "count it all joy when ye fall into divers temptations;" (James 1:2), meaning, or translated "various trials," which is directly related to the work of God's testimonies to souls that seek comfort. Do you have trials? Real trials, not American trials. Trials in the American mind are when your pool pump breaks, or your shovel breaks and you have to buy a new one; that is not what the psalmist is thinking about. Real trials, sickness, cancer, crippling diseases, poverty, enemies against you for your faith, friend and family members against you for your faith, afflictions brought in by corrupt governments and the like; spiritual trials, the wiles of the devil, spiritual attacks, fiery darts, mountains of sin that you have yet not removed by faith; real trials that need real comfort and direction.

The Spirit leads inwardly in such trials, by a secret motion on the heart attesting to the word, to consider what he has done with others in those same situations, as they are recorded in the bible, and he wants you to consider what he has done. David said, "but I will consider thy testimonies." He motions the soul to follow what he impresses on them as true in the word that they have considered it. He doesn't implant them into your head apart from you considering them. You will not have a trial, go to sleep, and the next day when you wake up, suddenly have comfort. He doesn't use sleep or negligence to comfort, he uses consideration of the word. He inclines you, presses you, even, as many of the old preachers used to say, woos you, to bend your wills to his word. When the Spirit directs or leads in this way, you are not forced against your will. Sons and daughters do not kick and scream against the Spirit to gain comfort; consider that for a moment. They are pliable to the Spirit's leading because they have been made that way by a frequent course of godly meditation. They are a considering people. "Thy people shall be willing in the day of thy power," (Psalm 110:3). Sons and daughters yield themselves willingly to be guided by the Spirit as they consider the word. Sometimes, it may not be pleasant. "My brethren, count it all joy," (James 1:2-3). James doesn't say *it is* joyful; neither did David. The parallelism, is set between trials and comfort. *The world is after me to destroy me and lies in wait to kill me; but I will consider your testimonies.* There is found the way of escape, and the ministering comfort of the Father, Son and the Spirit. "For the LORD shall comfort Zion: he will comfort all her waste places; and he will make her wilderness like Eden, and her desert like the garden of the LORD; joy and gladness shall be found therein, thanksgiving, and the voice of melody," (Isa. 51:3), speaking of the work of the Gospel on the soul. So, he leads them into truth, that they may, in spiritual power, reverse the affects of the fall, and be like the psalmist, who was like the Christ, in considering God's testimonies for his good. There worldly affliction and trouble were arrested and silenced by the comfort of the word of God. And because of this, in considering this, from the great variety of the subjects here, the scripture is very large, and reaches to several and various conditions of men in the world. There is nothing that the word of God does not cover, and so he says, "Thy commandments are exceedingly broad," (Psalm 119:96), which we will consider in the next chapter, and conclude our study on this passage.

Chapter 12: The Fallen Material World Rejected in Light of the Mysteries of the Gospel

"I have seen an end of all perfection: but thy commandment is exceeding broad," (Psalm 119:96).

David says, *I have considered and inspected the end and completeness of everything.* He's made it his job to consider things finite on the earth. At least generally speaking. He is making a contrast between limited human understanding and God's unsearchable and divine wisdom found in his law, and how far that law reaches. What does it cover? What is its breadth? From the variety or length of the subject here, the scripture is large, and reaches to all callings and conditions of people in the world. There is no situation, no group of people, no kind of person, no vocation, no hobby, no interests, no anything, that Scripture does not speak to. "Thy commandment is exceedingly broad," (Psalm 119:96). Why does he say *commandment*, and not *commandments*? The whole of Scripture can be likened to a single commandment, as Jesus taught. Love the Lord your God with all your heart, all your soul and all your mind. The Spirit of Truth testifies through the psalmist that the Law of God, (though only given in ten commands), is so perfect, that nothing may be added to it, and so large, that nothing may be compared with it; though it is ten, it is one. All human limitations in wisdom and perception of the temporary world fall to nothing in light of it. And even though the psalmist refers to the commandment, "thy commandment is exceedingly broad," and as it certainly includes God's Law, there is also a broader meaning from the whole psalm which includes all of God's word; for all the word concerns loving God. James Durham said, "it takes in the fulness and extent of the whole Law, in its obligation, as to all things, persons, and duties of all sorts."[51] Everything, from all of time, in any situation, is generally or specifically advised in the word of God. There is no thing new under the sun.   One theologian translated it this way from the original, "To all perfection I see a limit; but your commandments are boundless."[52] The boundaries of creation even in its perfection may be perceived, observed and found to be wonderous, but those of God's Law in its nature, application, and influence, are infinite. God's word is infinite, without bounds, without limitations, except by its nature. There is *no thing* in creation so perfect but that something is lacking to it, for it is limited in scope. God's Law is of infinite breadth, reaching to everything, perfectly meeting what everything requires, and to all times and places. In this

---

[51] James Durham, *The Law Unsealed: Or, A Practical Exposition of the Ten Commandments*, (Glasgow: printed by Robert Sanders, printer to the city and University, and are to be sold in his shop, 1676), 11.
[52] Roger Nicole, "Why I Am 'Comfortable' with Inerrancy," *Reformation and Revival 11*, no. 3 (2002): 120.

way, people can never outgrow the infinite word. They have, for example, as it pertains to the psalmist, a limitless storehouse of holiness to tap into. People in the world attempt to perfect their own things and bring them to their highest point; by human strength and ingenuity. But all these things cannot out-perfect the perfect word of God, and his commands to his people.

All temporal things come to an end; they have endings, and can be exhausted because they are finite, limited. But eternal things are eternal. Luther said, "He who by hope lives in the commandment and Word of God, having nothing in this world, craving nothing of these narrow things, surely lives in the broadness of spirit."[53] It is the same truth that the psalmist taught at the beginning of this section, that the word of God is not subject to change, because it is eternal and not temporal; it is settled and it endures forever. Calvin said, "He here asserts, that there is nothing under heaven so perfect and stable, or so complete, in all respects, as not to have an end; and that the Divine word alone possesses such fullness as to surpass all bounds and limits."[54]

The psalmist rested confident that such a word was comforting, and that God would minister to him, because it ministered to him in spite of all afflictions; no

---

[53] Martin Luther, *Luther's Works*, Vol. 11: First Lectures on the Psalms II: Psalms 76-126, ed. Jaroslav Jan Pelikan, Hilton C. Oswald, and Helmut T. Lehmann, vol. 11 (Saint Louis: Concordia Publishing House, 1955), 479.
[54] John Calvin, *Commentary on the Book of Psalms*, vol. 4 (Bellingham, WA: Logos Bible Software, 2010), 472–473.

matter what those afflictions were. There was nothing in the physical world he could turn to for comfort, because God's means of comfort is the word. And it did not matter what situation he was in, for God's commandment is exceedingly broad. The Holy Spirit testifies, that the Law of God, (though it is given in ten words) is so perfect, that nothing may be added to it, and so large, that nothing may be compared to it. The commands of God, are summarized by Christ, prophetically set in this verse, "Jesus said unto him, Thou shalt love the Lord thy God with all thy heart, and with all thy soul, and with all thy mind. This is the first and great commandment," (Matt. 22:37-38). The sense of the commandments are to be understood to be perfect. The law of God, to love God with all the heart, soul and mind, forbids all sins which the Lord condemns in his word; and commands all moral duties which he requires from his people. They show a man his sin, and the punishments due for them, that being humbled in themselves, they would seek Christ and his grace.

And that this word, this law may be a perfect rule to frame the entire life; that being redeemed by Christ, men may also be renewed according to the image of God, in true righteousness, knowledge and holiness.

Doctrine: The breadth of the eternal Word is in no way comparable to the fallen material world which vanishes like a vapor. David's testimony is from his own experience. The world is vain, and is insufficient to make man happy. Matthew Henry said, "David, in his time, had seen Goliath, the strongest, overcome, Asahel, the swiftest, overtaken, Ahithophel, the wisest, befooled, Absalom, the fairest, deformed; and, in short, he had seen an end of perfection, of all perfection."[55] Such things of the world do not last; for the glory of man is but as a vapor. In contrast, from his own experience, he knows the fulness of the word of God. It is sufficient for man, and God's commandment, to love him with all the heart, soul and mind, for the command is exceedingly broad. This is because no matter what situation man is in, the word of God reaches to all circumstances and situations throughout all of time. There is found in God's word, stability, and immutability, the same characteristics of the beginning of what David said in psalm 119:89-91. God's word never changes, is not ancient and out of date, it is unchangeable; it belongs to that sphere which is above the movement of time. What was good for Abel is good for Noah is good for Abraham is good for Joseph is good for Joshua is good for David is good for Paul is good for all Christians. All earthly perfection has its limits; God's law is limitless.

David says the same thing of the fleeting world in its ability to make man happy, that Solomon would later write, "Vanity of vanities, all is vanity." The world is only temporary. The things of the world are not to be doted upon. They end, they have limits, they are not that

---

[55] Matthew Henry, *Matthew Henry's Commentary on the Whole Bible: Complete and Unabridged in One Volume*, (Peabody: Hendrickson, 1994), 922.

which the heart must rest on. As Proverbs says, "beauty is vain," (Pro. 31:30); how quickly it fades; "but a woman that feareth the LORD, she shall be praised. Give her of the fruit of her hands; and let her own works praise her in the gates," (Prov. 31:30-31). Fleeting things, *flee*, and eternal things last. This may be said of everything in the world. God has a certain order in the universe so that the world doesn't explode in an instant and fall apart. The world abides by God's laws of nature, in which he set up the world in a way for it to operate. There are a good many things that believers can use while in the world. But all the things they use as tools for the glory of God, still, fade. They have a time, and then are no more. Think about all the industry of the world. Jesus said in Luke 16 that the sons of the world are *more* industrious than the children of light. They take advantage of the now, and they are set on making now pleasurable for them to the highest point they can because everything fades; eat drink and be merry *now*. But this is vanity, it is the madness of the world to rest, and think on, and be industrious, only in temporary fleeting things. What was Solomon's charge to this, even after he made an experiment in gratifying himself with all worldly things, and came away with this singular notion, "Let us hear the conclusion of the whole matter: Fear God, and keep his commandments: for this is the whole duty of man," (Eccl. 12:13). This is the same conclusion that is stated here in this psalm. "...thy commandment is exceedingly broad," (Psalm 119:96).

You see, the believer lays up treasure in heaven, not on earth; he does not look for satisfaction here, though things here may make life more pleasurable to the journey to heaven. Yet, they have their minds set on Christ above, who is seated at the right hand, not on the things of the earth. Their treasure is according to God's word, his broad word that encompasses their whole life, for all situations. Their treasure is according to receiving the Living Word, and following the living word, in obedience to God. Believers hope in Christ above all earthly things.

The word of God is unchangeable; its message is unchangeable. There is no conflict between any of the commands and / or patterns found by the faithful in the word concerning holiness. There is not one Law that contradicts another. There is not one disciple that taught contrary ideas in Scripture; there is no contrary teachings from the Old Testament to the New Testament. James 2:10 says, "For whoever shall keep the whole law, and yet stumble in one point, he is guilty of all." All God's commandments are *one*, for *thy commandment is exceedingly broad*. There is one character of God, and one Law which demonstrates his character. This Law requires submission and agreement to its obedience to God. Because in the Law, it gathers together all conceivable moral acts at once; rolled up all into one, love God. All duties God requires bind all rational creatures in comfort to it in character and conduct; to love him. Calvin said, "The divine law given to our minds, is the proper regulation of the principal requisite to a righteous observance of it."[56] Believers must righteously observe it, because the Law is always right, and it never changes; and it will righteously direct them into any good course before the face of God.

It is of perpetual obligation as Jesus said in Matthew 5:17, "Do not think that I came to destroy the Law or the Prophets. I did not come to destroy but to fulfill." Not only does Christ teach that he does not come to destroy the law, but he says those who are without the law or law-less must depart from him at the judgment. "Ye who practice iniquity," i.e. law-less, in other words, those who have abandoned the commandment to love God as God has revealed himself.

The Law is the rule of the Christian's life. They pray that the Holy Spirit would help them see things in the law, in the word, Psalm 119:18, "Open thou mine eyes, that I may behold wondrous things out of thy law." What do Christians find in the word of God in this way that cause them to disregard the limitations of the world for their happiness? They see the nature of sin. They see the nature of holiness. They see the need of Christ and his work and merit. They see the way of salvation. The Law is God's star in the firmament to lead one to Jesus Christ, and as the Magi followed the star to Christ so the people of God follow the commandment to Christ. They

---

[56] C. Matthew McMahon, eBook, *A Practical Guide to Primeval History* (Crossville, TN: Puritan Publications, 2016) The Establishment of Covenant Law in Genesis.

see that the Law demonstrates the righteousness of Christ's work fulfilled for his people. It causes them, then, to live accordingly, since Christ saves them and then uses the word, the Law, to make them more holy, no matter what affliction or tribulations they may be having in the world, or what questions they have in living before him. His law answers all of them in him. Hebrews 12:28–29, "Therefore, since we are receiving a kingdom which cannot be shaken, let us have grace, by which we may serve God acceptably with reverence and godly fear. For our God is a consuming fire." Can Christians use the Law for good? Most assuredly, 1 Timothy 1:8, "But we know that the law is good if one uses it lawfully." This is because it shows how rational creatures are able to mimic the Creator and love him through Christ, and, love others as well. God's word demands all good, and forbids everything that is evil. It shows the way of eternal virtue in Christ. The world may include things that have some virtue in them, but they are not as virtuous as the Law of God, and the word of God. The word of God, and his commandment, are holy because God is holy. His word answers his nature; it is as he is. It makes true Christians holy, because Christ sends his Spirit to use the word to change them and fix them and save them. David tells us, "Thy commandment is exceeding broad," (Psalm 119:96). It is of everlasting truth. Nothing shall be lessened or weakened from it. Nothing shall be changed or altered. It is broad for its usefulness, for it demonstrates the covenants of works and free grace. It extends to and covers all the circumstances of all men for all time. It will comfort men in distress if used in the right way. It has direction for men in happiness if used in the right way. It will lead one to be wise if used in the right way. It will show all things contrary to it to be foolish and vanity. It will teach men how to order themselves in every way possible, before God. It will either give them direct commands, or guiding principles. It presents men with the best ethics, economics, and politics in the world. It will make for holy and righteous families, flourishing kingdoms and prosperous nations; if one has interest in it. It makes them, as said in verse 24 of this psalm, a "delight" as they are the godly's "counsellors." The world would be blessed with holy families, holy husbands and wives, holy parents and children, holy magistrates and governors, holy people of all kinds if they heeded the perpetual word that is so broad, for the "beauty of the Lord our God" would "be upon us," (Psalm 90:17), for the commandment of God and the mysteries of the Gospel informed in it, would direct them in the right way under the governing of King Jesus. The Psalmist has entered into the sanctuary of God, and had understood the end of all things. What is the end of all things? What is the purpose of all things? Is it not, as Augustine said, "to excel in the kingdom of Christ, which hath no end?"[57]

---

[57] Augustine of Hippo, "Expositions on the Book of Psalms," in *Saint Augustine: Expositions on the Book of Psalms*, ed. Philip Schaff, trans. A. Cleveland Coxe, vol. 8, *A Select Library of the Nicene and Post-*

d) What is the broadest point, in all of the bible, in which hang all the Law and the Prophets? "Jesus said unto him, Thou shalt love the Lord thy God with all thy heart, and with all thy soul, and with all thy mind. This is the first and great commandment. And the second is like unto it, Thou shalt love thy neighbour as thyself. On these two commandments hang all the law and the prophets," (Matt. 22:37-40). Is it not to love God, and then to live out the commandment from another perspective, that is, to love one another, which is the same? It is an *old* commandment, that is it given in Exodus. Yet, it is a *new* commandment, in that it is to be patterned after the Christ who came and loved God and loved his neighbor perfectly, and so Christians are to follow his example.

Is there not an argument that could be made here from the psalm that the commandment, which is exceedingly broad reaches into the love of God and love of one's neighbor? That is the point of it. This is the broadness of the law; it is the heart of the Law, to teach men how to love God and love one another. This is the truth in which all other things pale in comparison; all of life hangs on this exceeding broad command. David had considered it and fell on the broadness of God's command; touching everything. It is as Augustine so well summarized, "Love God, and do what you please."

Nicene Fathers of the Christian Church, First Series (New York: Christian Literature Company, 1888), 575–576.

Love God and do what you please. Here one is devoted to the Word of God and to Christ. If one loves God, they do what pleases God which pleases them. If one loves God and does what one pleases, they do what God's exceedingly broad word teaches them to do.

The psalm is, overall, a covenantal concept and idea. It is no little or light matter to keep covenant with God; it is to love him. It is your evangelical duty to keep covenant with the God you profess to serve. But, to keep your covenant with God on your own is impossible in light of the fall. The children of fallen Adam are weak and wearied in their attempts at being righteous. This is because what God requires of you is exceedingly broad, because his word is exceedingly broad and requires from you much. And even "the much" he requires is to be perfect, without weakness or wavering; to its highest degree. If we consider what is required in the Covenant of free Grace, we find that it is very large in its substance, and it is difficult, even impossible for fallen sons and daughters of Adam to complete or uphold; they need a Mediator. In and of yourself you have no power and cannot perform it without grace from Jesus Christ. What is set within the bounds of these two words which you hear so often – believe and obey. Believe in Jesus Christ; obey King Jesus; to deny one or either is to contribute to the perilous nature of the day. To persevere in him, to overcome all temptations in him, to be continually faithful to him, to be overcomers and more than conquers in him is the remedy. To be faithful unto death that you may receive the crown of life. To do all we do for God, as being his servants, to devote all our whole selves to Jesus Christ, as those who are bought with a price, requires, care, diligence, and vigilance. Again, there are a great many duties laid on us in the covenant, and the precepts of this grand covenant are exceedingly broad. This is why the mystery of the Gospel is so grand, that Christ said without me you can do nothing. You need him at every step. Thy word is a light unto my path, a light for every step, was that not David's argument in this psalm? Every command that Jesus Christ gives you in his word is very full. There are duties to be done, sins to be avoided, afflictions and trials to be undergone, and comfort to find. God is to be believed in, and worshipped as prescribed by him in all his glory. Everything that you do is bound up together in what the word of God directs, guides and commands of you in. And every part of your being is under obligation to do them as you stand in relation to the Christ and his work for your never dying soul. Everything, loving God with all the heart, with all the soul, with all the mind; the will, the affections, ears and eyes and hands and feet and such, all owe obedience to the Christ who has paid the price for you and bought you, and ransomed you as a believer. We have our hearts to look after, and keep with diligence for God and his glory, "Keep thy heart with all diligence; for out of it are the issues of life," (Prov. 4:23). Our minds, ears, eyes, feet, hands, our tongue to order and keep within bounds, which must be well looked after, "I said, I will take heed to my ways, that I sin not with my tongue: I will keep my mouth with a bridle, while the wicked is before me," (Psalm 39:1). All your actions must be conformed to the exceedingly broad and perpetually unchangeable word of God, in all Christ's divine prescripts; bound in loving God. All our actions must be plumbed by the right rule of his word, and directed to their proper end, "Whether therefore ye eat, or drink, or whatsoever ye do, do all to the glory of God," (1 Cor. 10:31). Because the breadth of the eternal Gospel are in no way comparable to the fallen material world which vanishes like a vapor; the word lasts forever, where the world is fleeting.

The psalmist was very confident to trust in God's word, that all the issues of life are set down in his command to love God. This is not an indifferent thing you can take or leave. The psalmist was not making a notation on things indifferent. Nothing in the word is indifferent. If you believe what you like in the bible and throw away what you don't like, it's not the bible you believe but yourself. How can a person throw away part of the "one thing" – love God. The world is an indifferent thing in the context, it is fleeting and it is not lasting in comparison to the eternal word. It is not an indifferent thing whether you uphold God's word or not, to love him. If you would enjoy the comfort of the promise of Christ in the breadth of the Gospel, you must have the witness of your own consciences to his precepts. "If ye love me, keep my commandment," (John 14:15). The opposite of which is, if you don't, don't. It is one thing to be in the visible covenant of the church, and another thing altogether to have the promise of Christ in your heart with sincerity. People often think that they have no obligation to live as they should according to the word because 1 John 2:1, "If we sin, we have an Advocate..." They assure themselves, falsely, that Christ shall answer for all their sin no matter what they do, no matter how they act, no matter where they place their love; even if they love things in the fleeting world more than him. It makes little to no difference to them to neglect what God instructs them in his word, and to live carelessly before the means of grace; that argues spiritual declension and apostasy. But God will not be mocked in that, for his commandments are perpetual and unchangeable, and they are exceedingly broad to encompass the whole life of the believer. What will give you a better and more full view of yourselves then Christ shining his Spirt into your soul and comparing all that is there by his word and law? This argues your knowledge of it. You will never know what the broadness of the law consists and how you relate to it without being familiar with it. And it will not show you your corruption, those things to kill, and put to death for your good, if you do not consider it. Nor, will you know what will make you happy in Christ without being familiar with it. It is exceedingly broad, and it reaches to the smallest corruption, (Psalm 119:96). It is eminently spiritual, and searches the inmost corners of the heart, soul, and mind.

It is exceedingly pure, which can refine you in the fire of God's Holy-Spirit-work to sanctify you. It is exceedingly precious because it houses in it the promises of the Savior and his grand Gospel. There the believer finds all his ways directed and enlarged. There the believer sees the free love by which they "are thine" by the Father, given to the Son and redeemed by him, and empowered in the work of the Spirit in their soul. They know what it is to be saved, for they have sought out his precepts and considered his testimonies and looked into the broadness of his commandment. They know what it is to love God. There they find the precious blood of Christ's covenant for them, by which they were redeemed, and into which they are placed into service to him. They do not trust the world, for the world is fleeting; do not place your hopes in it. It endures only at God's discretion. One day it will be burned by fire. Riches, honors, pleasures, the estate that is most firmly settled by a man's labor and strength, are fleeting and will dissolve to nothing. This speaks also to David's words, I have seen an end of all perfection, but thy commandment is exceeding broad. There is a limit to what the world can do or offer; and it housed in the limits of that which is temporary. Lot's wife is remembered for her worldly lust, for loving the world more than she loved God; for her unbelief; for an everlasting monument of shame. It is so monumental that our Lord uses it as an illustration to sum up his teaching of his final coming and judgment. Remember

Lot's wife. Orpah did the same, going back to the heathen and to the devil in Moab when she was being pressed by Naomi about her intentions. Where will your eyes be? No, better yet, where is your *heart* now? For Lot's wife and Orpah and Judas and Demas and others, was it really a matter of mere sight on worldly things? For all of them it was their sinful disposition that caused all of them to love the world more than they loved God. Such is in opposition to the breadth of the Gospel, that Christ would come to save enemies, and make them friends. They did not want to hold onto God, being unresolved to dismiss all their earthlimindedness. They did not hold steadfastly to God's spiritual goodness, and the promise of blessing, and instead desired the sins of the heathen, and worldly things over the blessing of deliverance in the Gospel. They were more infatuated with the limitations of pleasures in the world than they were with God's word; they wanted to placate themselves, as all declining professing Christians desire to do. You must be forever willing to leave all the fleeting vanities of the world, of its supposed pleasure and profit, to forsake all for Christ and his Gospel; this is not an easy thing to do in light of the breadth of the word. Nothing will so powerfully quench earthlimindedness, inclinations to earthly things, as a desire and delight in higher and better things above where Christ is at the right hand of power in the throne room of God. You must be more content to be in heaven even while you are on earth in your thoughts, and hearts, and services to him. Because the breadth of the eternal Gospel is in no way comparable to the fallen material world which vanishes like a vapor. The word is sweet, and delectable, and satisfying, where safety is found in the Savior, where confidence can be had because all of it rests in Christ.

You must be committed to the truth of the Word, the exceedingly broad commandment, and look there for guidance. This is where Jesus is found; in loving God. I find it interesting when people say, "on such and such a day I found Jesus." Jesus wasn't lost; he was always right there in the word; did they just fail to look there? Do they fail to consider, to seek out his precepts, to consider his testimonies? And it is not enough to occasionally think about Jesus, but your minds must be set on him. It is a furthering of the psalmist's holiness as stated in Colossians, "If ye then be risen with Christ, seek those things which are above, where Christ sitteth on the right hand of God. Set your affection on things above, not on things on the earth," (Col. 3:1-2). Yes, Paul read psalm 119, because that *setting* is that *loving*, for it is that *loving God* and loving his exceedingly great and precious promises in the word. Guard very closely what your conversation and mind and heart and actions are taken up with. Pray to be committed to God's exceedingly broad commandment, the whole word, to love him with an earnest zeal. John Brinsley said, "Grow in heavenly mindedness. "Seek the things which are above," (Colossians 3:1). This is how the plant grows; and this is how the Christian should grow, upward, heavenward."[58] The Psalmist said, "How sweet are Your words to my taste, sweeter than honey to my mouth!" (Psalm 119:103). Such would never have occurred if he did not know the settled word, looked to its precepts, considered its testimonies and looked to his commandments, to grow up heavenward. Meditate on it daily, engage in divine contemplation of it. That is part of the substance of the whole psalm. Even in other psalms, Psalm 1:2, "But his delight is in the law of the LORD, and in His law he meditates day and night." Echoing this psalm, "Make me to go in the path of thy commandments; for therein do I delight," (Psalm 119:35). This is how people who love God, feed on Jesus Christ, by considering, seeking, loving, delighting in his eternal word that is very broad. And if we do not seek, consider, desire, delight, in God's commandment, we are not setting our minds on Christ and we are spiritually declining in our walk. Then, by default, they are set on sundry things of the world, like Demas, Orpah and Judas. And the psalmist is setting down a principle that is diametrically opposed to earthlimindedness. Because worldly people set themselves on that which is temporary and gratifying to the carnal nature; such things last only for a moment. The word teaches us, "that, denying ungodliness and worldly lusts, we should live soberly, righteously, and godly, in this present

---

[58] John Brinsley, eBook, *The Christian's Union, Communion and Conformity to Jesus Christ in His Death and Resurrection*, (Crossville, TN: Puritan Publications, 2016) chapter 8.

world," (Titus 2:12). Such is a distinction between temporary things of the world, in comparison to Jesus Christ who is the eternal word.

Things in the earth are not *bad* things, but when one is set to be earthliminded, then temporary things (which should be blessings as tools in service to King Jesus) are of no lasting value because they are attached *with a sinful motive* – not setting the mind on Christ first. To be taken up with the world and the earth is to look at earthly things as the greatest things of all. This can be any "thing" in the world. It can be apples, or houses, or jobs, or family, or money, or pets, or computers, or music, or anything. Earthlimindedness is set down in the Bible as *spiritual adultery*. It is placing a desire more on finite things, than on God's Christ; it is to replace loving God with other things. It's called idolatry for that reason. It is to have the heart make the world, things of temporary value, gods of a kind; things of the highest value in their own right. This the Lord condemns as sin. It is called enmity against God. "...know ye not that the friendship of the world is enmity with God? whosoever therefore will be a friend of the world is the enemy of God," (James 4:4). It makes men enemies of God instead of friends. Such worldliness was in context of this psalm as that which had limitations, to not be able to speak to that which God would *require* of his people; where the preacher calls it vanity of vanities all through Ecclesiastes. Apples, and boats, and houses, and money, and pets and other things of the world are not inherently bad in and of themselves. But if your mind is set on them instead of on Christ, they hold a sinful, worldly element in them. You are pinching your heart, narrowing your heart, so that you cannot love God and love your neighbor as you should. Such people are more interested in placating their own emotions and feelings, or, as Paul describes this, pinching their heart to restrict it. "Ye are not straitened in us, but ye are straitened in your own bowels. Now for a recompence in the same, (I speak as unto my children,) be ye also enlarged," (2 Cor. 6:12-13), which speaks directly to the largeness of the word. Where do you spend most of your time in your thoughts and actions and desires; that is where you find your god.

The mind and affections should never be wasted in focusing on the wrong things; which is why we are exhorted to redeem the time. Martha focused on hospitality if you recall, and she was upset that Mary sat at Christ's feet to hear him. Is hospitality evil? No. But if she was focusing on hospitality instead of on Christ, then she is not focusing on the one thing necessary, and that became evil and sinful for her. One thing, yes, one thing, one commandment. Priorities are misguided when they are not guided by the word and do not walk into the right course. Love God, *and do what you please.*

Placing a greater weight on the temporal than on the eternal, has always been the downfall of Christians, because the world is so enticing to the flesh; and they still carry with themselves the old man as a corpse. When the spiritual eyes of the believer are off the Christ, they are on something else. When the heart is not knit to the word as it ought to be, the mind is engaged in things of no profit, that are fleeting and worldly; they are knit to something else. There is no redeeming value in other things of the world. There is no value in anything outside of King Jesus. Certainly, by way of notation, Jesus can and will make things of the world helpful to the Christian, but this is not what the Holy Spirit through the psalmist is explaining. In his exceedingly broad, all encompassing, limitless command to love him, and take him at his word, he shows, explains, and directs his children how they may successfully accomplish all things in his service by the word. They must look there to know his mind. They must be able to say with the psalmist, "I have seen the end of all perfection." How did he see it? Was it that suddenly it just came to him? Or was it that he took time to perceive it? He looked and saw that nothing could compare to the word of God.

God's word regulates all of life, every portion, and not merely part of it. We can talk of partial reform, partial following, partial reformation, being cakes that are half turned, good for nothing, but to be thrown away. God determines, not just in church, but in every aspect of life, how sinners approach him, how they walk before him, how they live and move and have their being in him; how they live before the face of God which see them always, and is with them always. His word directs them. It is perpetual, all encompassing, will never fail them, and is a light to them for all time. It makes paths straights and takes them *out* of crooked ways.

And living life *in view of* God's word, *by* God's word, is always successful in light of God's exceedingly broad commandment; to love him more than anything else; it will yield success. It is a mark of a true disciple in this, "If any man come to me, and hate not his father, and mother, and wife, and children, and brethren, and sisters, yea, and his own life also, he cannot be my disciple," (Luke 14:26). This is a very hard saying in scripture, directly linked to this passage in the psalm, that the world is fleeting, and the word of God is enduring, and all things in comparison to the word are vanity. It even applies to things that we think are, as Christians, important; where we might place a greater importance on them while we live in the world. And what is more important to many people than family and how families feel, live and act? In comparison to Jesus, all other things, even good things, are considered as *hated* in light of him. That's harsh isn't it? Yet, the breadth of the eternal Word of Christ is in no way comparable to the fallen material world which truly vanishes like a vapor.

If the happiness of Jesus Christ found in the word of God is truly full and satisfying to believers, it should then purge our desires in the pursuit of things that are here below. Jerome said, "Let them favor earthly things who have no interest in heavenly promises."⁵⁹

It is a very strange and uncomely thing for a Christian to say they have a desire after heavenly things, after the word of Christ, and yet, continue to run after the vain and empty pleasures of the world in whatever form they come. The psalmist is implying: where is your treasure, where is your crown, where is your Savior? Where is your violence for heaven and heavenly things in comparison to the fleeting pleasures of the world?

And what a foolishness it is who trade true happiness in Christ through the eternal word that is perpetually satisfying, for empty gratifications that last but a moment? One of the blessings that makes heaven so great, in that there is nothing mixed there, but only Christ, where the saints are blissfully happy into all eternity. All these short pleasures of this realm, now, in its fallen state, will be turned into sufferings for the wicked. Happiness in fleeting things of the world are changed into the endless sighing's in hell for them; they stand as a witness against them forever, and gnaw at their conscience. There is no ease associated to them in such worldly things. And worldly things are often distractions from the sweet deepness of the Gospel of Christ and the word. They often *cause* Christians to forget God.

---

⁵⁹ William Spurstowe, eBook, *The Sermons of William Spurstowe*, (Coconut Creek, FL: Puritan Publications, 2012) sermon 1.

Why would you want to forget God? *Forget him you ask?* Of course; to set the mind on the world, on transient things, fleeting things, is to *forget* the happiness that you can have in Christ. It is to turn from eternal things to fleeting things. It is worldliness and earthly-mindedness. Why do you think sin is so repetitive? It is fleeting. It is not satisfying. If God is not the object of a man's thoughts, something else is. They find other things to take up their time, and they forget God and shut him out of their thoughts because they don't have enough time to do what he wants them to do. "Many walk of whom I have told you often, and now tell you even weeping that they are the enemies of the cross of Christ, whose end is destruction, whose God is their belly, and whose glory is in their shame, who mind earthly things," (Phil. 3:18-19). Earthly things are far more important to them.

Consider the positive ending to this section to the Psalm. What do you need to know about the Christian religion? Everything is contained in God's word. "...thy commandment is exceedingly broad," (Psalm 119:96); Jesus summed this statement up by saying, *Love God*. True religion has never existed, and never can exist, where the truths revealed in the Bible are unknown. The word of God is not only necessary to salvation, but it is also divinely successful and useful to the accomplishment of salvation, as well as the sanctification of the believer. Remember, saved, being saved, will be saved. Jesus said, "Go ye therefore, and teach all nations, baptizing them in the name of the Father, and of the Son, and of the Holy Ghost; teaching them to observe all things, whatsoever I have commanded you: and, lo, I am with you always, even unto the end of the world. Amen," (Matt. 28:19-20). The apostles and disciples went everywhere preaching Christ, by the word. To the Corinthians Paul says that "it pleased God by the foolishness of preaching to save them that believe," (1 Cor. 1:21). The writer to the Hebrews said, "The word of God is quick, and powerful, and sharper than any two-edged sword, piercing even to the dividing asunder of soul and spirit, and of the joints and marrow, and is a discerner of the thoughts and intents of the heart," (Heb. 4:12). What does the word do to you? What discernment do you find in it? What discernment do you find in it about you? What kind of diligence do you give to it?

The Bible, with its breadth in the mysteries of the Gospel, is complete, and equally, accessible to you; it was not so much for David. The character of the Scriptures, taken in connection with being inspired by God, without error and that they will never fail you, proves their divine origin as a whole book, and in every chapter and verse, and you can buy one in Walmart. It is God's mind that you can find for a few dollars in a store today. There is nothing else to be added to that book; love God and do what you please; and if you love God, what you please to do is what God is pleased you do. "What thing soever I command you, observe to do it:

thou shalt not add thereto, nor diminish from it," (Deut. 12:32). "According as his divine power hath given unto us all things that pertain unto life and godliness, through the knowledge of him that hath called us to glory and virtue: Whereby are given unto us exceedingly great and precious promises: that by these ye might be partakers of the divine nature, having escaped the corruption that is in the world through lust," (2 Peter 1:3-4). The Bible is God's word to man and furnishes us with sound and true and exceedingly broad words about him (*theology*). *The 1647 Westminster Confession of Faith* (1:6) says this, "The whole counsel of God, concerning all things necessary for his own glory, man's salvation, faith, and life, is either expressly set down in Scripture, or by good and necessary consequence may be deduced from Scripture: unto which nothing at any time is to be added, whether by new revelations of the Spirit, or traditions of men. Nevertheless, we acknowledge the inward illumination of the Spirit of God to be necessary for the saving understanding of such things as are revealed in the Word; and that there are some circumstances concerning the worship of God, and government of the Church, common to human actions and societies, which are to be ordered by the light of nature and Christian prudence, according to the general rules of the Word, which are always to be observed," (Gal. 1:8-9; 2 Thess. 2:2; 2 Tim. 3:15-17; John 6:45; 1 Cor. 2:9-12; 1 Cor. 11:13-14; 14:26, 40).

The word is clear. When we deal with the clarity of the Scriptures, we are dealing with understandability (perspicuity). Are the Scriptures so clear that anyone can pick them up, read them, and find salvation? The answer to this is a resounding yes. Can an infinite God communicate to finite men and make himself understandably clear in preaching? The answer to this is "yes" but it is a qualified "yes" in that God communicates himself via an accommodating means. Certainly there are mysteries taught in Scripture (the Trinity, Christ's hypostatic union, *etc.*); but as a believer, you can understand clearly what salvation is if you read your Bible and hear the word as David did; the breadth of the Gospel is set there, and all the duties that Christ requires of you are set there. His commandment, love God, is exceedingly broad in this. Calvin said, "For by a kind of mutual bond the Lord has joined together the certainty of his Word and of his Spirit so that the perfect religion of the Word may abide in our minds when the Spirit, who causes us to contemplate God's face, shines; and that we in turn may embrace the Spirit with no fear of being deceived when we recognize him in his own image, namely, in the Word."[60]

The word of God is eminently sufficient, exceedingly broad, covering everything you ever need to know. It is the only rule of faith and practice. It is exceedingly broad in comparison to the fleeting

---

[60] *Institutes of the Christian Religion*, 1:9:3.

limitations of the world. The Scriptures are the fountain by which God conveys to us the knowledge of his will about what we are to believe concerning him, for faith, and what duties he requires of us, for practice, without exception. This means that there is no other source by which we obtain knowledge concerning salvation, or our obedience of Jesus Christ, or of the Gospel, but by the word.

In this, the blessed mysteries of the eternal Word are in no way comparable to the limitations of the fallen material world, which cannot make anyone happy, or satisfy anyone, which vanishes away like a vapor; *so says the Holy Spirit by the psalmist.*

Concluding Thoughts

You have considered, with me, this section of the psalm and have *all* the tools you need to live righteously before God, as the psalmist did, in the grace of Jesus Christ; to magnify him at and by his word. What glorious things we have considered from Christ's mouth! The eternal nature of God, the glorious promises of Christ, how all things are under his Kingship and kingdom, (even you!), his providences and his ordained afflictions, his salvation and the way he saved you. Now, when times of affliction come, you can say with the psalmist, and with Luther, "I am thine, save me!" May it be so for you in your walk before Christ's face in holiness all your days. Amen.

Other Works by Dr. McMahon at Puritan Publications

The Ten Commandments in the Life of the Christian
This work takes Christ's Ten Commandments, the commands of King Jesus, and not only expounds their basic teachings, but also how those commands apply to the life of the Christian.

I Am for You: God's Power in Supporting His People
This volume is a spiritual journey through five important Scriptures: Jeremiah 3:1, Mark 5:25-34, Luke 16:4, 1 Samuel 17:34-35, and Ezekiel 36:9. It demonstrates the cultivation of true assurance that Christians can sincerely have as believing Christians, if they trust in the work of Jesus Christ.

The Kingdom of Heaven is Upon You
Jesus preached, "Repent: for the kingdom of heaven is at hand," (Matthew 4:17). This is the Gospel. But what did Jesus mean by preaching in this way?

The Five Principles of the Gospel
We may hear preachers say, "believe the simple Gospel of Jesus Christ and be saved!" Is the "simple Gospel" contained only in that single short phrase? Or is there more?

5 Marks of Christian Resolve
If Christians resolve to do "something," and never actually get around to doing it, what good is that? If Christians desire to glorify the living Christ in their kingdom service, then such service does, truly, come in light of a real biblical resolution turned to action.

Christ Commanding His Coronavirus to Covenant Breakers
Why is the coronavirus plaguing the world today? Is Christ in control of it? And how does it affect the church?

Joseph's Resolve and the Unreasonableness of Sinning Against God
How much do you hate sin? Joseph was resolved to cast off all wickedness as he lived before the face of God. Do you?

5 Marks of Devotion to God
Mark 1: Daily Bible Reading and Study, Mark 2: Daily Meditation, Mark 3: Daily Prayer, Mark 4: Fasting, Mark 5: Family Worship ... Do you desire a closer walk with Christ?

Walking Victoriously in the Power of the Spirit
Are you walking victoriously in the Spirit? Are you baptized by the Spirit, indwelt by the Spirit, walking abundantly in Jesus Christ by the Spirit? Do you even regularly talk this way?

5 Marks of Biblical Reformation
Everybody loves to claim the magisterial reformation for their own! Everyone wants to be a reformer in that way. But take God's principles of a Biblical Reformation and apply them to the church in practical daily living, then that's a different story all together.

www.ingramcontent.com/pod-product-compliance
Lightning Source LLC
Chambersburg PA
CBHW030102170426
43198CB00009B/461